FOOTY'S
Greatest Players

Edited by

Stephanie Holt

Garrie Hutchinson

COULOMB
COMMUNICATIONS

Published by:

COULOMB
COMMUNICATIONS

PO Box 751
Port Melbourne 3207

National Library of Australia Cataloguing-in-Publication entry:

Footy's greatest players.

  ISBN 0 9580737 3 2.

  1. Australian football players—Biography. 2. Australian
  football—Biography. I. Hutchinson, Garrie, 1949 –. II.
  Holt, Stephanie, 1961 –.

  796.3360922

Every effort has been made to acknowledge the source of all photographs reproduced in this
book. If any acknowledgements have been omitted, please contact the publisher and these will
be rectified in subsequent editions.

Front cover image: Gary Ablett, courtesy of Getty Images.

CONTENTS

FOREWORD

Ron Barassi

Beauty they say is in the eye of the beholder. Greatness (in the footy player sense) is very similar – it's in the eye (opinion) of the beholder (the enthusiast).

So Stephanie Holt and Garrie Hutchinson's latest footy book on this very quirky subject – football's greatest players – will, if history is any guide, bring about a chorus of discussion, dissension and dismay.

This clamour will be matched by those who agree with the authors.

The common thread among the greatest players are club Best and Fairest awards, AFL team of the year nominations, State representation (in ye olden days), captaincies, battles against the Irish, Brownlow medals, media awards, recognition in club and AFL Halls of Fame, etc.

Fair enough, but I believe that while the 'greatest' moniker is any fan's individual assessment, there must be some thought given to the following three traits:

1) Longevity – our choice must play for some years (with John Coleman a definite exception) and with regular distinction.

2) Presence – equally as surely, one's greatest players should have this quality.

And the last trait, I reckon, which is a must if considering any great, is:

3) Prominence when the pressure is on – our hero must rise to the occasion in the big matches, in the must-win games, in contests where the club's pride is at stake.

All of the above guarantees an ongoing discussion topic at the local, at family BBQs, the workplace – anywhere. It's part of footy culture and a worthy part to boot.

In these animated talk-fests, one regular accusation will come out, I bet you. It is, of course, 'You're biased.' Fair enough, but just tell me, how the hell does one know (for certain) that they have purged their brain cells of this 'poison'?

I would probably be accused of bias myself, because I would name players I have coached in my line-up of greats: John (Mopsy) Rantall comes to mind – he hardly ever let his team down, no matter what size of defensive task he was given; and I'd definitely put Carlton's John Nicholls and Alex Jesaulenko on my list, I don't care what people will say.

One thing I should make clear on this whole subject: when it comes to footy, I like the idea of a player being 'the most valuable', not 'the best'. And sometimes there *is* a difference. This player is the first picked.

In this context, the greatest player that I've ever seen is Leigh Matthews.

INTRODUCTION
(Some of) Footy's Greatest Players

Stephanie Holt & Garrie Hutchinson

Who are footy's greatest players?

'Greatness' is a much overused word in football. Not a quarter goes by without a commentator or barracker calling out in admiration or irony that a player has taken a great mark, thumped a great kick, laid a great tackle or snapped a great goal. And any game won by a kick or less is, naturally enough, hailed as a great game.

In the heat of the moment, passionate supporters and excitable commentators may be closer to the mark than they realise. The dictionary allows that 'great' things are those of a size, amount or intensity considerably above the normal or average. But is a player who is only considerably above the normal or average truly 'great', or just (on their day, in the games we happen to see) very good?

Reflecting over the history of football – without argument, a great game – we looked for something more than this. And when we cast our eyes over the current crop of players, we wondered which ones would provide the next chapter of football history. Which will be remembered? Which immortalised in images or barracker cries or carefully retold stories?

Great things, the dictionary also suggests, may be 'distinguished', 'of extraordinary powers', or 'very admirable'. These terms, we can be confident, describe the players we have profiled here, though they would apply to many more. One way to approach making a list of great players would be to assess those who exhibited 'great' skills on a regular basis. But that may not be enough. There are plenty of spectacular players who took a lot of great marks and kicked a lot of great goals – Tony Modra, Mark Jackson, Warwick Capper spring to mind – but who wouldn't qualify as truly great players. Because greatness – in *our* minds, and therefore in this book – has something legendary and inspirational about it.

Legends live in the collective storytelling memory of fans, like a Daicos kick, or a Greg Williams handball, or Darrel Baldock's run. At the MCG in 2003, a not-yet-great player attempted an end-over-end, swerving, dribbling goal. 'There's only one Peter Daicos,' came a comment from the crowd. And everyone around knew exactly what that meant. Daicos and what he could do lives on in that succinct story.

The deeds of the great are passed down the barracking generations: a grandfather shares with a grandson his despair at the felling of John Coleman; mothers and fathers tell a wide-eyed child watching David Rodan weave some magic inside 50 that they should have been there when Michael Long won a Grand Final with some kind of mesmeric force. These assessments are, necessarily, one-eyed views.

The moments that really live, for a Carlton supporter, are Carlton moments: when Brent Crosswell kicked the goal that put the Blues in front in the 1970 Grand Final; when Greg Williams cleared the centre square in 1995 and received his own pass, or seemed to; Stephen Silvagni's moments of tear-inducing courage too numerous to mention. Among the greatest of the great, John Nicholls and Alex Jesaulenko.

And a St Kilda supporter will treasure memories of Tony Lockett marauding around the goal square at Moorabbin or coming perilously close to Fred Fanning's all-time-record bag in his later days; or Nicky Winmar cutting a swathe through the field in the 1996 Ansett Cup; or Bob Murray marking in defence to secure the Saints their first premiership.

Every barracker for every club has their own list, celebrates their own greats. That is exactly as it should be. Those passions and biases give our game part of its endless fascination.

The footballers in the AFL Hall of Fame are inducted because they have made a 'significant contribution to Australian football at any level since 1858, on the basis of record, ability, integrity, sportsmanship and character'. Behind that carefully worded criteria, however, even this is a subjective, slippery definition. It has allowed 176 players to enter the Hall of Fame to date, and seventeen – Ron Barassi, Kevin Bartlett, Haydn Bunton Snr, Roy Cazaly, John Coleman, Gordon Coventry, Jack Dyer, Polly Farmer, Peter Hudson, Leigh Matthews, John Nicholls, Bob Pratt, Dick Reynolds, Barrie Robran, Bob Skilton, Ian Stewart and Ted Whitten – to be enshrined as Legends. There is no question that these are great players. They had long careers, most of them played hundreds of games. They kicked goals. They were matchwinners for their clubs over long periods. Some of them even won Brownlow medals – but not all of them.

Ron Barassi was (no perhaps about it) the greatest impact player of them all. He won six premierships as a player for Melbourne, but never came close to winning a Brownlow, and 'only' won a couple of Best and Fairests for Melbourne. Ted Whitten came closer to the Brownlow. He was third, once, and also won five Best and Fairests for Footscray. But Barassi and Whitten didn't need medals to live on in the memories of every football fan across Australia. They were football characters, giants of the game.

So you'll find Ted Whitten in *Footy's Greatest Players*, and Barassi, too, who wrote the foreword. Barassi, of course, was also a great coach, and features, as do most other players who excelled at both arts, in our companion book, *Footy's Greatest Coaches*. And is excluded, only by reason of space, from a fuller profile in this one.

There are some non-footballing tests applied to official AFL Legends, which is why the truly legendary Gary Ablett is not (yet) in the Hall of Fame. But he's on the cover of this book. We don't believe Ablett's sad off-field actions should exclude him from consideration. We want to celebrate and remember and understand his game. He inspired football fans of all persuasions. We were enthralled by his spectacular skills and intrigued by his self-effacing, enigmatic demeanour. His football lives on. He is among the greatest ever.

Judging players of generations years ago is almost impossible, but there were giants in those days, and we've made a stab at resurrecting a few of them, on the basis that they had the qualities of today's greats, and were so judged by their contemporaries. 'Pompey' Elliott, Dave McNamara, Albert Thurgood, Roy Cazaly from the early days are here; Jack Dyer, Haydn Bunton, Gordon and Syd Coventry, Polly Farmer, Darrel Baldock and Kevin Murray from the good old days are also given a run.

We remember best the players we've seen perform the improbable on a regular basis, and who live on the hard disk of footy memory. So there's a bit of a bias here towards players of the not-so-distant past. Dermott Brereton, Peter Daicos and Tony Lockett are included, as are some of those champions who endeared themselves especially to the fans, including Leigh Matthews, Robert Flower, Don McKenzie, Nicky Winmar and Bruce Doull.

Of contemporary players, Martin Flanagan would only allow four as great: Nathan Buckley, James Hird, Andrew McLeod and Michael Voss. We have added Robert Harvey and Wayne Carey. We have perhaps seen the best of all of them, but that best is as great as anyone who has pulled on a boot.

A 'truth in labelling' title for this book would be *Some of Footy's Greatest Players*. In the end you just can't fit all the evocative writing on all the great players into one volume. And one set of memories, one series of arguments for greatness, will surely provoke others. We could easily set to work on another three or four books of this size.

PIONEERS
of the Game

From its earliest days, football produced great players.
Their deeds, if not their names, may be forgotten now, but
they were honoured by their peers and celebrated by their
supporters. The newspapers of the day extolled their virtues.
They took themselves and their sport seriously. Although the
low-scoring, stop-start games of the past might be
unrecognisable today, these players perfected some of our
game's distinctive features, from the leaps of Roy Cazaly to
the kicks of Dave McNamara.

1

'HARD AS NAILS'

Jack Conway and the
Early Days of Football

by Mark Pennings

J.J.A. 'Jack' Conway is one of the forgotten heroes of the early days of football. Accounts of this period have been dominated by the mighty deeds of T.W. Wills and H.C.A. Harrison, but in newspaper reports of the time, it's apparent that Conway, too, was a household name.

Following his death in 1909, the *Australasian*'s obituary provided a colourful description of Conway as a man 'as strong as a house. Forty-three in the chest, with thighs, calves, biceps and forearms to match, he was a formidable opponent to shoulder in a football field.' So proud was Conway of these blessings from nature that in his later years, when coming across old friends, he would, according to the *Herald*'s obituary, 'close his hardened fist and, beating a great chest, would make the proud declaration, "Hard as nails, no embonpoint, no adipose tissue, all sinew and strength."'

Conway was said to possess a 'lustiness of personality' and was of a 'frank and generous disposition'. As an athlete he was a man of exceptionally fine physique and vitality, with great strength and powers of endurance. He was not a rule maker, like Wills, nor an influential administrator, like Harrison, but his importance as a player during an era of football 'warriors' should not be underestimated. He was the first great captain of the Carlton Football Club and was one of Harrison's most formidable foes in those glorious football battles of bygone days.

Conway's association with Australian football began at the game's genesis. Born at Fyansford, near Geelong, on 3 February 1842, he was one of the first generation of Victorian-born Europeans and was educated locally, becoming a foundation pupil at the Melbourne Church of England Grammar School in 1858. Conway took great pride in his nationality. While managing the first Australian Test cricket tour of England in 1878, an Englishman had the temerity to enter the Australians' enclosure speaking pidgin English – Conway tossed him over the pickets. By this time, Conway had enjoyed a long career as a participant in Melbourne's sporting life; he had been a successful footballer and cricketer, and was also a respected sports journalist.

Conway's love of sport was inculcated during his teens when he lived in Melbourne. It was the late 1850s, the very time when football first organised in the colony. Melbourne had a large population of young British-educated gentlemen, and English-style public schools were being founded in the colony for native-born members of the elite who had the time and inclination to play sport on the weekend. These men and boys, including Conway, were the first to play football regularly in Melbourne throughout the winter. Conway's school, Melbourne Grammar, played an important role in the development of the local football code, due in large part to its headmaster, Dr J.E. Bromby, who was an enthusiast, advocate and organiser of early football matches. It is therefore likely that Conway participated in the historic first football games between Melbourne Grammar and Scotch College, in 1858.

Melbourne Grammar also played football against St Kilda Grammar on 5 June 1858, a month before T.W. Wills' famous letter in which he advocated forming a football club and drawing up a code of laws. On 31 July that year, when cricketers like Wills, W.J. Hammersley and J.B. Thompson were participating in scratch football games in parkland next to the MCG, a group of St Kilda men were playing Dr Bromby's schoolboys in parkland near St Kilda. (Unfortunately, there are few details about the nature of this St Kilda 'club'.)

Although cricketers had begun organising football matches in the Richmond Paddock, the games played by the schools seemed to have been more organised – the celebrated games between Melbourne Grammar and Scotch in August and September that year were adjudicated by umpires, including T.W. Wills. Melbourne Grammar probably played more games than any other football team or group in 1858, and as a pupil of the school, with an outstanding career ahead of him, it is likely that Jack Conway was involved in these contests.

In September 1858, twenty-seven gentlemen from South Yarra challenged a similar number of 'Melbourne' players to a football contest. As Conway's school was located in the South Yarra district, the team probably contained some of its schoolboys. These gentlemen played at Richmond Park and it was reported that the South Yarra players brought a set of written rules, which were:

> generally agreed to, but, due to the different laws to which the players had been accustomed in their school days, and the long-forgotten excitement of the sport, they were 'more interested in the breach than the observance'.

This game was played before the Melbourne Football Club was formed, and although Melbourne cricketers were among the first to actively promote football in Melbourne, the contribution of Melbourne Grammar (and its South Yarra connections) to the development of the game also deserves recognition.

By the age of 17, Conway, like others from Melbourne Grammar, such as Bromby's sons, Christopher and Ernest, was playing football for the South Yarra side. Many famous early footballers represented South Yarra at the time, including George O'Mullane, Henry Hale Budd and W.J. Greig. In those days it was not unusual for players to represent several clubs during the season, and from 1860 to 1862 Conway played with South Yarra, St Kilda, Richmond and Melbourne. From 1863, however, he seems to have played exclusively for Melbourne, and in 1865 he was often mentioned among the best players in their games against clubs including South Yarra, Royal Park and Geelong.

By 1866 Conway was playing for Melbourne and the new Carlton club, which had been formed in 1864 and had begun playing games in 1865. Conway was one of a number of captains for Carlton in 1866 and 1867, but became its sole leader in 1868. He also played the odd game for Emerald Hill and Albert Park during this time, as he lived in Albert Park and captained the South Melbourne Cricket Club and was occasionally 'roped in' by these clubs.

Conway achieved his greatest fame at Carlton. He took his captaincy very seriously, and was an 'ever-active' leader of fine teams that included legendary players such as Tom and Billy Gorman, 'Lanty' O'Brien, Jack Donovan and Harry Guy. Conway's significance can be measured by the work he did above and beyond his role as captain, for he was the pivotal figure who established the proud character of the Carlton football club. In the 1876 edition of the *Footballer*, 'Old 'Un' claimed that Conway was 'the man who made Carlton what it is, though they never properly acknowledged it'.

Indeed, Conway grafted his lifelong motto – 'Game first, self last' – to the team spirit of this club, and was also described as the embodiment of Carlton's club motto: *Mens sana in corpore sano* ('a healthy mind in a healthy body': a classic ethic for muscular Christianity). He was thus the ideal Victorian athlete, displaying a discipline and selflessness that high-lighted the best instincts of the sons of the British Empire, whose indi-vidual needs were sacrificed to the larger interests of club or country.

During the 1868 and 1869 seasons, Conway reached the peak of his football career and was acknowledged as the driving force behind Carlton's rise to power. He was invariably reported as one of that team's best players, and his goalkicking ability was among the best in the colony.

As captain, Conway was always prepared to defend Carlton's reputa-tion. After a tough victory over Melbourne in late 1869, H.C.A. Harrison used the end-of-game ritual of three cheers for the opposing team to proudly boast that Carlton were the second-best team in the colony. Conway responded to this mischievous act in a letter to the *Australasian*:

> I have been requested by members of the Carlton FC to contra-dict a statement made by Mr. Harrison, the Melbourne Captain, at the termination of the recent match between Carlton and Mel-bourne, in reference to the much-vexed question as to which club is to be awarded the palm of superiority in the football field. Mr. Harrison ... took occasion to state that the Carlton club was, after Melbourne, the best club in the colony. This statement naturally gave rise to a deal of surprise and dissatisfaction in the minds of the Carlton players, who justly think themselves, by their previous performances, when pitted against Melbourne and other clubs, if not superior, quite equal to their rivals ... In conclusion, I beg to state, on behalf of the Carlton club, that they are both willing and ready to meet the MFC when and where they please, before the season expires.

Harrison and Conway had a great rivalry on the football field, and their battles were important elements in the hard fought games that occurred between these two clubs. This competitive spirit also helped to push football to the forefront of the Melbourne sporting public's attention. Harrison once acknowledged Conway as the 'brilliant captain of one of our greatest rivals', and the contests between these two and their clubs were the cause of great interest and admiration.

One spectator who recalled those times wrote:

> It was something to be remembered when that grand and fearless footballer, the great old skipper of the reds, H.C.A. Harrison – lithe, sinewy, well conditioned, strong and hard as nails – sprang panther-like bound against the Herculean captain of the blues, solid as a rock, waiting for the charge. The impact was so tremendous that the very ground seemed to tremble with the shock.

Of course in the 1860s and 1870s football was very different from today. Goals were rare in those days, and final results resembled today's soccer scores. The game was contested by a group of heavyweight 'followers' who were generally engaged in congested scrums. The whole exercise was based on rushing the ball forward and spilling it out into the open spaces, from where it was hoped the 'goalsneak' would kick that much-coveted goal. The game was also known for its 'purlers', in which great fun was derived from knocking a player onto the earth in a way that made them slide along muddy ground.

The *Leader* provided a highly entertaining and vivid account of Conway and Harrison's feats in a game between Carlton and Melbourne at the Richmond Paddock, just north of the MCG, in June 1870. It portrayed these men as warriors on a battlefield, and reveals Conway's sartorial flair:

> The contending forces file out of the gate behind the pavilion, mingling for the time in noisy fraternity … The captains are not on the field yet, but make their appearance in a moment or two amidst more cheering. Harrison is known by his red jacket, and Jack Conway by his zebra-striped cap.

Unfortunately, all is not as it should be for the Carlton playing list, and the captain uses his powers of authority to rectify the situation:

> Conway, upon whom rests the honor of Carlton, looks anxious as he surveys his squad, for some carpet knights of the first twenty would not venture abroad today … Only fifteen yellow caps stand

around. Jack shades his eyes with his hand, and casts a rapid glance along the crowd to spot out some recruits who will make up his weight, at all events. Suddenly he shouts out first to one, then to another, and the appeal is not in vain. After a little hesitation, two of the spectators leap into the arena, and rush across to the pavilion, where they divest themselves of uppers, and come up prepared for the fray. Ready!

The game then proceeds and players run hither and thither in order to gain whatever advantage they can, but there are many scrimmages. At one of these, the reporter describes the players 'all in a heap, with Harrison and Conway in the middle, gallantly singling out each other as the only worthy foe'. On another occasion, when the pace of the game picks up, a Melbourne player grabs the ball and runs for dear life towards the Melbourne scoring end, until:

> The Carlton captain happens to be raging in the neighbourhood, and renders good service by placing himself in front of one of the best Melbourne runners, who is so intent on the game that Jack is able to bring him up with a buster three or four times, by simply standing in his road.

After Melbourne scored a much-treasured goal, an intense struggle was undertaken and the players worked hard, straining every muscle to ensure victory or the chance to even the score. The journalist noted the epic nature of this conflict and explained that:

> If the battle field lacked the neighing of steeds, the shouting of the captains was not wanting at all events, and the vigour of the troops seems unabated ... The strife waged until the shades of evening began to draw in, and the pale radiance of the moon, visible by glimpses through the masses of clouds overhead, gave token that it was past sundown.

Coincidentally, Conway and Harrison each played their last game in the same bruising encounter at Albert Park on 7 October 1871. This was the final and most important game of the season, for the winner would claim the South Yarra Challenge Cup and the premiership for that year. Conway played his part in a 2–0 win, which was Carlton's first premiership and marked the most successful year in their short history. Conway played in some Carlton scratch matches at the beginning of 1872, but was 'incapacitated by an accident' and subsequently retired, aged 28.

Conway therefore finished his football career at the top, having helped make Carlton the strongest team in the colony. He also played a major role in shaping its attitudes and ideals. His heroic deeds were not forgotten, and he was fondly remembered in 1876 by 'Old 'Un', who published this poetic tribute to Conway and his famous playing days in the *Footballer*:

> There's gladness in remembrance, John,
>   of rivals you had few,
> When o'er the Melbourne's rugged ground
>   you led the famed Dark Blue,
> You've joined in many a gallant charge
>   after the flying leather,
> And I often think of the good old days
>   when we were boys together.

Mark Pennings is an art historian and Essendon supporter who worked on the AFL's centennial art exhibition in 1996 and now lectures at Queensland University of Technology.

'"Hard as Nails": Jack Conway and the Early Days of Football' is derived from a book being compiled by Mark Pennings and Trevor Ruddell: 'The Pennings/Ruddell Compendium of Nineteenth Century Football.'

2

ALBERT 'THE GREAT' THURGOOD

Thurgood's Match

by 'Observer' of the Argus
introduction by Garrie Hutchinson

Introduction

Essendon's Albert Thurgood was the James Hird of his day – the greatest centre forward of the 1890s. He was fast and athletic, and could run a hundred in even time. At just over 180cm and less than 80kg, Thurgood was a lightly framed cruiser compared to the lumbering dreadnaughts who usually played in set positions in those times.

Observers noted that he was as nimble as a hare, but was tough with it. Footy historian Cec Mullen, who saw him play, thought he strode the turf as if he was lord of the manor, a general inspecting the troops, a description that suggests a combination of Hird and Wayne Carey at his imperious best.

Thurgood was a tremendous kicker of the footy – he was the longest kicker in an era of prodigious punters. Punts of over seventy metres were a regular feature of his game. In 1899 he roosted a measured place-kick close to a hundred metres – 107 yards 2' 1" to be exact – with slight wind assistance. No-one has kicked a footy further. He could drop kick over eighty metres.

Playing mostly at centre half-forward in the last three of Essendon's four consecutive VFA premiership years, 1891–1894, he topped the goalkicking table with 56, 64 and 63. At the height of his powers he went to work in Western Australia, where he played for Fremantle for three years, from 1895.

Essendon managed to win the first ever VFL premiership in 1897 without 'Albert the Great', and a permit wrangle forced him to stand out of VFL football for season 1898, but he was welcomed back during the 1899 season.

In 1900, Thurgood headed the VFL goalkicking list with 26 goals, and Essendon were back playing in the finals. In 1901 he was the dominant player in a premiership year, being named Champion of the Colony by Melbourne's sportswriters (an honour equivalent to today's Brownlow medal) for the third time, following wins in 1893 and 1894.

In a 1901 semi-final against Fitzroy, he kicked five of Essendon's six goals, and shepherded the sixth one through. He played centre half-back when his team was kicking against the wind, and also took a turn in the

"PAST & PRESENT CHAMPIONS."

(7) A. J. THURGOOD, 1892-1901.
ESSENDON FOOTBALL CLUB.

Albert Thurgood 'drove the spectators mad with admiration'.

ruck. In the Grand Final, against Collingwood, he kicked six goals, three of them against the wind, one of which, a place kick, was later measured at over ninety-three yards.

The 1901 season was his greatest, and effectively his last. In 1902 he was suspended for striking, and played only a handful of games, including the losing Grand Final. He played another handful of games in 1906 before resuming his interests as a bookie and racehorse owner. He died after a car accident in 1927.

Thurgood's Match

Once again Essendon have been completely, soundly and scientifically thrashed – up to half time. When the resting-time came on Saturday, Fitzroy had five goals to one, and though Essendon's followers said afterwards, 'We must give them a bit of encouragement to begin with,' they were none the less in a state of painful anxiety during the whole of that first hour. For Fitzroy had done everything in the game immeasurably better than their rivals, and simply walked round Essendon with the superiority of their little-marking.

Then came Essendon's pet term, and with it Fitzroy's complete discomfiture. One ineffectual rush by Fitzroy and then Essendon simply took possession of their goal – and stuck to it as pertinaciously as a sheriff's officer.

Wright was the first to score, and then Thurgood, the invincible, played a lone hand that simply drove the spectators frantic with admiration. He had played back, forward, and on the ball, everywhere with infinite credit; but the four successive goals in a few minutes was the coping-stone – and one of those special feats of which Thurgood alone seems capable.

Three of his four goals were splendid ones, and he had a couple of shots in addition quite eighty yards out that covered the whole distance, and were only a trifle out in direction. Unquestionably we have never had such a goal-kicker as Thurgood – save and excepting always a number of those pioneer marvels to whom we gladly give the distinction of being all that they claimed to be. It saves argument.

At all events, Fitzroy saw their well-earned lead disappear in a few minutes before the remarkable capacity of one man, and by this time they were so exhausted by their tremendous efforts in the first half that all chance of a recovery had gone too.

Though the game was interesting to the close, Essendon having once got the lead kept it. The goal to Forbes should, I think, have been a free kick to Banks, but it did not affect the main issue. While one never expects an umpire to do all that the unreasoning barracker asks him – such a thing is not within the range of poor human ability – Schaefer's umpiring in this match was by no means his best performance.

Essendon's triumph is summed up in one word – Thurgood. He may not boast, 'Alone I did it' – in fact, he is not one of the boasting type – but none the less it would not have been done without him. Captain Dick now fully realises that he has command not merely of a phenomenal goal-kicker, but a fine all-round footballer, and when Essendon were playing against the wind he did not waste him forward, but sent him to more responsible posts.

Early in the game Banks undertook to watch him, but seemed to tire of his task and wisely assumed that he could do better for his side else-where. Essendon's defence was particularly well looked after by that fine, manly footballer, George Stuckey – Officer being given an outlet for some of his energy in the ruck. Further out Finlay and Grecian were a most capable pair. In the early stages it seemed that George Moriarty would hold his own with Finlay, but later on the dashing Essendon centre-man defied all opposition. In the skirmishing line Wright was, next to Thurgood, the most valuable man to the side – his high-marking and clever passing being especially noticeable. Ball, Kearney and Watson did splendid work in the ruck – the last-named a bit better than his average form for the season. Of course there were many other Essendon men prominent in the game, but those named should be thanked for special services.

'**Thurgood's Match**' is an edited version of a match report by 'Observer' in the Argus, 13 August 1894.

3

FRED 'POMPEY' ELLIOT
The Champion Who Gave His Name to a Hero

by Ross McMullin

The earliest surviving film footage of the VFL provides a fascinating glimpse of the 1909 Grand Final. Particularly prominent in the grainy celluloid exchanges is Carlton's 31-year-old captain-coach, Fred 'Pompey' Elliott. The origin of Elliott's nickname is unclear, but there is no doubt about his football pre-eminence. A champion at Carlton during one of its most successful eras and an outstanding leader, he captained the Blues to a premiership and later captain-coached the club. He was also the first footballer to play 200 VFL matches.

Elliott was a talented, sturdy and scrupulously fair onballer who read the play well, had admirable stamina, and was good in the wet. According to *Melbourne Punch*, he had a 'ravenous appetite for the bag of wind' and was 'as solid as asphalt and as resilient as prize rubber'. His skill, courage and leadership are evident in the footage of that Grand Final.

Pompey Elliott was one of the earliest VFL stars during the pre-1914 era, when league football firmly established itself in the hearts and minds of Victorians. However, like many Australians, Elliott found life after 1914 very different.

Elliott was born in Carlton and never really wanted to play anywhere else. He came under notice after playing for various local teams during the final years of the nineteenth century, but sloppy administration saw him slip through Carlton's fingers. Invited to present himself at Carlton's annual general meeting with other potential recruits, Elliott turned up full of expectancy. To his bewilderment, nobody spoke to him. He was too shy and modest to initiate a conversation himself, and went home crestfallen.

Melbourne showed more initiative, and persuaded Elliott to join the Fuchsias. He played his first game for them in 1899, the year he turned 21, and played thirteen more in an impressive debut season. Carlton's administrators, eager to atone for their previous negligence, became seriously interested. Elliott was receptive to their overtures. He transferred to the Blues the following year.

On 5 May 1900 Elliott played his first game for Carlton. It was not a memorable year for his new club – the Blues finished the season second-bottom with only five wins. 'Carlton have of late years appeared as though they expected defeat in every game,' concluded the *Argus*. Melbourne, the team Elliott had left, won the premiership.

The next year was worse. In 1901 Carlton finished second-bottom again, but this time with only two wins. After these discouraging first two seasons at Carlton, Fred Elliott decided to venture to Western Australia. Many Victorians, footballers and non-footballers alike, had been doing so for years. The Victorian economy was still in the doldrums following the catastrophic 1890s depression, but the West was thriving after extraordinary gold discoveries. The contrast in employment opportunities and overall prosperity was stark. In 1902, Elliott played for North Fremantle.

But better times were in store for Carlton, thanks to the advent of Jack Worrall. A top-level footballer before the formation of the VFL and a former Test cricketer, Worrall became the first official VFL coach when the Carlton committee placed him in charge of their under-performing team.

Worrall made an immense difference. An opinionated disciplinarian, he demanded absolute control. The captain, the committee and the general manager had previously shared responsibility for tactics, training, selection, recruiting and team management. Not any more. Worrall took control of everything. He was determined to change Carlton profoundly, to transform the reputation Carlton had developed for being inconsistent, individualistic, lightweight, and lacking in discipline, cohesion and tactical proficiency.

Lax training methods became a thing of the past. Worrall ruthlessly removed players who failed to measure up to the standards he demanded. 'Boys, booze and football don't mix,' he declared, 'You've got to cut out one or the other. Players who prefer beer to eucalyptus will be struck off the list.' He scoured Victoria and beyond for the kind of players he wanted, preferably big and strong but, above all, committed goers with a good team ethic.

Fred Elliott fitted perfectly into Worrall's vision for the new team he was creating. Although not tall, Elliott had a solid frame and a straight-ahead, robust, committed approach that were well suited to the long, direct style Worrall preferred. Moreover, the sense of excitement Worrall was generating, the feeling that Carlton was going somewhere at last, was infectious. Elliott wanted to be part of it. He returned to Carlton for the 1903 season, joining other notable Worrall acquisitions in Jim Flynn from Geelong and Mick Grace from Fitzroy.

In Worrall's first season the Blues had managed a significant improvement, with seven wins. Their progress was even more pronounced in 1903. After the first five rounds Carlton was undefeated and on top of the ladder. Untimely injuries to Flynn and others at the business end of the season contributed to narrow defeats in the finals. Carlton finished third; under Worrall they had clearly become a side to be reckoned with.

Elliott had been a notable contributor to Carlton's rise. He had established himself as a leading onballer, playing in effect as a ruck-rover (though the term was not to be used for decades to come), combining well with his ruck partner, Flynn, in particular. Visionary set plays at stoppages were part of the Carlton onballers' repertoire.

In 1904 Elliott consolidated his reputation with his best season yet. When Carlton defeated Essendon by three points to advance to a VFL Grand Final for the first time, ecstatic Blues fans carried Elliott off the ground in triumph. However, their mood was different after the biggest game of all. In the Grand Final Elliott was again outstanding and Carlton was in front at half time, but Fitzroy won by four goals. The following year Fitzroy was again Carlton's tormentor, defeating the well-fancied Blues convincingly in the Preliminary Final before going on to win another premiership.

Carlton finished the 1906 home-and-away matches on top of the ladder. Hopes were high that this could be the big breakthrough at last. Opposed to them in the Grand Final, aiming for their third premiership in a row, was Fitzroy. Would the Blues' nemesis of recent years strike again?

Not this time. Carlton bounced out of the blocks with sustained brilliance and vigour. At half time Carlton was 7.4(46), Fitzroy 1.7(13). A spirited Fitzroy revival saw the margin reduced to fourteen points, but Carlton steadied and powered home with six goals in the final quarter.

Elliott kicked two of them. 'Pompey Elliott kept prancing with the spheroid till the bell,' enthused *Punch*'s colourful report. 'Time after time he kept trespassers off the happy hunting-ground and drove them away to the swamps.'

In this premiership side Elliott was selected as first rover, a position Worrall had switched him to earlier in the season when the first-choice rover was injured. At the time Worrall had acknowledged that this 'is an

Fred 'Pompey' Elliot flanked by Vin Gardiner and an orange boy, *courtesy of Carlton Football Club*.

experiment that we are trying, but I think it will be effective'. It was. 'This change brought Elliott out from the thick of the ruck to the fringe of it where he was entirely in his element and where he proved himself unapproachable in power and resource.' While both roving and resting up forward, Elliott 'excelled all others with the constant brilliance of his labours'.

Though still a perpetual-motion player, the heart and soul of Carlton's on-ball grunt, Elliott had polish and finesse to complement the fearless bulldozer style that first brought him to attention. According to the *Australasian*'s football writer, 'Elliott has gained enormously in finish since I saw him last year and is now an artist as well as an untiring, vigorous worker.' He was, in later footy parlance, now suited to being an outside midfielder as well as an inside one, while maintaining his outstanding work rate and hard-ball gets. As always, he read the play astutely and adapted well to wet conditions. Despite his fame he remained humble and down to earth.

Carlton's 1906 premiership team was a very special side. Legendary umpire Jack Elder, who was still officiating in VFL matches in 1922, claimed it was the finest team he ever saw. Spectators enjoyed watching the Blues. The attendance on Grand Final day was 44,437, then a record MCG crowd, and most were euphoric Blues supporters. No team had ever attracted such support. The *Australasian* concluded that, thanks to Carlton, football in 1906 'has been far more popular than in any previous year in its history'.

Pompey Elliott was now entrenched as a household name in Victorian football circles, as were his illustrious teammates Flynn, Grace, 'Mallee' Johnson, 'Bongo' Lang, Fred Jinks, 'Hackenschmidt' Clark and a dazzling centreman with astonishing evasive skills, Rod McGregor. At 28, Elliott was in his prime, a leading member of this popular champion team that Worrall had recruited and moulded. He was appointed its captain in 1907.

Complacency was evident in 1907, but Worrall cracked the whip and Carlton was well placed again with the finals imminent. But a spiteful encounter with South Melbourne enraged Blues supporters. A South player notorious for vicious violence ran amok. When the umpire did not report him, Carlton used its prerogative to do so, aware that the VFL wanted to remove unbridled thuggery from the game. South retaliated with a counter-report, citing three Carlton players including Elliott.

The hearing was a farce. South's offender confirmed his proclivity for violence and intimidation in a series of physical clashes with witnesses, and was given an appropriately hefty penalty. But Elliott and a teammate were also suspended. This was a miscarriage of justice to rank with the nine-week suspension Greg Williams incurred in 1997 for inadvertently pushing umpire Andrew Coates, who insisted a report was unwarranted. The umpire who officiated at the Carlton vs South game gave emphatic evidence that Elliott had done nothing wrong. This umpire, former St Kilda ruckman and captain Jim Smith, who had played against Elliott many times, was adamant that he had a clear view of the alleged incident. Despite this, Elliott was suspended for the rest of the season.

Smith was so incensed by the injustice of Elliott's suspension that he resigned from umpiring. Elliott, who valued the reputation he had maintained over a long career as a fair and upright player, was scarred profoundly. The suspension ended the run of 106 consecutive matches he had played since returning from North Fremantle. Moreover, because Carlton managed to narrowly defeat bitter rival South Melbourne in a tense Grand Final, it deprived him of the thrill, satisfaction and honour of being a premiership captain.

Elliot rectified that in 1908. The mighty Blues went through the season almost undefeated. They lost only one game, a mid-season thriller in atrociously boggy conditions. Their rivals that day, Essendon, pushed them hard in the Grand Final when a fierce wind ensured that conditions were again poor. Pompey Elliott's superb leadership was very evident as he stationed himself as a spare man in defence against the gale, moved his forwards closer to the midfield, and urged his defenders to stay staunch. They did, and Carlton held on to secure its third successive premiership.

Worrall and numerous observers were convinced that more premierships would follow. The team he had created had a significant edge over its rivals in talent, power and, with him as coach, tactical guidance. However, these perceptions were shattered in 1909. Some players wanted more money and were fed up with Worrall's autocratic discipline. Disgruntled players submitted a petition to the committee calling for Pompey Elliott to replace Worrall as coach. Teammates loyal to Worrall refused to sign. Worrall, sensing that the friction was intractable, resigned on 29 July, and the committee appointed Elliott as captain-coach. Although the team was good enough to keep winning, dissension and rancour plagued the club.

Pompey Elliott was now Carlton's most experienced player by far. He had the utmost respect from his teammates as a footballer and captain. But Worrall's masterly coaching was no easy act to follow, especially for someone who had never coached and, unlike Worrall, was still playing and had high personal standards to maintain on the field at the same time.

Still, the Blues sailed into the finals in excellent form. Six convincing victories in a row following Worrall's departure landed them in another Grand Final. Between them and a fourth flag was South Melbourne. It was a fierce contest. Scores were close throughout. Carlton was severely hampered by injuries. This was well before the introduction of bench players to come on as replacements, and for much of the match Carlton had only sixteen effective players. After a desperate struggle Elliott's Blues lost by two points. Although Carlton's injuries had obviously harmed its prospects, some pundits concluded that the strong favourites had also missed Worrall's tactical dexterity.

Elliott, bitterly disappointed, said he would retire, but he changed his mind and saddled up again. During the intervening summer there was further internal strife, which led to an extraordinary general meeting on 17 March 1910. Pompey Elliott addressed that meeting to inform the members of his grievances against Worrall. It was the start of yet another turbulent year for the Blues. Several key players, dismayed by Worrall's departure, had left the club. Elliott told those remaining that Carlton was still talented enough to do very well if they maintained their focus. They did. After fifteen rounds Carlton's solitary defeat had been by one point. Another premiership looked likely.

Sensational controversy intervened. For some time league football had been tarnished by the twin evils of on-field thuggery and alleged off-field corruption. Media hysteria about the violence produced erratic, disproportionate disqualifications. Carlton forward George Topping, who had a reputation as a talented and fair player, was reported on a striking charge after coming to the rescue of a besieged teammate during a fierce 1910 contest against South Melbourne, and for this solitary offence was suspended for two years. Harder to deal with were the persistent and sinister corruption rumours.

These murky insinuations surfaced dramatically just before Carlton's semi-final clash with South Melbourne. Blues stalwarts Bongo Lang and Doug Gillespie, together with dashing young forward Doug Fraser, were all late withdrawals from the Blues side after arriving at the ground ready to play. Lang protested. Rod McGregor declared that if they weren't playing he wouldn't be either. Amid consternation in the Carlton rooms, Elliott told his stunned players that the omitted trio had apparently been bribed to sell out their mates. The allegations were not yet proven and would be carefully investigated, but in the meantime the Blues could not risk selecting anyone whose commitment might be questionable.

Information that some Carlton players had been implicated in corruption had been passed to the club committee. The committee satisfied itself that these suggestions did seem to have substance, and decided to clandestinely pursue evidence that would incriminate the perpetrators. Long afterwards Elliott told one of his grand-daughters that Carlton officials had directed him to go to a certain restaurant on a certain evening, and told him that if he went inside and hid behind a particular Chinese screen he would hear things. He went, and he did hear things, things that influenced him to make those late changes.

These sensational developments disrupted Carlton's finals campaign. Elliott and his players prepared for the Grand Final amid swirling allegations, searching inquiries and blaring headlines. Pompey urged his players to focus on the imminent battle against Collingwood, but team morale and cohesion had been undermined. It proved to be one of the most controversial and notoriously vicious Grand Finals. Carlton lost narrowly. After the corruption inquiries, Lang and Fraser were suspended for five years, while Gillespie was exonerated.

So Carlton had played in five successive Grand Finals, losing the last two narrowly under captain-coach Pompey Elliott. He had played a key role in two premierships and suspension had unjustly deprived him of a third; it could easily have been five in a row. In 1911 Carlton was again a premiership contender, but lost a crucial final to Essendon, now coached by the legendary Worrall, who not only guided his new club to a flag but repeated this feat in 1912.

After the 1911 season Pompey Elliott decided to retire. A champion player, an outstanding leader and a VFL legend, he had played 197 games for the Blues. He should surely have been selected in Carlton's Team of the [20th] Century. Including his Melbourne matches in 1899, he had become the first footballer to play 200 league matches. He had shown striking durability over a long period in the centre of the action. Elliott's evidently enviable ability to carry injuries had helped, but he was now 33 and not getting any younger.

Adjusting to retirement was not easy. Elliott was persuaded to play briefly in the VFA, and a busy family life eased the adjustment. He had married Florence Windsor, an award-winning singer, and they had three daughters. The first, Marjorie, had been born a few weeks before Fred led Carlton to the 1908 premiership.

Elliott's fame was indirectly revived after Australians rushed to enlist for service in the Great War. Enlisters from Carlton comprised a company in the 7th Battalion led by a charismatic commander, Harold Elliott. During training in Egypt, before the landing at Gallipoli, some of his men conferred the Carlton champion's nickname on their colourful colonel and started calling him 'Pompey' Elliott. It stuck. By the end of the war this military Pompey Elliott had become a household name as Australia's most famous fighting general, more celebrated even than Pompey Elliott the footballer.

Fred Elliott's life by then had been tragically transformed. He had enlisted early in 1916. The enlistment form described him as a 37-year-old Carlton-born timber-stacker with grey eyes and thinning brown hair that was turning grey. (Previously, while playing for Carlton, he had been employed as a slater.) He began the customary weeks of pre-departure military training, as many prominent sporting identities had done before him.

But something went terribly wrong. It is unclear what. Perhaps he simply could not adjust to military life. Perhaps a vindictive superior decided to make the life of the formerly famous Private Elliott a misery. Some relatives have speculated that he may have been pressured to enlist by the receipt of white feathers. 'I have no idea how a man could kill another mother's son,' a grand-daughter remembers Fred saying decades later.

By late April 1916 Elliot was drinking heavily. He started to complain that he was being persecuted. He was hearing abusive voices and buzzing noises in his head. Fred was a gentle, affectionate father, but in this disturbed state his daughters meant nothing to him. Doctors later concluded that he was suffering from delusions triggered by the stress of being on military service.

He kept drinking. His hallucinations grew worse. It all became too much. On the first day of May he cut his throat. Help materialised in time, and doctors were able to repair his throat. But after this incident there was no place for him in the army, and the medical authorities assessed him as too disturbed for civilian life as well. Fred was admitted to the Lunatic Asylum in Kew. He remained there for decades.

The Elliotts still owed money on their family home in Moonee Ponds when he was admitted to the asylum. The Carlton Football Club quietly donated what was owing. It was reported in 1922 that an appeal had been established for the wife and family of the former Carlton champion, who was described as 'gravely ill'. The VFL itself made a notable contribution. Apart from this modest publicity intended to maximise donations, the newspapers were apparently silent about Elliott's real situation.

'The whole family was never the same after Fred's breakdown,' his grand-daughter concluded. Florence reacted to the news of her husband's attempted suicide with such hysterical screaming that her beautiful singing voice was never the same again, and that terrible night's screaming left their eldest daughter, Marjorie, with an enduring nervous condition.

Florence did not visit Fred in the asylum, and when he was at last released, he lived in a bungalow at the rear of the matrimonial home. Marjorie eventually feuded with her sisters, left her daughter Peggy, then 15, and moved to Mount Gambier with the new man in her life.

Fred would collect Peggy at her workplace and walk her to and from her nearby grandparents' home each day for lunch. His grandchildren remember him as a shy, polite, kind, supportive and well-dressed gentleman who read prolifically, enjoyed gardening and walked long distances, especially to watch Carlton play. Around his neck was a collar-shaped scar like a bracelet.

Honourable to the last, Fred kept insisting, even on his deathbed, that his 1907 suspension had been unjustified.

Ross McMullin is a Melbourne historian. His most recent book is his biography of General Harold 'Pompey' Elliott (2002). His other books include *Will Dyson*, and *The Light on the Hill*.

4

DAVE MCNAMARA AND THE LIONS OF HIS DAY

by Dave McNamara
with an introduction by Garrie Hutchinson

Introduction

Dave McNamara, if he is remembered at all today, is remembered as one of the longest kickers football has ever produced. Many who know nothing of his career will recognise the oft-reproduced photograph of McNamara mid-kick that sublimely captures the powerful grace of our game.

The greatest 'kickist' of his age, McNamara had first played for St Kilda between 1905 and 1909, kicking four goals from five on debut for an unexpected Saints win, and helping propel his side to the VFL finals for their first time, in 1907. He was the champion of the 1908 Jubilee carnival for Victoria, but football was as fractious in the early years of the twentieth century as it has been ever since, and McNamara fell out with the club in the middle of 1909 and crossed to the Essendon VFA team, Essendon Association.

McNamara was a class above everyone in the VFA. He played in Essendon Association's 1911 and 1912 premiership teams and kicked eighty-one and 107 goals in those seasons, becoming the first player to kick over a hundred goals in senior football. In one match for Essendon, he kicked eighteen goals from centre half-forward.

By the time the champion goalkicker had been forgiven by St Kilda, it was 1913, and he was wanted as captain-coach, but the VFL wouldn't grant him a clearance. He was forced to stand out of football for the

1913 season. He would surely have won the Saints their first premiership had he played – they lost the 1913 Grand Final to Fitzroy by thirteen points.

Early in 1914, a columnist named 'Oriel' wrote the following in the Melbourne daily the *Argus*:

All is well now. Dave McNamara, after a long struggle, which every section of the world not living in heathen blindness has followed with breathless interest, has secured a permit from the Association to play football with St Kilda. As soon as the permit was granted, rain fell and the farmers became jubilant once more. 'Oriel' may not take some passing interest in the Home Rule question – until the football season opens, at any rate, but it is difficult to arouse much enthusiasm in that struggle after the McNamara affair, and a settlement is sure to be arrived at in a day or two when the news of the satisfactory solution of the great Australian Football Problem is digested in the House of Commons.

Very soon we may expect to see Lord Roberts and Major McInerney, each wearing St Kilda's colours, shaking hands and swearing eternal friendship. Those foolish fellows the State Premiers, it is true, still sit in conference. Mr Agar Wynne as president of the St Kilda Football Club should certainly break the news to his brother Ministers, Federal and State. All Mr Wynne need announce to the conference is 'Don't argue, old fellows it is all right; St Kilda has got that permit for Dave McNamara.' After a minute or two of impressive silence the conference would quietly break up, and the visiting Ministers, with all their problems packed away in their portfolios, would unostentatiously depart to their respective States. A champion footballer has got his rights at last so what need is there to bother about State rights? And, anyhow, what is the question of the hour? Not Home Rule, the double dissolution, State debts, the Felton Bequest pictures, low necks, and split skirts. The question is, 'What chance St Kilda for the premiership?'

McNamara played from 1914 to 1923, except for the World War I years, 1916 and 1917, when the club didn't compete, and 1920 when he broke his leg. He kicked ten goals in 1922.

Usually a left-footed place kicker, McNamara was famed throughout his career as a tremendously long kicker of the football, though in later life he said he never did kick over a hundred yards. He beat the rugby league legend Dally Messenger in a long-kicking competition in Sydney in 1914, with a kick of eighty-nine yards, two feet, and claimed a world record, with a kick of ninety-three yards, at St Kilda in 1923.

But McNamara's abilities went beyond his almost freakish kicking ability, and he proved himself not only a match-winning player but an astute analyst of the game. During 1913, the year he stood out of football, he wrote a fascinating book with his thoughts on the game and its players, nominating the greatest players, the 'lions', of his day.

Dave McNamara and the Lions of His Day

First of all, let it be considered what the necessary qualifications are in obtaining the ability to play the game up to the standard demanded by the leading clubs of the day. A player must undergo a very thorough preparation before he enters the field.

Those unacquainted with the manner of sending out a team in good fettle have no idea of the careful attention that is bestowed on each man. Your footballer must be physically strong ere he tackles the game. It may be said, and with truth, that some very clever players of the present day are not so. 'Tis the exception, and not the rule. These men make good by original and brainy play that which is lacking in strength.

I am going to deal with the successful 'bailer' – the paragon of all those who desire to play the game as it should be played. All the leading clubs are fortunate in the possession of several such players – men who stand out of the 'ruck'. Strength, it will readily be admitted, is a valuable and most essential asset. Alone, however, it is of no avail. The following example will clearly prove this:

Place the Herculean Sandow on the football field and allow him ten minutes' strenuous work battling for the ball. He would need a rest, and would probably sit down and have one. It would be impossible for him, tower of strength though he be, to maintain the pace and dash which we are so accustomed to see and enjoy. Our footballer undergoes a special preparation, which enables him to withstand the strain for a much longer period than five minutes.

Alf Gough, the sturdy Essendon Association follower, is a worthy example of this. He is an exceptionally strong man, and in many a hard game he has battled and fought strenuously in the ruck for four quarters.

Certainly he would be tired at the finish, but not so distressed as to be unable to play another quarter should it be required of him. Gough would make Sandow look foolish on the football field, just as surely as would Sandow discomfort him on the wrestling stage.

Having undergone the necessary preparation, our man must assuredly possess the qualifications of a footballer. The game is not what it might appear to the uninitiated: that of a given number of strong and fleet-footed athletes striving for some end, without a well-defined purpose.

Strategy takes no small share in the prospects of a game. The opposing camps have mapped out their respective intentions, and each man playing is a component part of a well-designed plan. He is a capable footballer, but his prowess is of no avail should he elect the hazardous task of losing his place on the map in the endeavour to defeat the opposition 'on his own'.

As the application of brain power is of vast importance I propose to enlarge on this qualification by showing the various effects it produces.

The captain is the man who designs the plan, and has complete charge of it. He governs its method of attack and mode of defence. Such necessarily vary as the game alternates, and the good captain is always quick to remedy the faults which are apparent in any part of the field. To be successful he must have the team completely under control, and each man must know that it is his absolute duty to do exactly as instructed. Should the captain be wrong at times, it is just as necessary for him to be obeyed. The following example will show the reason for this obedience:

Supposing orders being carried out are proving ineffective, and various players notice it. Their ideas would, no doubt, be varied. What would be the result if each man acted on his own initiative? Pandemonium would prevail, such as happens – our women folk can tell – on the opening day of a big bargain sale. How difficult a matter then for the captain to get the team in hand again. It would not be so hard should the fault be in the one direction. But the result of the above mentioned fallacy would make for a very decided variety of faults. Instead of playing as a combination the side would be utilising as many plans as our Parliament in its proposition to build a Federal capital. Would success be achieved? It certainly would, as surely for a football side as for a Federal Parliament, if one plan be adopted, and all concerned are prepared to act in concert.

It would be appropriate to mention here an example of football generalship, and it is to Jack ('Dookie') McKenzie, my old friend and opponent, to whom I would refer. He is the cleverest and coolest captain it has ever been my lot to contend with. I have often played against him, and at times under his direction, and it has always given me pleasure and excited my admiration to study his tactics.

In important representative games in which I have had the honour to take part I have seen his influence as captain so exercised as to have absolutely dominated and won games which were apparently lost to us. I am speaking of the Interstate matches, in which we were opposed by South Australia.

These games, in which Victoria has been represented by both League and Association teams, have often provided very close and exciting finishes. I have discussed them with leading men of both sides, who have been convinced of McKenzie's cleverness. An almost certain defeat did not affect Dookie, who never gave in. He would quickly form a plan, instruct his men, and, setting the example himself, often left no doubt as to the result.

It will be noticed that in discussing captainship I have departed somewhat from the path laid down. The relation, however, is close, for the captain is the fountainhead, from whose source the players should drink, and, having drunk, made use of all the brain power at their disposal in bringing about any desired result.

It is evident, then, that the successful player must utilise all the forces he possesses in this direction.

One has only to watch the game closely to be convinced that the men who play best play 'with their heads'. How advantageous is it to be able to kick and 'mark' a ball well! Yet how many splendid footballers have we seen who are only moderate in these departments! An example of one or two will evidence this contention.

Jim Smith, of the St Kilda and Brighton clubs, was a very poor kickist, and only moderate at marking, but what an effective player he was! 'Hughie' James, the brilliant Richmondite, kicks very badly. He is one of the best followers at present playing our game. 'Billy' Payne, of the Essendon Association (or 'Lollylegs', as he was humorously termed), was a very poor exponent of the art of kicking; nevertheless he was a clever and capable player. Several others could be mentioned, but the examples given should suffice to emphasise the vast importance, of exercising one's brains to the utmost.

Having had a thorough preparation, and being also well forward in the tactics of the game, our footballer has other qualifications to achieve ere he reaches the front rank.

The manner of playing nowadays makes it a necessity for a player to possess 'dash' to be of good service to his side. Pace is not 'dash', as surely as 'dash' is not swearing. 'Dash' is the desirable thing acquired by acting on the very instant an opportunity arises. Having secured the advantage, it is naturally followed up and the desired objective gained. The advantage gained by the application of 'dash' gives for a player the very security his opponent loses by the non-application of this very salient feature.

Control of one's feelings is inseparable from success. The game is one of hard bumps and heavy falls, usually brought about in a fair and legitimate manner, much as may be said to the contrary. He who receives a fall and seeks revenge is not the man who is wanted on the football field. The game offers in this respect splendid opportunities for the young man to exercise self-restraint, and is a useful nursery for character building. You will notice that the man who takes good-naturedly all the knocks inseparable from the game is the most successful at it. Many a good footballer has cut short his career through inability to restrain his temper. On many occasions I have seen men capable of showing magnificent football lose splendid opportunities in endeavouring to get even with opponents who have happened to cause them heavy but perfectly fair falls. This desire to get even often succeeds, but in a very different manner to that anticipated. The powers that be do all the 'evening' that is required, and the miscreant finds himself on 'even' terms with the subscribing public – that of being permitted to look on for a very modest charge.

'Bert' Busbridge, the Essendon League champion, is a worthy example of what a player should be in this respect. He is universally admired for his fairness of play, though he is big and strong enough to roughly handle any man should he so desire. But, no; he conserves his strength for a better purpose. Never is he to be seen doing an unfair thing, or seeking redress upon a player who may have 'roughed' him. What a champion he has proved!

'Charlie' Hardy, the North Melbourne rover, is worthy of mention in this respect. Roving, as he often does, throughout a game, and receiving his full share of hard bumps and nasty falls, he never troubles about the man who caused them. The ball is his sole objective, and therein lies the success of a very capable footballer. The clever Essendon (Association) rover, Jack Hoare, is also a player of this class.

Courage is an indispensable factor. The player who goes right ahead, devoid of fear, in spite of solid opposition, possesses a wonderful asset.

How often has it been said of a player that 'he is afraid.' In some cases it may be right to say so; but in others, though appearances make for the belief, it is totally wrong. Some players go ahead without caring what harm befalls them; others do so only when it is necessary, but judiciously avoid trouble if by steering clear of it the purpose in hand is as readily effected.

George Topping, of Carlton, and 'Teddy' Kennedy, of the same club, may be instanced as examples. Topping is a wonderfully game and clever player, and, though small of stature, he is considered to be one of the best players of his class. He does not appear to know the meaning of fear, and takes all the risks, often paying the penalty.

'Teddy' Kennedy, the brilliant wing player of a few seasons back, adopted very different methods to those of his bold club-mate. He was as effective a player as one could desire to see, always on getting possession of the ball making the best use of it. In conversation he told me that

Dave McNamara launches a long distance left footer.

running into trouble did not appeal to him if he could effect his purpose as well by avoiding it. All football enthusiasts know how well he effected it. What a magnificent centre line was he a component part in, with George Bruce and Rod McGregor completing the line! The combination was in its best days very hard to beat. They were all players of the same nature avoiding trouble if it proved as profitable so to do. This principle is certainly the better, and for evident reasons. It serves to open out the play, which is at all times desirable; also to become incapacitated during the progress of a game is of no assistance to the player or his side.

Having dealt with the chief qualifications essential to the make-up of a footballer, let me summarise them: Strength, Brain-application, Obedience, Self-restraint and Courage. Some excellent footballers possess the majority of these attributes, but a combination of them all marks the champion. Systematic practice, of course, is imperative, as it is in all athletic pastimes.

It would be appropriate just here to list the names of some men who, in my opinion, have proved themselves lions in the game. Also my readers are invited to study the question, and see how far the aforesaid qualifications are embodied in the players named. The names of men still playing and of others recently retired are as follow:

Jim Sharpe, Fitzroy and Collingwood.

Henry Young, Geelong.

Charlie Ricketts, South Melbourne and Richmond.

Ernie Cameron, Essendon League.

J. [Jim] Marchbanks, Carlton.

'Mallee' Johnson, Carlton and North Melbourne.

['Vic'] Cumberland and [Victor] Barwick, St. Kilda.

Lindsay Maine, Essendon Association.

Dick Lee, Collingwood.

Fred Stancliffe, Brunswick.

[Frank] Langley, Melbourne.

The late Mick Grace, of Carlton.

These are in addition to the players previously mentioned. It will be noticed, also, that the men who have played the game as it should be played have remained in the arena for an exceptionally long period.

'The Lions of the Day' is extracted from Dave McNamara's 1914 book, 'Football'.

5

'UP THERE CAZZER!'

by Hec de Lacy

Back of beyond, back of the Barcoo, an Aboriginal stockman chased a buckjumper round a corral while his mate, Tommy, hung with knees and thighs to the heaving and pitching back of the untamed flea-bitten horse-flesh dynamo. Jerry chased him round and round, slapping the side of his leg with an old felt hat and yelling to urge the brute on: 'Up dere, Cazzer! Up dere, Cazzer! Don't know who dis plurry Cazzer is – up dere, up dere you plurry beaut!'

South of Hobart they cried with delight, 'Up there Cazzer!' West of Wyndham they took up the cry, 'Up there Cazaly', though it's pounds to peanuts plenty who used the phrase could not tell you who 'dis plurry Cazzer' was – flesh, fish or vegetable. To the colourful adaptability of the language of our people we gave the cry of the football partisan, and doing so we added lustre to the name and memory of one of our greatest footballers.

It all had its beginning round the football grounds of Melbourne – particularly on the South Melbourne ground, where the local-born Roy Cazaly answered the cry of encouragement from a thousand one-eyed Southern barrackers by flinging himself into the air, high above the opposition, to gather an amazing mark. 'Up there, Cazzer!' – the great Southerner, poised in the air, hung there as if his elbows were getting purchase for his hold on the air itself, then with a graceful bend forward he picked the ball off the outstretched fingers of the pack. The best was never good enough to check the brilliance or upset the uncanny judgement of this man, who seemed to be able to make the very air itself support his flying body.

'Up there Cazzer!' they yelled – the rucks rose for the throw-in. There was a clever turn in mid air. A little man with his stockings over his boots moved like a flash to accept the gift ball from the follower and South Melbourne's fortunes sped on. Do you remember them – Roy Cazaly and his rover, Mark Tandy, with the burly frame of Fred Fleiter to barge a way for 'Cazzer' to work? These three formed one of our most famous rucks.

Today, Roy Cazaly plays the greater, if less spectacular, role of coach, and just how capably he does it is reflected in the performances of the young Camberwell side, who a fortnight back beat Williamstown in their great struggle to make the Association finals. If I wanted a young football side to be developed in all the fundamentals of winning football – if I wanted them taught how a great game should be honoured in the playing – I would get Roy Cazaly and persuade him to handle the batch of colts.

With one exception – an unfortunate three years at South – Cazaly has had a most outstanding success as a coach. It is my opinion that at South Melbourne Cazaly was hindered rather than helped by people who believed they knew more about how a football team should be handled than did even this great player with nearly thirty years' experience in football and coaching. Even today, I see in the South Melbourne ranks players who have Cazaly to thank for the remarkable improvement in their play.

I have always been a firm believer that the coach of the side should be the team manager and sole selector of the side. He should not have his plans and his ideas overruled by the vote of a committee. If I were asked to support my idea, I would use the example of Cazaly at South Melbourne as one of my strongest arguments. However, the work that Cazaly has done in a single season at Camberwell has answered his critics at South.

It was as a coach I first came into direct contact with Cazaly. After a period in Tasmania he had returned to Melbourne to take charge of Preston, then very inconsistent. One day they turned on brilliant football: the next they were scarcely able to provide opposition.

After watching them for some weeks, Cazaly sacked half the team and amazed the critics by taking the field with a lot of boys gathered from the local paddocks. I was among those who sniffed, 'What does this fellow think he is at?' Seeking him out at Preston, I put it bluntly to him that if the experiment failed he and the 'bird' would become very close friends.

'I'll take a chance,' he said. 'I've got eighteen fighters behind me now – not one of these kids cares whether he is playing on the Preston ground or away from home. He'll go down fighting. I can do something with kids like that.'

He had to win some thirteen matches straight to win the premiership. He won twelve of them – a dozen brilliant odds-against victories with youngsters who were mere tyros yet were fighting it out like seasoned players. He went down finally to Northcote – an experienced team built on half a dozen league champions – on a blustery north wind day – just the one day in a score that would upset a team of inexperienced juniors and suit the veterans. Watching the rise of that young Preston team, I saw many things that caused me to admire the great qualities of this foot-baller. I knew why he was a champion, even though in those days he was not the player he formerly was.

Many a callous old head started the day's proceedings against a Cazaly fledgling by giving the youngster a belt or two to put him off his game. Immediately the first blow was struck, that youngster got a temporary move and Cazaly took over the 'whacker'. Before many minutes, it was the bully who was calling for the trainers. I recall a game at Preston when a big follower stood off and threw a punch at a clever little wingman. Cazaly left the forward line, ran the big fellow to earth, spun him round and with his open hand smacked him across the face. While this was going on, another player, a former league man, ran up from behind, gave Cazaly a rabbit-killer and dropped him.

He was up in a split second.

The ball was kicked into a bunch, in which Cazaly and his assailant were principals. Despite my closest watch, all I can report is that Cazaly came away with the ball, loping in that long striding way he had, while the assailant had his tongue hanging out over his cheek and was evidently seized suddenly with some form of violent spasm. The rough stuff was stopped in a trice.

With the opposition trying to play real football, Preston triumphed. So in other games, Cazaly let no man deal with his colts. He literally took on all the bullies – not in the crude bash and wallop ways of a street fighter, but quietly, unobtrusively – yet very effectively. I asked Cazaly regarding this phase of football, Did he agree with it? Did he condone rough play? 'No, I don't. I never will' – he was quite definite on the point – 'But years of experience in all grades taught me that the fellow who wants to win by bashing your best players is, in the show-down, chicken-hearted':

I came into the league at 15 – a big lump of a kid of twelve stone – but nevertheless a butt for everyone who thought the best way to beat me was to bash me. I soon came to the conclusion that most of these fellows were curs underneath, and were only punching and kicking because they were lacking confidence in their own football.

I can say I never once hit a man in a game of football without he thoroughly deserved it. But I did find out – early – that the best protection a young player, or any player, had from these bashers was to give them a real good one back soon after they started the rough stuff, and adding a little advice like 'There is one or two more where that came from if you are still feeling the same about knock-ing me.' Never once did these tactics fail to stop a rough house.

In one league game, a chap chased me all day, and finally cut open my eye. When I returned to the field with my eye stitched and started to give him a bit back, he lay down on the grass without being hit. Just fancy: without even being hit! There are plenty of fellows in the game today who will tell you that story.

Cazaly, therefore, was a colourful player. He survived among a race of hard players because he had skilled himself to be hard along with the hard. He matched an electric mind, a sense of split-second imagination, against the more obvious tactics of the roughneck, that misguided fellow who considers that his prime role in football is to punish the more skilful into submission.

Punishment never took the edge from Cazaly's efficiency because he snapped off the threats of the bully like the head of a ripe carrot.

Cazaly was born at Albert Park in 1893. He began his football with the local school team, graduated through junior teams until he got his big chance with St Kida at the very young age of 16. He did not want to play with St Kilda, and he certainly did not want to play with South Mel-bourne. He says that he always had a soft spot for Carlton, and that it was his ambition as a kid to play for the Blues. In fact, he joined Carlton's second eighteen, but sustained a bad shoulder injury. Because of some oversight, he did not receive the attention he expected, and he left Carlton rather disappointed.

His chance came at St Kilda. He jumped into the team. Despite his tender years, they played him in a man's role – follower and half-forward. He stayed at St Kilda for eleven years, during which period he became captain of the first eighteen. However, in 1920, internal troubles had St Kilda in their grip. Cazaly, tired of the wrangling, asked for a permit to play with Carlton. However, under the league district football scheme, he

Roy Cazaly shows Laurie Nash how to hold a footy.

was prevented from doing so. St Kilda wanted Cyril Gambetta, on whom South had a hold, so it was fixed up to switch Cazaly for Gambetta. Sid Campion was largely responsible for his appearance with South.

Cazaly played like a champion during 1921, '22, '23 and '24, gradually building up the great ruck force that stimulated the side. In 1926 he crossed to Minyip as playing coach, but for the two years following he was back again with South, and the cry 'Up there, Cazzer' again echoed and re-echoed.

About this time, City club, Launceston, asked certain football officials in Melbourne to find them a man who could mix in with a rather difficult personnel, inspire them and lead them to a premiership. City badly wanted a premiership. This small committee decided that Cazaly was the man. He went across and became as famous a figure in Tasmanian football as he had been in Victoria.

He stayed at Launceston for three seasons, and City won two of the three premierships contested. The North, under the leadership of Cazaly, triumphed over the South – and that means quite a lot in Tasmania.

In 1931, he returned to coach Preston, and I have related something of his experiences there. The following year he returned to Tasmania, this time to Hobart, where he led North Hobart for two seasons, in one of which they were premiers, beating Canenore, led by Albert Collier, in the Grand Final. Then he transferred to New Town, and led them to their first premiership in fifteen years.

After two years at New Town he was invited to coach Fitzroy. However, South Melbourne had prior claims on his services, and he was forced to reject the Fitzroy offer. The next three years at South were among the unhappiest of Cazaly's career.

Cazaly had some remarkable experiences in the game. He told his story four years back in these columns [in the *Sporting Globe*] and it made such colourful reading and provoked such keen discussion that some accused him of drawing the long bow. These people can be assured that everything Cazaly said in his articles was confirmed at a later date, by people associated with an incident, writing to the office supporting the story.

For example, he told the story of how early in his career at St Kilda he and Vic Cumberland exchanged blows, even though Cazaly was a kid and Cumberland a grown man. When the story was told I received letters saying that Cazaly as a kid would not have stood two seconds against Cumberland. I was reading these letters when a visitor called with two members of the South African rugby team. He wanted to see a picture of Dave McNamara kicking. He had told the South Africans about McNamara's kicking, he said, and wanted to show them his action.

I got the picture, and in course of conversation he said how much he was enjoying Cazaly's articles. 'Do you know, that story he told about himself and Cumberland fighting at practice brought back happy memories to me,' he said.

'You are a Victorian, then?' I asked.

'Victorian? Of course I am. I was St Kilda's fullback in those days, and I helped to hold that young kid away from Cumberland. He was fighting mad.'

It was Wally Grant, who was fullback for St Kilda for many years, but had been resident in South Africa for some time. I introduced him to Cazaly again and they spent the rest of the afternoon yarning over old times. So with every incident Cazaly related.

Cazaly was a member of the Victorian Carnival team that visited Perth in 1921, and was again in the Victorian side in that much discussed roughhouse match at Hobart in 1924, when Victoria just beat the Westerners.

Yet Cazaly has the greatest admiration for the football of Cumberland. 'He was the perfect physique of a man', he told me this week, 'and taught me all I knew about ruck work. Cumberland never wasted the ball and always passed it on to a teammate. He was a big man and a big-hearted footballer – one of the greatest the game has produced.'

When Cazaly was learning the game, he jumped week in and week out after a ball swinging on a piece of elastic. He learnt how to swing himself in the air to meet its varied flights. Going home through the park at night, he would run slap up against a tree trunk, turning or swinging at the last minute to avert crashing into the trunk. His skill in avoiding opponents was perfected by those tree trunks. He perfected his kicking. He worked for his success.

To back up his football, Cazaly has some telling philosophies. Chief among these is one I will never forget – A man is only as game as he is fit. How true it is – the confidence of physical fitness.

For his own part, Cazaly neither smoked nor drank alcohol. He was something of a faddist in his eating. He banned the frying pan. He would not eat a fry to please anyone. He took the most extraordinary care of his body, particularly his feet: 'If you want to know when a man is washed up, watch his feet,' he said, 'If he can't lift his feet, he can't lift his game – his heart might still be willing, but his best will be second-rate.' He never played a game of football, or for that matter, took part in any sport, without at its conclusion carefully bathing his feet in a saline bath and thoroughly massaging them. Few Victorians know that in Tasmania Roy Cazaly is a registered masseur, and practiced there for many years.

Of Roy Cazaly I can only say this: If I wanted a boy of mine to be taught the finest points of football and to be set the example of manly bearing in a hard, relentless game like football, I would not hesitate to ask Roy to handle him. I know that any boy would be the better for the example and instruction of this man.

Hec de Lacy was a leading sportswriter in the 1930s and 1940s, especially in the *Sporting Globe*, where his match reports reinvented the formula.

'Up there, Cazzer!' first appeared in the *Sporting Globe* in 1943.

GREATS from the Classic era

For almost twenty years, during the ’50s and ’60s,
football was dominated by two players – Ted Whitten Snr,
and Ronald Dale Barassi. For a time they vied for the
moniker 'Mr Football', and if opinions varied over which
of them deserved it more, certainly no-one else ever
challenged for the title. Along with other greats
from that era – Graham 'Polly' Farmer, Kevin Murray,
Darrel Baldock – they transformed the game, brought
it to eager TV audiences across the country,
and inspired football fans everywhere.

6

TWICE THE VALUE
Collingwood's Coventry Brothers

by Michael Roberts

Gordon Coventry

There are many images one can conjure up of the league's second-greatest goalkicker, Gordon Coventry. But that of a nerve-ridden, insecure young man unsure of his ability and too afraid to try his luck in the big time is not likely to be among them. Yet that is just the picture the burly Coventry set as he stood at Victoria Park station on his first night of training at Collingwood. Indeed, had the train service to Diamond Creek been a little more frequent, the chances are that Gordon might never have donned a Collingwood guernsey.

Gordon – or 'Nuts', as he was known to his family, apparently because he had a disproportionately large head as a child – had been playing since age 13 with Diamond Creek, as a centre half-forward in the Heidelberg competition. In August of 1920, when Diamond Creek played off unsuccessfully for the premiership, Gordon Coventry began to prepare himself for another summer on his parents' orchard, dominated by more cricket and more tennis. But the next day Collingwood officials Ern Copeland, Jack Joyce and Jack Peppard were on his doorstep; his excellent game in a losing side had so impressed a Magpie scout that he was asked to train the following Tuesday and promised a game the next Saturday – in the Collingwood seniors.

Coventry duly turned up on Tuesday afternoon but was rapidly becoming a nervous wreck. The youngest of the seven Coventry brothers was halfway down the ramp that led from the train station to the football ground when he was overcome with stage fright, turned around and went back. He sat on the platform for some ten minutes, mulling over his decision, and admitted later that if a train had come along during that period he would have got on it.

In the end, the deciding factor was the fear of the ribbing he would get from his brothers at home if he 'piked' it. 'I decided I would sooner face what was in store for me at Collingwood than go home and tell my brothers that I was too nervous to enter the dressing room,' he wrote in the *Sporting Globe* some years later. Thank heavens for a little bit of sibling pressure.

Gordon's early experiences at Collingwood did little to make him believe he had made the right choice. In fact his first training night actually convinced him he had made the wrong choice. Coventry could mark and kick but not much else. He was slow, awkward and cumbersome. He spent the whole night watching players do things he could not, such as blind turning and left-foot kicking, and returned home thoroughly demoralised.

Nevertheless, and much to his amazement, he was chosen at centre half-forward for that Saturday's game against St Kilda. Unfortunately he fared even worse there than he had at training. The nerves took hold of him again and he managed only one kick. The following week's *Football Record* said Coventry appeared 'stage frightened' and did not shine. Coventry was a little more harsh on himself. 'I saw hundreds of lads having their first League games thereafter, but none was so inglorious as mine,' he wrote.

Coventry was dropped for the next game, but was asked to continue training. He actually told secretary Copeland that he felt he was out of his depth, but Copeland did not listen. Much to Coventry's bemusement, he was back in the team for the last home-and-away game of the season. By this stage he thought the selectors were 'barmy', but managed to kick three goals anyway.

If Coventry was amazed to be selected in his first game and bemused to be chosen for a second, he was simply shocked when chosen for his third – a final. 'To be candid, I did not want to be selected,' he wrote. 'I felt that the task would be beyond me.' This time Coventry was even more nervous than he had been in his first game, but the match against Fitzroy was played in a quagmire and Coventry went home disappointed with the standard. After his next game he went home determined to give league football away.

Gordon Coventry, 1299 career goals.

The game was against Carlton, and Coventry, this time less troubled by his nerves, kicked five goals. The trouble was that for each goal he kicked he also lost a tooth. Coventry took a hell of a hammering that day, mostly from Paddy O'Brien, and was so sick and sorry for himself by the end of it that he did not want to know about league football. His parents initially supported him in his disaffection, but the lure of an invitation to play in the Grand Final was too much. Despite his doubts, despite his nerves and despite his bruises, Gordon Coventry was hooked.

With those doubts gradually overcome, Coventry set off on one of the greatest careers of any player to have taken the field in VFL football. He was not an immediate success, and took some years to firmly establish himself, but his ultimate record was staggering. It is now almost too well known to bear repeating, but the sheer magnitude of his achievements makes it impossible to ignore.

His career total of 306 games stood as the highest by any Collingwood player until it was eclipsed by Tony Shaw in the mid 1990s, and he was the first VFL player to reach the 300-game milestone. He kicked 1299 goals in his league career – a record that stood for more than sixty years until broken by Tony Lockett. He was the first man to kick a hundred goals in a season and achieved this four times. He kicked a hundred goals against every VFL team bar one. He kicked fifty or more goals in a record thirteen consecutive seasons. He was the VFL's leading goalkicker six times; Collingwood's leading goalkicker sixteen times. He was the Copeland

Gordon Coventry: he used one pair of boots over his whole spectacular career.

trophy winner in 1933. An interstate representative on twenty-five occasions, he kicked a hundred goals in interstate games. He kicked a record 111 goals in finals games. His two highest individual match tallies, seventeen and sixteen, were both records at the time and earned him £50 'rewards' from John Wren, who considered Coventry his favourite player.

Given his reluctant, doubt-ridden start to life as a VFL footballer, it is clear that Coventry's was not a career based on brash self-confidence and unshakeable belief in his own ability. Rather, it was built around a strong physique, a vice-like pair of hands, superb judgement, a steely determination and a great Collingwood team, into which he fitted perfectly.

Coventry's play bore little resemblance to that of either his predecessor in the full-forward post (Dick Lee) or his successor (Ron Todd). He did not possess the artistry or ability of the former, nor the leap and agility of the latter. Where Lee and Todd were spectacular, Coventry was solid and workmanlike. He was neither fast nor brilliant, but he kept on kicking goals – most of them, remarkably, with the one old pair of boots that he would neither polish nor replace.

Coventry was a large man with strong, square features. He had a determined mouth and a jaw that looked like it had been set in concrete. So stern was his countenance that once he was taken in by police in Sydney, who thought he was a wanted criminal. He stood just on 183cm (6ft) and weighed about 83kg (13st 1lb), with huge shoulders, a big rump and massive hands. One critic wrote that Coventry was like a rock: 'No man ever ran into Gordon Coventry without hurting himself.' He was a master at out-positioning defenders, who often found themselves with virtually no way of getting to the ball around his enormous frame.

Richmond's highly rated fullback, Donald Don, once said in the *Sporting Globe*:

> Once Coventry gets in front of you it is very hard to pass him with his ungainly run, his body wobbling and his arms and legs sprawling. He is also a very hard man to mark against. He has the knack of fending you off. And when his hands close on the ball it stays put, locked in a grip of steel.

Wal Lee, Collingwood's veteran trainer, said Coventry had one of the hardest bodies to unbalance he had ever seen. 'He could take a buffeting and seldom be knocked off his feet,' he said. 'And once the ball hit those hands of his that was it – it was all over.'

Coventry's use of the body was one of the outstanding features of his play. He did not always use it to kick goals himself. He became very adept at simply blocking defenders out of the play, thereby allowing one of Collingwood's smaller brigade to nip in and score. Coventry was also one of the first players to develop the skill of marking the ball with his hands well in front of him. With his substantial rump stuck out and his arms extended he was a difficult man to counter – a little like Brian Taylor or Jason Dunstall at their best.

Coventry was neither quick nor mobile. He did not really need to be. H.A. (Hec) de Lacy, in the *Sporting Globe*, once described him as a flat-footed footballer who moved less distance either up or out than any forward he had seen. He rarely strayed far from goal, and Collingwood knew how to play to him. When he did leave the goal square he developed a jinking, stuttering sort of run that confused defenders. Combined with his uncanny positioning and immense body strength, this was usually enough to give him the space he needed. His judgement was so good that he usually did not have to run far. And, as Donald Don and Wal Lee have commented, once he got his hands near the ball it was 'good night'.

His kicking had always been outstanding; as a lad of 15 he could comfortably punt the ball about sixty yards (55m). In the best tradition of country footballers he could also do it bare foot – he hated wearing boots or shoes of any kind. When he came to Collingwood he became a better-balanced kick, which actually cost him a little yardage but improved his accuracy.

Despite his physical attributes and talents, Gordon struggled for quite a while in league football. The problem appears to have been psychological. He was really the archetypal country lad: quiet, shy, gentle, easy-going, laid-back to the point of almost comatose. He said little to teammates, even less to opponents. Nothing seemed to bother him much, and on the field his play clearly lacked devil. Early in his career this casual manner was often interpreted as indifference to the task at hand or a lack of determination. He developed a reputation for laziness, and critics frequently attacked him for poor, erratic or inconsistent play – often comparing him unfavourably with his brother Syd.

Gordon struggled to make a major impact, and by 1924 there were some beginning to doubt his ability to make it in the big time. Prior to that season he had accepted a coaching job in Tasmania, but wisely thought better of it later. Early in 1925 Gordon found himself dropped from the team and with his career at the crossroads. Fortunately, he returned with renewed determination, a few good performances boosted his confidence and his attitude was never again questioned.

Nevertheless, he remained very much a gentle giant. He frequently took a fearful hiding from opposition fullbacks but never retaliated. Well, almost never. The one time he did hit back prompted one of the most celebrated tribunal cases of all time. It was in 1936 against Richmond. Coventry played with a crop of painful boils on the back of his neck and, after repeatedly being struck on them, hit out at the Tiger defender responsible. Despite it being his first report in more than 280 games, he was harshly suspended for eight weeks – the remainder of the season. A public furore erupted, but the sentence stood.

Coventry subsequently apologised to Collingwood fans for 'forgetting my good manners' and retired. But he decided he did not want to leave the game on such a note, so returned for the 1937 season – when he kicked a total of seventy-two goals to win the league's goalkicking title for the sixth time. This was a more suitable note on which to retire and that he did, going off to coach in the amateurs and leaving the goalkicking to his protégé, Ron Todd.

Coventry left behind a staggering series of records. Yet he did it all with a humility and modesty rarely seen in football, let alone in one who has achieved so much. He was a warm, gentle man who was loved by all who knew him – a reaction that would have been the same had he never kicked a football in his life.

It was a sad day indeed at Victoria Park when Coventry died in 1968 – ironically, the same year in which Dick Lee passed on. The records he left secured his place in football history, because they stamp him as one of the greatest full-forwards of all time.

Syd Coventry

Over the years there have been almost as many ideas about what constitutes the perfect pre-match meal as there have been pre-match meals.

These days, with most clubs having dieticians to strictly control players' food and drink intake, it is a lot more scientific. But in the past players have been left to rely on a variety of ill-informed theories that were in effect little more than fads. Some recommended eating nothing at all, others said pasta or food drinks, still others suggested a hearty steak. None ever advocated eating a kilogram of chops and steaks for Saturday lunch. It is just a pity nobody ever mentioned that to Syd Coventry.

Once, fairly early in his career at Collingwood, Syd was 'batching it', his wife being in hospital. He invited brother Gordon around for lunch before a game. Syd always felt his wife served too light a lunch on Saturdays, and was determined to rectify the situation.

'We'll have a slap-up feed today, Nuts,' he assured Gordon. And so they did. A couple of hours, a pound of steak and a pound of pork chops later, Syd and Gordon took the field – to put in two of the worst games they ever played. They were sluggish, short of breath and completely ground-bound. By the time their digestive organs began functioning properly, Collingwood was too far behind to make up the difference.

Syd and Gordon were suitably ashamed, and any thoughts Syd might have had about a career as a dietician were cut short then and there. The episode is remarkable not just because of the sheer naivety (or should that be stupidity?) involved, but also because it has to be one of the rare occasions – perhaps the only one – on which Syd Coventry let Collingwood down. The club has had no better on-field leader in its history, and much of the club's success in the 1920s and 1930s can be attributed to his influence.

Syd joined the Club in 1922 and quickly established himself as one of the premier players in the competition. Although older than Gordon he joined two years later, and settled down much more quickly. Indeed Gordon, despite his two-year head start, was still trying to establish himself while Syd was winning acknowledgement as one of the best ruckmen and followers in the game. Syd was much more consistent than his brother, and he played with greater vigour and devil.

As a footballer, Syd was a near-complete unit. He stood only 180cm (5ft 11in) but weighed around 86kg (13st 8lb) and was magnificently proportioned. Initially tried in a variety of positions, it soon became clear that his greatest value lay in the ruck with spells in defence. In only his second season he was already recognised as a matchwinner and one of the strongest, most versatile and most talented big men in the game.

Syd had strength way above the average and threw himself into the most fearsome crushes with abandon. Gordon once said that one of Syd's greatest assets was that he knew how to use his weight more effectively than anyone else in the game – always fair and usually productive.

This was particularly so in the ruck, as one sportswriter in the *Sporting Globe* noted in 1927:

> He provides the strong, rugged work with a vengeance. Syd seems
> to be electrical in his movements and a mass of energy, unsparingly

throwing himself into the vigorous ruck work. Those strong shoulders of his are never idle, and he literally forges his way through anything. He takes some terribly hard knocks, but gives them back equally hard.

There were times when Syd carried the Collingwood ruck single-handedly, and it was most often left to him to slow up the big men of other sides. When following, Syd rarely crossed the half-forward line, preferring to wait behind the play and gather kicks around the centre of the ground. Teammates say he became a master at this, winning hundreds of kicks through his precise judgement of where opposition defences would direct the ball.

When the ball did come his way, the basics of his game rarely let him down. He was a magnificent high mark, with a good spring and splendid

Syd Coventry, Collingwood Captain was 'born to lead'.

anticipation. When the ball hit the ground he was not lost either, and was seldom beaten by other followers in a race for the ball. He was a long drop or punt kick, and was described as having 'the kicking power of a healthy horse'. Dick Lee was once moved to brand one of Syd's drop kicks at training the best he had ever seen. With such power, it is perhaps not surprising that Syd was not fond of short passing. His only obvious weakness was his left-foot kicking, which sometimes left a little to be desired. Such were his skills and his dominance of matches that, in 1927, he became the first Collingwood player to win the Brownlow medal.

But Syd Coventry's value to the team could never be measured in marks or kicks alone, or even through the hard work he did in the clinches. His inspiring leadership, which is next to impossible to quantify, was perhaps his most valuable quality. Gordon once said that Syd seemed 'born to lead' in football, so naturally did it come to him. Certainly, no man did more as a player and a leader to inspire those Collingwood teams. His determination, fearlessness and will to win frequently lifted the team to greater heights. 'A few words from him, if we were not shaping like winners, usually had the desired effect,' said one former teammate. 'He shepherded our small men in a manner that won him reverence and loyalty from all members of the team, and he never asked his men to do a job he wouldn't do himself.'

The power of Syd's leadership is well illustrated by the fact that the team won premierships in each of his first four years as captain, 1927–30. Victoria also fared well under his captaincy, not losing any of the many interstate matches for which he was in charge.

As Gordon pointed out, Syd's leadership qualities were evident from early in his football career. That career began at age 13 with the Diamond Creek team, where he was joined at different stages by most of his brothers. He played six years with Diamond Creek and captained the team. As many as six of the Coventry boys played with Diamond Creek at the same time, but both Gordon and Syd were convinced that the VFL never got to see the best footballer among the Coventrys; that honour they bestowed on another brother, Norman, who was killed in World War I.

The Coventry boys worked in the mines around Diamond Creek, and Syd spent two years in a similar job in Queenstown, Tasmania. While there he had been approached by several VFL clubs and signed with St Kilda, to play with them on his return. Gordon had started with Collingwood in his absence, and had told them about Syd. Fortunately the lure of brotherly love – together with the prohibitive distance from Diamond Creek to St Kilda – proved strong enough to have Syd renege on his contract with the Saints. St Kilda officials were justifiably peeved, and when the VFL's Permit Committee refused his application to play at Collingwood for the 1921 season he was forced to delay his entry to league football for a year, playing instead with Collingwood District.

Once he was ensconced at Collingwood, the lure of greener pastures occasionally tempted him away. Only the club's determination to keep him stopped those attempts from being successful. Prior to 1925, for example, he did pre-season training at Horsham and intended to captain-coach there.

A few years later Footscray tried unsuccessfully to get Coventry to the Western Oval, and a year after that he actually applied for the coaching job there. On each occasion, the club refused to clear him, and Coventry stayed.

Eventually Footscray was rewarded for its persistence when Coventry became its coach in 1935 – but only after a written agreement had been reached between the clubs that stipulated he would not be able to play. There was never any doubt, however, that Coventry was Collingwood to the core. His two years at Footscray were neither successful nor particularly happy and he came back to Victoria Park soon afterwards, acting as vice president from 1939 to '49, and as president from the turmoil of 1950 through to 1962.

Coventry's years in administration only served to reinforce his revered status at Collingwood. Although much livelier and apparently more alert than his laid-back brother, Syd shared Gordon's warmth and kindness. He had a delightful sense of humour and was regarded by most of his former colleagues as 'a truly great man'. He was also a truly great footballer. He played 227 games in thirteen seasons, captained Collingwood for eight seasons, won the Brownlow medal in 1927, the Copeland trophy in 1927 and 1932, represented Victoria on twenty-seven occasions – many of them as captain – and was widely acknowledged as one of the greatest players and leaders to have taken the field in VFL football.

Syd Coventry will always have a special place in Collingwood history. His achievements on the field ensured him an exalted place in the record books, while his outstanding personal characteristics ensured him a special place in Magpie hearts. Collingwood has had many champions throughout its history, but few are held in greater esteem than Syd Coventry.

Gordon and Syd Coventry, brothers in arms.

Michael Roberts is a Melbourne writer, editor and football historian with an addiction to Collingwood. His books include *A Century of the Best*, *Collingwood at Victoria Park* and *Heart of the Game*.

'Twice the value: Collingwood's Coventry Brothers' draws on earlier versions of the Coventry stories from *A Century of the Best*.

7

HAYDN BUNTON
Best and Fairest

by Jack Dyer

I got one of the biggest shocks of my football career during a game against Fitzroy in the early '30s.

If there has ever been a one-man team, it was Fitzroy in those days – and the man was the great Haydn Bunton senior. At that stage, with a couple of Brownlows under his belt, Bunton was the number one player in the league. He was one of the best ball-handlers I've seen, and it was sheer delight to watch him in action.

Brownlows are awarded to the Best and Fairest players, and it's no wonder he collected three. Although it's debatable whether he was the best player at that time or not – I certainly thought he was – there was no question about his fairness. Haydn Bunton is the fairest player the game has produced.

He was a true sportsman on and off the field. He just absorbed any knocks he received – and there were plenty of them. He never squealed and never showed he thought they were unfair. I only ever saw him hit back once. And that's when I received my great shock.

It was my job that day to take care of Bunton. If you beat Bunton you beat Fitzroy. Every coach in the league opened his remarks before a Fitzroy game saying: 'Only one player can beat you and that's Bunton. I want him under lock and key for the day.' So there it was. It was Captain Blood's job. But it wasn't only me who was pushing, pulling and shoving him. Every other Richmond player who got close enough did the same.

It was in a pack and I was making sure Haydn wasn't feeling as comfortable as he would have liked to be. And then it happened. That one second in his entire football career that he lost his cool. *Wham ...* My nose was flattened in a bloody mess. I was dreaming!

I didn't believe it. But there was no doubt the mighty blow came directly from Haydn Bunton's fist. I didn't complain, because the blow was fully deserved, but Haydn didn't do those things. Here I was, the big tough man, being dealt with right and proper by the biggest gentleman in the game. I just walked away shaking my head and feeling my nose.

Haydn had to put up with those same tactics every match, and as I said, I only saw him explode once. He was the target for every football charger in the business. Plenty of times he copped it and always with a delightful baulk or twist he would gracefully glide out of the way. I've seen opponents trying in sheer desperation to down him, but he had remarkable balance and always sidestepped out of trouble. He could make the most elegant footballers look like three-legged elephants. He was a true artist. With his long stride and athletic build, he was a joy to watch.

There have been very few footballers that have given as much to football as Haydn. He lived for the game. When the ball was bounced he knew nothing else; he gave his all. He could play at top speed all day and still be a champion at the finish. It was no wonder he was usually the most conspicuous player on the field.

His dominance was unbelievable. He knew where he stood and he let everyone know – and that was right on the front line, the number one player. He was the key to Fitzroy. He didn't tell them. He showed them how. Haydn could play a team almost on his own.

Fitzroy was not strong in that era, which meant a great call on his stamina. But he never relaxed in his concentration. You couldn't stop Bunton. He was too clever and he won enough votes to win three Brownlows.

Although he is one of the best players I have seen, I can never concede that he was the best player in the history of the game. But then again, I still don't think we found out how great he was. This is the tragedy of Bunton. He was a star in a feeble side. He shone like a beacon.

Even in the umpire department he had finesse. I remember him going up to an umpire after the Lions had been beaten by about twenty goals and saying: 'That was one of the finest umpiring performances I've seen.' No man's vanity could resist that. I'll bet he got four votes that day.

By 1937 Bunton was Victorian and Fitzroy captain and had served a term as Fitzroy captain-coach. After 117 VFL games and 205 goals, he switched to Subiaco, and set new standards for West Australian football.

He promptly won three Sandover medals in four years.

He reappeared briefly with Fitzroy in 1942 while in the army, and by 1945 was playing with Port Adelaide. He appeared in the first Grand Final of his senior career. Port lost. The next year he was a South Australian umpire, rated one of the best ever, but he retired in disgust after being passed over for a Grand Final. A coaching term with North Adelaide in 1947–48 finished his active interest in big football.

Bunton had his football triumphs, but also his share of tragedy in private life. Part of it centred around the childhood of Haydn junior, who was crippled for four years, from the age of seven, with a hip disease.

Haydn Bunton, triple Brownlow medallist.

It seemed he would never walk properly, let alone play football. But Haydn Bunton wouldn't have it. All his energy went into helping his son recover, which he did.

In 1954 life looked sweet. He was a top insurance salesman, and his son was making a big football name. But on Christmas Day, 1954, his wife died suddenly. Nine months later, he was fatally injured when his car ran off the road into a tree. He lingered some days and before he died told his son: 'Play the best you can on Saturday.'

When he died, his great rival and friend Dick Reynolds said: 'Bunton was a great footballer and a great man. He was the best ball-handler I ever saw.' This tribute came from a man who had played a record number of 320 VFL games, coached Essendon into the finals sixteen times, and produced four premiership sides.

Jack Dyer, former Richmond great, was a prolific writer and media figure on radio and television from the 1950s to the 1980s.

'Haydn Bunton: Best and Fairest' first appeared under Jack Dyer's byline in *Football Heroes*, 1975.

8

JACK DYER
1981, and going on with business

by Geoff Slattery

Ten years ago, when he was a football columnist with the *Truth*, Jack Dyer was called to give evidence in a Victorian Court. In the case, a defamation suit against the paper's boxing writer, 'The Count', the court was having difficulty finding out the defendant's identity.

Dyer took the stand. His police days helped him race through the oath; then he was asked the identity of 'The Count'.

'I don't know, sir,' he replied.

The court was flabbergasted.

'You mean you've worked there for so many years, and you don't know who a fellow writer is?' asked the counsel for the aggrieved party.

'Yes sir,' said Dyer.

'Well,' continued the barrister, 'who are some of those you work with?'

'Aaah,' said Dyer, 'there's Mopsy, and Pogo, and Bluey, and Big Steak and ...'

The judge cut him short. 'Mr Dyer,' he intervened, 'you are turning this hearing into a Roman Holiday.'

The phone rang for ages before the familiar voice answered: 'Dyer speaking.' We exchanged a few wisecracks before we got down to what Dyer likes to call 'business'. It was time for the Jack Dyer story to be reconsidered. After all, it was sixteen years since his life story, *Captain Blood*, had been published. And the legend is bigger than it's ever been. Dyer was momentarily taken aback. 'After all these years,' he said, 'someone wants to talk about me.' Then he laughed. Dyer can't be serious for long these days.

We began at South Vermont, where Dyer has been living for the past two years. Wide, quiet streets, rolling hills empty of life, big cars in big garages, brown bricks sitting in clay, and a day's march to the nearest pub. Dyer lives out here with his daughter Jill, son-in-law Warren and their three children. It couldn't be farther from Dyer's Richmond.

Two pairs of low-cut boots stand drying on the front porch, immediate evidence of the tradition continuing. A dedication dominates the flywire screen: 'Bless this house, Oh Lord we pray, make it safe by night and day.'

Again, a long wait before the door opens. Dyer never worries about haste or time. 'Hello-how-are-you-are-you-well?' he says. It's a typical Dyer greeting, covering the lot in one mouthful. Ten years earlier, when I met him for the first time, he used exactly the same words. And nothing else about Dyer had changed. Not the wide nose, big ears, grey sideburns supporting the brushed-back steel-grey hair, the kind eyes, the fast-moving mouth, the slow laugh, the delight in stories from the past.

Dyer was cleaning the potatoes, getting things ready for tea. It was strange to watch the vegetables treated so tenderly in those big, rough hands. But that's Dyer – the Captain Blood part of him started and finished on the football field.

The invitation to start from the beginning was all he needed. 'Right,' he said, 'right from the start – Yarra Junction State School.' Then came the Dyer definition of education in the '20s. Like most things Dyer says, nobody could put it better. 'Mum wanted us to go on, so she sent me to Richmond. Put me into St Ignatius's, to see if I could play football and cricket. Brother Peter was the sportsmaster. He took me straight down to Surrey Park and arranged a scratch match. He was very happy with the performance. We went on to win the premiership. He said he had only wanted a ruckman. After six months at St Igs, he was transferred to De La Salle, so he took me with him. He said, "We might as well go on with the business."' That last line sounded more like Dyer's than Brother Peter's.

Memories of schooldays for Dyer don't go much further than footy and fighting. Big wins and big losses, interspersed with tales of hiding college cap and blazer as he came home to Richmond, for fear of 'mobs waiting for you on the corner'. They were the Depression days and, whether he liked it or not, Dyer had to leave school after his Intermediate year to provide for the family. You get the impression it didn't worry him too much. 'I wasn't a bad scholar, but I lost interest,' he said.

It's probably fortunate that Dyer went into the workforce at 14. Had he taken the option of a scholarship to Xavier, and perhaps further, his great broadcasting lines would never have caused so much mirth for so many. It doesn't worry Dyer in the least that his quaint use of the English language – his so-called Dyerisms – create so much humour. Last year we took great delight in publishing quite a few lines from the man's broadcasts. Did he feel we were ridiculing him? Not at all. In a pub in North Melbourne last week he said: 'We were starting to slip away a bit. They put us back on the map.'

Dyer's amazing ability to slip the tongue has lasted as long as the man himself. He started on radio in 1952, three years after his retirement from the game, after much persuasion from Phil Gibbs, now sports director of Channel 10. 'He wasn't keen to do it,' said Gibbs:

He reckoned he couldn't speak on radio. So we finally convinced him to have a practice first. We went to a game at North Melbourne. Jack was terrible. Even then he had a language of his own. I'll never forget him saying: 'Pass the benicolars, Phil.' But we went back and listened to the tape, and despite it all, you could tell even then he had that quality about him.

Part of the deal with Gibbs was that he would teach Dyer the art of radio if Dyer would teach him the finer points of football. 'The lesson started at a social match at Keilor,' said Gibbs:

All the old stars were playing. Jack told me to play in the ruck with him. We were waiting for the first bounce and Jack said to me to take the knockout. Up I went, and I felt this whack across the ear. It nearly knocked me out. Dyer had hit me a beauty. I couldn't believe it. I said to him, 'What was that for?' He replied, 'Now you know what it feels like.' It was part of his teaching.

Dyer doesn't teach football with such fury these days, but according to Gibbs his radio style hasn't changed in those thirty years. 'He is certainly more confident, but nothing else about him is different'.

'More confident' is verging on gross understatement. Gibbs used to run a Saturday night football show called *Pelaco Inquest* in those days; naturally he wanted Dyer on the panel. Again Dyer resisted, saying he

Jack Dyer, media star with a language of his own.

couldn't possibly speak on a game for five minutes straight. The answer was simple. Immediately after the match 3KZ would send a typist to Dyer who would recount the story of his game. She would type it out 'in English' and, at 8 o'clock that night, Dyer would read it out on air. Twenty-five years later he was using the same methods to record his morning footy talks for 3KZ's breakfast show. (Despite the need for 'on air' scripts, Dyer is rated one of Melbourne's best after-dinner speakers.)

Of all his media activities – radio, TV, newspapers – Dyer prefers radio. 'It's just like playing the game,' he says, 'you're always with it, and you can abuse the umpire.' People listen to Dyer not for what he says about the football but for how he says it; some find him infuriating, most don't. Dyer's knowledge of football also causes debate. It's safe to say he knows more about players than about the modern game. 'Nothing new has happened in football,' he says, 'they are just a bit more polished. In the old days they all bounced the ball, and kicked it, and handpassed it. They thought just as quickly.'

What doesn't provoke debate is discussion of Dyer's football prowess. He is universally agreed to be a champion, in the real sense of the word. In the foreword to *Captain Blood*, the late Hec De Lacy, of the *Sporting Globe*, wrote of Dyer: 'Jack Dyer, Richmond's giant, was the greatest big man in Australian football. He stands supreme, he's the greatest of the great.' Not surprisingly, Dyer rarely polled in the Brownlow medal, although it is not generally recognised that he finished fourth (with seventeen votes) to Marcus Whelan (with twenty-three), in 1939. (Dyer was also a very good cricketer. Before football took over early in the '30s, he had scored a double century in the mid-week league. His most prized trophy is a cup that names him 'best all-round athlete' of St Ignatius.)

Dyer will be 68 in November. He is fit and strong, and looks years younger. There is no hint of the illness that, in the late '50s, had him close to death. He was more than 108 kilograms (17 stone) then – now he is under 83 kilograms (13 stone). He is in the fiftieth year of the sport he loves. 'The most satisfying thing in my life is to be able to have kept in football,' he admits, 'and the ultimate was life membership of the VFL.' Dyer puts that above his 311 games with the Tigers, and above the fact he played and coached the Tigers in premiership years.

There is more to Dyer's life than football, but it needs considerable prodding to get it out of him. Ask Dyer about football and he'll talk forever. Ask him about his family, his friends, his other life, and he just smiles, mumbles a few lines and then looks blankly at you, waiting for the next question. His wife of more than thirty years, Sybil, died ten years ago. His friends say her death left him flat. Says Dyer slowly: 'Everything was all nice until she died. Suddenly it was ...' His family kept him going. 'I'm pretty lucky,' he said, 'I've never had to live by myself.'

But it's plain that Dyer could not be happier with life. He is forever smiling, joking, always relaxed. He will talk to anyone about anything, and is forever confronted in pubs by people talking about football. He is never more content than when he is holding forth at the bar with friends or, more likely, drifting acquaintances. Dyer knows some by name, others by nicknames. Those who know him are always amused by his inability to remember names. The story of Dyer in court is no different when Dyer is at work, at the pub or in the street.

Every week Dyer makes the trip to Richmond for lunch at Craig McKellar's pub in Swan Street. It's there he picks up all the gossip, maintains the links. If it were up to him, he'd rather live in Richmond. 'But the kids love it out there,' he says. When he retires from the media round ('I'd like to stay in it forever, but the mind won't let you. The mind takes over') he'd be happy to 'get right out of town. A bit of shooting, a bit of fishing … beautiful …'

Dyer's closest friends remain the men of his playing days, men like Ted Rippon and Laurie Nash and Lou Richards, although Dyer says: 'Don't say that. He's my bread and butter,' and Richards says: 'You're writing about Jack. That'll take about three paragraphs.'

Dyer and Richards are the two who have kept TV's longest running programme, *World of Sport*, from tedium. Ron Casey, the show's compere and HSV-7's general manager, describes Dyer as 'the gentle humorist'. But there is nothing gentle about a battle of wits between Richards and Dyer after a Collingwood vs Richmond contest.

The popularity of the duo can be measured in the number of advertisements they do together, and the number they knock back. Richards says Dyer is 'the funniest bloke in the world to do advertisements with':

He's forever changing the script in midstream. We were doing an ad for a chainsaw, and I'm saying something like 'You use it with your partner,' and Jack's supposed to reply with: 'Is it any good for camping?' And lo and behold, he adds after camping 'and fishing'. I nearly fell through the floor. I had to ad lib to Jack's fishing line. I ended up saying 'Yes, it's great if you catch a whale, it really makes the filleting easy.' The funny thing is, whenever he throws in these lines, the ad is always much better.

Casey is another at *World of Sport* with undisguised affection for Dyer. 'Every year,' says Casey, 'at the end of the football season, Jack says he's got to have holidays. He says he's suffering "industrial fatigue".' Casey never says no, and so Dyer goes for his annual holidays, fishing at Bemm River, through Albury, up to Queensland.

One year, Casey recalls, he wanted Dyer to do some promotion for Channel Seven:

> He wasn't on the phone, so I sent an urgent telegram to ask him to come to the studio. We received no reply, so I sent another. Still no answer, so in the end I went over to his house in Richmond. I knocked on the door, hardly knowing what to expect, and Jack answered. Behind him, on the mantel, I could see the telegrams – unopened.
>
> I said to him: 'Jack, I sent you those urgent telegrams, why didn't you open them?' Straight away he replied: 'Oooh, I never open urgent telegrams, you never know what might be in them.'

Most of Dyer's stories have been heard or read before. One he told me on Tuesday seemed a new one:

> We were playing out at Carlton, and I had to catch the train to the ground. You had to in those days. I only had a deener, and I caught the train out there. Then I looked out the window, and I couldn't see any houses. I thought 'This is not Carlton.' Eventually the train stopped at Reservoir. I didn't know what to do. Eventually a bloke put me on the right one, and I arrived just in time.

On to the field he went, getting into the game:

> I was so riled up, I had a lovely time. Blokes were going down everywhere [despite the nonsense, Dyer appears to have a genuine delight in recounting stories of on-field violence]. Anyway, we won easily, and I've left the ground feeling marvellous. On the train again – and you wouldn't believe it – the carriage was full of Carlton supporters. They never stopped abusing me – kids, old ladies, the works. One bloke said to me: 'You must have eaten your babies, Dyer.' I said to him: 'Me. I'm gentle. I go to church on Sundays.' The train stopped. I was out like a shot, and into the next carriage. It was full of Richmond supporters. The rest of the trip home was lovely.

No story on Dyer would be complete without a few of his lines: The following come from his account of the 1978 Grand Final between Hawthorn and North Melbourne:

On the kickout, it's out towards the wing position, the pack fly
again, over the top of the pack and a good mark has been taken
here. It looks like … it is … Cowton with the ball. He immediately
handballs it in the air, away they go as Henshaw comes down the
ground. He's going for the short pass. It's not a good one at all.
It's punched away by Martella [*sic*]. Another punch up in the air.
In goes Demper … dipter … ier … domenico … in after it again.

And:

Up they go in the air, it goes over the top of the pack and the mark
has been taken. Here's a handball going across, gets it across to
Moore, Moore has one bounce, two bounces, comes right up the
field. He's looking for a kick here to Ablett, Ablett makes position
beautifully too, and he's got the ball Ablett, right on the wing
position again, here's the kick by Ablett, sending it right up. He's
getting pushed out of the road, Moncrieff again. It goes down to
the ground. In they go in after it. A chance for a handpass, gets it
across to Russo, Russo lines 'em up, kicks into the man coming
towards him. Knights comes in, he's showing plenty of pace, too,
Knights, at this stage. He picks it up, he's tried to play on, he got
pulled by the leg, the umpire gives a handpass to Hendrie …

Can't you just hear him saying that? Richards has heard Dyer for thirty
years, but he never tires of the man. 'You couldn't buy what he's got,' he
says, 'you couldn't make it up.'

Despite his years, Dyer remains a busy man. During the week, the
Herald tried to trace him to get him photographed with the new
Premier, Lindsay Thompson, an avid Richmond fan. Dyer wouldn't be
in it: 'Don't they know I'm a Labor man?' he wailed. On Tuesday, he
was up at dawn, filming a commercial for Tattslotto with Richards.
('That's the first time I've seen a million dollars,' he said. 'We tried to
pinch some, but they had two armed guards.') Then out to St Albans to
present some guernseys to a primary school on behalf of 3KZ. Then to
North Melbourne to do his column for *Truth*. ('It's getting harder.
Once upon a time there was only one writer you had to beat. Now there
are thousands.')

Then to Richmond for some photographs. We met at McKellar's
pub. The old blokes around the bar cheered when Dyer arrived, forty

minutes late. Dyer was prepared for anything. We went from one bar to another, then for a walk down Swan Street. Dyer was self-conscious as he posed outside Dimmy's.

Several people went past. He knew none of them. Occasionally one would greet him.

'How-are-you-are-you-well?' asked Dyer.

Geoff Slattery was a journalist at the *Age* in the 1980s and is now director of Geoff Slattery Publishing and AFL Publishing.

'Jack Dyer: 1981, and Going on with Business' first appeared in the *Age* in 1981.

9

THE APOTHEOSIS OF 'CAPTAIN BLOOD'

by Gavin de Lacy

In 1932 Jack Dyer was nicknamed 'Bing' by his teammates at Punt Road. Dyer had a fine singing voice and his popular smoke-night number was Bing Crosby's 'Where the Blue of the Night', a song from *The Big Broadcast* (1932). The title of another moving picture was the source of his better-known nickname, 'Captain Blood'. Starring Errol Flynn as the eponymous pirate hero, *Captain Blood* screened in Melbourne from 11 April 1936 at Hoyts Regent Theatre.

In his 1965 autobiography, *Captain Blood*, Dyer wrote that:

> While Errol Flynn was butchering film extras as Captain Blood in 1935 [it was actually 1936], I was being accused of even more brutal carnage on the football field. Scribes at the time claimed I was littering the fields with as many broken and bloodied bodies as Flynn in his films.

Reviewing the 1936 round 4 Carlton vs Richmond clash, *Age* football writer John Ludlow ('Forward') wrote that 'Dyer has developed a straight-ahead, full-chested rush that has no counter. In one effort he simply ran "through" Cooper and goaled.'

Herald journalist Alf Brown argued that Dyer was nicknamed Captain Blood 'after one particular hectic game'. The hectic game was probably the 1936 round 9 Richmond vs South clash, although Dyer remembers it as a Fitzroy game. Dyer also wrote that Ludlow was the first to call him Captain Blood, but Ludlow did not make this claim. Writing in his column on 29 June 1936, Ludlow noted that Dyer was 'styled "Captain

Blood" by Richmond enthusiasts because of his amazing strength and fierce courageousness'. This is the earliest record of the nickname.

The nickname was used occasionally in the newspapers in the late '30s, including a reference in the local *Richmond, Hawthorn, Camberwell Chronicle* on 4 September 1936. The terrific description of Dyer is worth quoting in full:

Consistently conspicuous this season, Jack Dyer, Richmond's 21-year-old bull dog battler of the rucks, has been in rare fettle ... Six

Captain Blood by Barry Dickins.

feet one inch tall, with his weight gradually approaching the four-teen-stone mark, Dyer, with his limbs of steel, grim aggressiveness and strength of a lion, must develop into Australia's outstanding follower. Incredibly fast for a heavy man, he makes the ruck type all club officials pray for. Opponents find the young giant a tough proposition, and if the opposition want the heavy stuff ladled out he can hold his own with the hardest. Dyer crashes his way through ground packs, plays the long, driving game, punches mightily from the ruck, skittles aerial opposition with staggering bumping, and drags down amazing marks with a grip that plays havoc with opponents. Imperturbable, fearless, dashing and all-powerful, this young giant, nick-named 'Captain Blood' by his admirers, may easily develop into one of the champions of all time.

Dyer later flattened many opponents, fortifying his Captain Blood persona. 'When the fans took up the cry,' Dyer wrote:

I was stuck with it for life. The reputation that went with the name made me a target for the abuse of hostile fans. I was never to run on to a football ground again without being jeered, heckled, hooted and even spat on.

In the '40s, prominent football writer Hec de Lacy popularised the nickname in sympathetic pieces on Dyer in the *Sporting Globe*, including those of 21 September 1940 and 27 August 1949. Lou Richards, who coined many football nicknames, attributes 'Captain Blood' to de Lacy.

Dyer later used the nickname as a by-line, and for the title of his autobiography (written with *Truth* journalist Brian Hansen). He also broadcast football with Ian Major on 3KZ as 'The Captain and the Major.'

His is the most famous of all football nicknames.

Gavin de Lacy is a Richmond fanatic and co-editor of *Paper Tiger*.

'**The Apotheosis of "Captain Blood"**' originally appeared in Richmond fanzine *Paper Tiger*, no. 11.

10

TED WHITTEN
The Making of Mr Football

in his own words

It was my father who made me decide to have a go at Footscray: 'You might never get another chance.' And it was Charlie Sutton, Footscray's playing coach, who went to work on me. 'There's an opportunity there for you,' he said.

So in 1951, I saddled up in Footscray's practice games. I was given a run in the centre and at centre half-back against Jack Collins. I put everything I had into every moment of training. They didn't bother telling you whether you were a certainty to make the final training list, only that you were going all right. Footscray recruited tremendously well that year, with players like Peter Box and Herbie Henderson, and I wasn't sure I could make the grade. In the final practice game, Vice-captain Wally Donald said: 'Fire today and you're in.' The next morning I went down to the ground to see them post the list. It was one of my greatest thrills to see my name there. But then came another anxious week, waiting to see whether I would make the senior side.

On the Thursday night my family huddled around the radio when the Footscray team was announced. My heart was in my mouth and my stomach in my boots as the broadcaster read through the team until he reached the half-forward line: '… centre half-forward … Whitten,' and there was a wave of cheering from the family.

My first opponent was the Richmond badman, Mopsy Fraser. From the moment the Footscray team was announced, football fans told me Mopsy would kill me. 'He'll kick your head off,' everybody said, as a gambit congratulating me on making the senior side.

Before the game, Charlie Sutton didn't bother to tell me how to come at Fraser: 'Just play up to your practice form and you'll be right,' he said.

As I ran down the race and circled the field, all I could think of was Mopsy. The crowd was forgotten and I started to shiver and shake. Teammate Merv Laffey came over to me: 'You're shaking, but don't worry. You proved yourself the best kid in Footscray. Now go and show them you're the best here.'

'What about Fraser?' I stammered.

'Don't worry, we'll look after him.'

A player's first kick in big time football should be one of the cherished memories of his life, but not mine. My first kick in the game came from Mopsy – a fierce boot in the ankle.

As the coin was tossed, Mopsy Fraser had joined me. I got a big shock. As we came face to face he looked like a mad gorilla. His curly hair was hanging down his face, he kept gritting his teeth, there was hair sticking out everywhere and he was smothered with oil. It was an awesome sight, but I had been taught to be a sportsman and I offered to shake hands.

Crash ... went his boot, and as I hobbled around he snarled: 'That's just a starter.' There was more to come. As the ball bounced, a Footscray player grabbed it and shot it towards me. I went for the mark but Mopsy crashed into my back like a ton of bricks. Ump Jack McMurray gave me a free and with my first legitimate kick in league football I kicked a goal.

Mopsy was raging mad: 'You've made a mug out of me. You won't do it a second time, because you won't see the game out.' He was right. Just before three-quarter time, I raced in for the ball. As I came from the pack I saw Mopsy, teeth bared, charging at me like an express train. In horror I knew I couldn't get out of the way. A wave of agony, and the next thing I recall was being carried from the ground on a stretcher. I had to go to hospital, the first of many trips, but apart from sore ribs and a few aches I was all right.

Off the field Mopsy was a good bloke. On the field he was a villain. However, he was a brilliant footballer. After speaking to Mopsy the day after the game and finding he was part human, I seldom worried about an opponent again.

I was born in Footscray in 1933 and my earliest football recollection is kicking a paper ball around Centennial St. We broke more than our share of windows. My father, despite the damage to his pocket, encouraged me and my brother Don to play. When we were kicking the paper ball thirty yards, he declared: 'When you can kick it forty yards regularly I'll buy you a ball.' It wasn't long before we dragged him to the street to measure our distances and we got our new football.

The real foundation of my football was laid at St Augustine's Christian Brothers School in Yarraville. The school sports coach, Brother Greening, took a personal interest in his athletes. He taught me many techniques that were to be a great advantage in later years. Centre was my position in the school team and I was very light, but Brother Greening was confident I would make the grade as a footballer and spent as much time with me as possible. His main principle was to play the game and play it clean. I've followed this as closely as possible, but the road you walk in league football calls for strong action at times. There were tough games even in the Christian Brothers inter-school football.

I was a mad football supporter even then. Every training night I would go with some mates and watch the Footscray players in action. The Footscray side had some great players – Charlie Sutton, Billy Wood, Norm Ware, Harry Hickey, Joe Ryan and Arthur Olliver, who was my idol. The technique of Olliver was the one I decided to follow.

When I left school I joined Braybrook, in the Footscray District League. Jim Middleton was coach. He was more than 60 but trained me as hard as I've ever been trained. The Footscray District League was pretty tough. One bloke with the Carlton Stars played regularly with his arm in plaster and gave me some tremendous whacks with it. Against Miller's Rope Works I ran into a fellow and he split my jaw. I didn't have a clue how to protect myself. He brought his knee up in a pack and I didn't know how to get my head out of the way.

I played half a season in my first year and that was in the centre, but the following season I often played at full-forward. There was a golden streak for me, and in one game I kicked fifteen goals; in another, fourteen. I finished with ninety-three goals for the season. Fred Goldsmith, playing with Spotswood and later to win a Brownlow with South Melbourne, was the only one to beat my goal tally for one match. He kicked eighteen.

The following year I played full-time centre and met Goldsmith, Bill Gunn and Ron Stockman, all of whom later played for South. I tied with Bill Gunn for Best and Fairest in the league, and won on a countback. Roy Evans, the first captain to lead Footscray into the finals and coach of the Bulldog thirds, watched me in action at Braybrook. He was the one who got me my invitation to train at Footscray.

In that first game for Footscray, playing against Mopsy Fraser, the critics had placed me among the best players until I was injured.

Footscray's selectors decided to keep me in the side for the following match. It was another ordeal. My opponent was Carlton's Bert Deacon, a gentleman on and off the field. I went on to the ground knowing I was against a classy Brownlow winner, but knowing I could settle down and play my own brand of football. How wrong I was. He took me apart and I had only two kicks for the match.

With that display I was scared I'd be dropped from the side, so I had to spend another anxious week. We gathered around the radio again on the Thursday night. My hopes sagged as the commentator read out the half-forward line and my name was missing. Then I heard him say: '… full-forward … Whitten.' I was still in business, but another ordeal was coming up. We were playing Fitzroy, and my opponent was rough, tough fullback Vic Chanter, backed up by Fitzroy's version of Mopsy Fraser – Norm John-stone – who played just as hard as Fraser but lacked his polish and skill.

After playing against Chanter that day you'd have thought I had shaved my legs. He pulled all the hair off one leg as we jostled for posi-tion throughout the day. In the first quarter I had five simple shots at goal and missed the lot. I tried a drop kick, a punt, a drop punt, a torpedo punt and a floating punt. I finished the match with 2.7. Chanter didn't talk much. He had the habit of punching the ball away and every now and then he missed the ball when it was close to my head. It was very disconcerting.

After the game Norm Smith, then Fitzroy coach, asked Charlie Sutton to introduce me to him. He asked why I had tried such a wide variety of kicks when shooting for goal. I told him I was trying to find a kick that worked. Norm said:

Don't worry about that. Your ground play and marking are good. When you come to kicking, always give yourself another chance. You've got your team mates striving to get the ball down to you and you don't want to waste the opportunities they create. Give yourself a chance. Persevere with the one kick for a while and see how it goes.

I appreciated Norm's genuine desire to help a youngster, even if he did play for another club.

My form was patchy but good enough to keep my position in the side and the selectors persevered with me in key forward positions. Against Melbourne they switched me to the centre on George Bickford. In a hectic go, I followed Bickford through a pack. Our ruckman, big Dave Bryden, set him up for a perfect shirtfront. As Bickford burst into the open I was at his heels and Bryden was thundering head-on at him. Bickford was an old head and at the crucial stage he side-stepped. I froze with horror and Bryden couldn't stop his charge. He trampled me into the ground.

A flash of agony and I was out like a light. Again I was carried off on a stretcher. This time things looked grim. I was in a coma. Seventeen hours later I woke in a bed at the Royal Melbourne Hospital.

When I was ready to train again Charlie Sutton ordered simple kick-to-kick training for me. During the practice Bryden grabbed the ball, wheeled for a hard drop kick, and I stuck my head right into it. Another flash of pain and I was out again. I came to in hospital nine hours later.

From that stage, Charlie Sutton worked like a Spartan, teaching me to protect myself and the art of going into and coming out of packs. He did his job well, because from then I was able to avoid serious injury and missed games only through pulled muscles and an occasional broken nose.

In '51 we confounded the critics by making the finals with a side full of youthful recruits. Late in the season I looked like missing out on foot-ball – the Army called me for National Service. They gave me one week

Ted Whitten, takes a classic mark in front of the Gasometer at Arden Street, North Melbourne.

in three to play for Footscray, but when the big week came for the First Semi-final against Essendon, the Army refused point blank to let me play. It was the biggest disappointment of my life.

I was picked for the side but there appeared no hope. Footscray secretary Roy Russell phoned me in camp on the Friday night before the game and said: 'Leave has been refused but there is one more chance.' He didn't say any more. It was a pretty desperate last chance, as it turned out. The next morning I received a telegram from the Prime Minister, Sir Robert Menzies, telling me he had intervened to give me special leave. He said he had gone to a lot of trouble but wished me the best of luck. I was selected to play on the half-forward flank.

It was an awe-inspiring occasion to run on to a field in one's first league final. The atmosphere is completely different from anything you have ever experienced. By comparison, home-and-away games seem like park football. That ground gets bigger and bigger when you are losing and that's what happened to us that day. I had only four kicks. Still, we hadn't done such a bad job in making the finals.

Season 1952 was an education year for my football. Sutton had spent a lot of time building up my physique. I was still trying to find my natural position and they started me in the centre against Essendon's Alan Dale. My form was fair enough to hold that position. We started the season well and looked like carrying on where we left off the previous season. The second-year recruits were playing well. By the time we played Fitzroy, I had convinced myself the body-building exercises had strengthened me so much I could stand up to anybody.

There was Fitzroy's big Bert Clay, fifteen stone of muscle and strength, coming through a pack. This was my chance to prove myself. I went straight at him, intent on stopping him. He put out an elbow on his way through and flattened me like a tack. The body-building had not been as effective as I thought. Charlie Sutton was still at me, trying to teach me protection. He said: 'I'm sick and tired of having you hurt. Just have a glance before going into a pack. You're not being a squib or a coward having a look. Don't stop, just keep going, but know where the danger lies.'

I replied: 'I want to do it the way you do it. You don't look first.'

He snorted: 'You do as I say, not as I do.'

Against Collingwood that year I clashed with the famous Twomey brothers, Pat, Mick and Bill. I was playing centre half-forward and Mick forged through a pack. He was disposing of the ball when I caught him with the full force of my shoulder. He dropped like a log. Before he'd hit the ground I was smothered in Twomeys. Pat had me by the throat and Mick by the scruff of the neck. One of them roared at me: 'That was our brother you hit. We'll kill you.' All of a sudden there was a blur of red, white and blue. One guess: Charlie Sutton.

He was wild-eyed and frothing at the mouth. He scattered Twomeys everywhere. Out of the confusion emerged Mick with a free kick. As he went back, Sutton said to me: 'That's exactly what I want you to do. You've got to give a little bit back. Don't just keep copping it.' I've given a lot back since and taken a lot.

Charlie played it hard but I've never seen him do a foul thing on or off the field. He never told his players to do anything unfair. He was a tower of strength for the Footscray youngsters. We were precious cargo as far as he was concerned.

Bob Rose, Collingwood's brilliant rover, was playing at his peak then. He was a brilliant ball-player and a quick thinker. Playing against him at Victoria Park, I tackled him as he took the ball. He could have dodged away but instead allowed me to grab him. A fraction before I did, he punched the ball away and a free was awarded against me for holding the man. Rose goaled and turned to me: 'That's experience, son. You'll learn it as you get older. We needed that goal so I wanted you to grab me.' Football was instinctive to Rose.

I played on Murray Weideman in his first game and this time I had the experience. I was giving him a bit of a bath and he couldn't win a kick. Herb Henderson was kicking off at one stage and I turned to Murray: 'Come on, you'd better be in this. Come over and see if you can get a kick.' It must have upset him. As I raced in for the mark, Weideman soared head and shoulders above me and took a screamer. He didn't look back after that. He was a great footballer for Collingwood and a great bloke.

In the middle of the season we struck a slump. The second-year recruits lost touch and confidence. From good things to make the finals we were slipping out of calculations. Charlie didn't panic and he worked like a beaver on us. He didn't rant or rage but went about trying to rebuild our confidence.

In the game against Fitzroy, Alan 'Butch' Gale flattened a Footscray player and spun around to have a go at me. I gave him one slap across the face with an open hand. You could have heard the smack in the grandstand. Both our mouths gaped in amazement. A bit bewildered by my own effrontery, I stammered an apology: 'I'm sorry Butch, I didn't mean it.' After the match Butch approached me: 'There was only one thing you did wrong. You didn't close your fist when you hit me.'

Footscray got going again and figured in a photo finish, but unluckily missed the finals. We'd never have finished so close without the patience of Sutton, who, in this period, was infusing more fire into my play. I realise today just how much I owe him. He was a dynamic player and wouldn't ask any man to do anything he wouldn't do himself. There wasn't much he wouldn't do, of course. He gave out plenty of hard but fair knocks. And when he was knocked down himself, he never squealed. He always got up laughing – if he could get up.

Sutton paved the way for the younger players and looked after them like a mother hen. I will always remember playing Melbourne that year on the MCG and receiving a couple of hard knocks and going down for the count. Charlie burst through the pack, pushing players everywhere and picked me up in his arms. He was like that with all the young blokes, and they'd have laid down their lives for him.

Charlie was always thinking ahead. In later years I became aware that in addressing players, and in most aspects of coaching, he always looked straight at me, making sure I was absorbing every detail. He had decided that one day I would replace him as coach.

Mopsy Fraser and I saddled up for our second round when we met Richmond again. I was running for a mark on the boundary with big Ray Poulter thundering behind me. He gave me an almighty push and I went straight over the fence into the crowd. As I got up, a woman wielding an umbrella screamed: 'You dirty big mug, Poulter!' She lashed at him with the brolly, missed, and collected me instead. Poulter just laughed: 'That's one you've saved me from.'

No matter what commotion occurred on the football field the umpires always headed straight for Mopsy. During this game Bill Scanlan fell and Mopsy stumbled across the top of him, getting both feet in his chest as he stumbled. I thundered in and fell on Mopsy and in the confusion gave Mopsy one on the jaw. Mopsy got up spitting mad and set to kill. The umpire rushed in: 'Do that again Fraser, and I'll report you.' No wonder Mopsy got mad at times.

Season 1953 saw the birth of Jack Collins as a full-forward. Against Collingwood, Frank Tuck was assigned the job of minding Collins. He niggled at him all day. Quarter after quarter, he jostled, pushed and pulled at him. He did his job well. Finally, when play was at the opposite end of the ground, there was a commotion and right in the middle of it were Collins and Tuck having a punch up. Both were reported. They tried valiantly to clear themselves at the tribunal but each was rubbed out for four weeks. Collins was the kind of footballer who could take only so much niggling before squaring accounts.

We expected to go well that season, but the Collins suspension and the loss of fullback Herbie Henderson through chicken pox were severe blows. Yet Collins was to do a memorable job. When we played the Dons we were desperate for a way to hold Coleman, and Collins was given the job. He did an amazing job with the freak forward. It was no mean feat limiting the champ to four goals, one of them from a free.

Anyone who saw Coleman knows how hard he was to beat. He could lead like a greyhound, and to keep pace with his slippery turns you needed to be a magician. If that wasn't enough, he had tremendous spring and could come from behind the pack to take beautiful marks. His judgement was uncanny, and he was a long and deadly kick for goal – seven kicks would bring him six goals. The problem then was to confine him to four or less kicks for a match, and few players achieved this. Coleman could have won kicks in any era, and with talented players getting the ball to him, it was no wonder he knocked up so many goals.

We overcame our bad luck in '53 and made the finals. We won the First Semi-final, but Essendon finished our hopes with an easy win in the Preliminary Final. We weren't disheartened. We were exhilarated at making the finals.

The big thing was to win a premiership, but winning a State guernsey is one of the great thrills of the game. I was on the verge of State selection one week when I made my old mistake at training of not protecting myself and collided head-on with a Footscray big man. I went down for the count and wound up in the Footscray and District Hospital, once more with a tremendous black eye. It was so bad I had to go to a specialist, who advised against the game with South Melbourne. Meanwhile, the interstate selector, Roy Russell, told me I had only to do well against South to be a certainty. The specialist was adamant: 'You shouldn't play. A knock on the eye and you could go blind.' The Footscray selectors left the choice to me. I decided to give it a go.

Early in the match I was apprehensive and guarded my eye at every opportunity. But as I warmed up, I worried less about the injury and started to play well. Late in the game I dashed into a pack … *crash*. I reeled back from a tremendous jolt to the eye from Keith Browning, a South defender. My head felt as if it had exploded, as searing pain shot through me. As I wobbled around waiting for the stars to clear, I realised with relief that Browning had caught me in the good eye. That night I was nursing two black eyes. But I had achieved my object and was in the State side.

In 1954 we entered the season full of confidence and a will to win unequalled in the club history. Sutton was the dynamo, and goal to goal we had no peers. Herbie Henderson, Don Ross, Peter Box and Jack Collins were formidable players, and I made up the numbers at centre half-back. Another of our great strengths was the overall defence. In all matches that year, including the finals, fewer than a thousand points were scored against us – a record for a VFL series.

Peter Box was moved from the centre to centre half-forward and couldn't strike form; he considered himself a centreman and nothing else. We made the Grand Final, and were to play Melbourne for the premiership. When the selectors met to pick our side, they left the selection room without having picking Peter in the side. In the throes of saying goodnight, they noticed a figure still seated at the table – Charlie Sutton. 'I've got one problem I want to talk over with you fellows,' he said. They went back, sat down and selected Box at centre half-forward. Sutton's judgement was vindicated when Peter played superlative football.

The game was the most heart-pumping I have ever experienced. There is no feeling like that Grand Final feeling. No matter how seasoned a campaigner you are, the nerves twitch in your stomach as you wait in the dressing room to hear the coach's address. And the gladiators at the Colosseum could not have been more apprehensive than a footballer hitting the turf of the MCG to the roar of a hundred thousand spectators. The thrill lasts all day.

The ball was bounced in brilliant sunshine and we attacked from the outset, with Don Ross dictating play from the centre. Charlie Sutton played a fanatical role from the start, looking after Jack Collins at full-forward, minding John Beckwith, and having short bursts on the ball. Beckwith was in the back pocket and Charlie gave him a roughing up. In the meantime, Collins was leading well from goals. He kicked a few early and we were on top. You could sense the crowd was with us.

There were a few heavy clashes with Geoff Collins. Sutton had planned to have only five-minute runs on the ball, but he couldn't help himself and all day ran backwards and forwards shouting and encouraging: 'Your names are going down in the history books. You're

Footscray's first premiers,' he shouted again and again. It must have been annoying to the Demons but it was a great spur to the Bulldogs. We piled it on and never looked like losing.

In the last quarter Collins had seven goals on the board and needed only one more to equal the record for a Grand Final. We did everything to get the ball to him, and finally he took a mark, well within kicking distance. Then, to our amazement, he made a short pass to Brian Gilmour, who was closer to goal. We had the game won but he was such a team man that he put the club ahead of his own individual records. On players like these you build a premiership side.

When the final siren sounded, we must have gone mad. We had known from half time that we would win, but the magic moment still comes only when the final siren sounds.

We hot-footed it to Footscray, where a mayoral reception was held, and Charlie Sutton was installed as mayor for the night. Then down to the club rooms for the big celebration, but what a let-down that was. Most of the players were dog tired, but somebody had passed the word around to supporters to bring their own glasses and free liquor would flow all night. There were ten thousand people there, no liquor, and ten thousand empty glasses. The players couldn't get in, some tried to climb through the windows, but eventually most went home. It was all a horrible bungle and very disappointing. Still, it couldn't take the edge off winning that premiership.

In 1955, after winning the premiership, we were overconfident. It was incredible that such a good side as the '55 Bulldogs should have missed the finals. I believe it was because we became complacent. We had achieved the goal of winning our first premiership and there must have been a mental letdown because, if anything, we should have been a better team for the experience. Possibly we took some games too easily. It must be realised that premiers are the number one target for all teams. The opposition plays against them as if a premiership is at stake. We lacked the opposition's will to win.

In 1957 I hit my peak. Sutton and club officials were at loggerheads, but few of us realised how serious the differences were. Midway through the season came explosive news: 'Sutton's been sacked. You're the new coach of Footscray.' I couldn't believe my ears. I wasn't even captain of Footscray. Even more unbelievable was the sacking of Sutton – the man who had done more for Footscray than any other player. I was flabbergasted. I had always wanted to be captain of Footscray, but never dreamed I would be playing coach. My mind churned. I wasn't even captain. How would Harvey Stevens take it? He was captain.

I told the committee: 'I won't accept it until I speak to Charlie.' I went to Charlie's home but couldn't find him. The committee wanted my decision that night. I went back to them and they pointed out that if I didn't take the job they would get an outsider. Charlie Sutton was definitely out. That clinched it. 'All right, I'll take it,' I decided.

Next day I went to see Sutton and he had a lot of old players gathered at his hotel. He took me upstairs and said: 'You can do the job. If ever you get into trouble, get on the phone and I'll be down in a second.'

Our next match was at St Kilda. I went to bed on the Friday night tense and excited. I could not sleep. That pre-match address went over and over in my mind. The reaction of the players was a big worry. They were tremendously loyal to Sutton and I didn't know if they thought I was involved in some plot against him.

There was tension in the dressing room before the match, and I could feel the eyes of the officials, players and supporters on me as I stumbled through my address. It was a pathetic speech, and I was aware of repeating myself over and over and over. Five or six minutes after I started, a little figure emerged through the doorway: Charlie Sutton. The room went still and chill. The first fellow he headed for was me: 'Good luck, son. In future take your time when you talk to the players.' He was still coaching me.

'**The Making of Mr Football**' is an edited extract from the 1968 edition of Jack Dyer's *Wild Men of Football*, and is used with the permission of Brian Hansen.

11

GRAHAM 'POLLY' FARMER
Redefining the Ruck

by Steve Hawke

Commentators have always argued over the relative importance of ruckmen to the game. 'Big men win big games' is the preferred cliché of the pro-ruckman brigade in Western Australia, whilst in Victoria they say 'a good big man will always beat a good small man.'

'It doesn't matter who wins the knock, what matters is who comes away with the ball when it hits the ground,' is the favoured response.

The two arguments show the tendency of romance on the side of the ruckmen and science in favour of the on-the-ground ball-getters; and in the modern era of statistics and scientific analysis, the trend is in favour of the latter.

But the clash between the ruckmen is also bound up in the psychology of the game. Like no other position on the field, there is a personal and physical confrontation between the two lead ruckmen who contest the opening bounce. There is the formalised combat of the ruck contest that demands that the two confront each other over and over again in a direct, head-on clash.

Psychology aside, though, it is also logical that a dominant ruckman will give his side a significant advantage on the field of play, even before any contribution he might make around the ground with his marking and general play. As well as the centre bounce-downs to start each quarter and after each goal, the ruckmen go head to head at boundary throw-ins and each time play halts on the field but the umpire does not award a free kick. Depending on the scores and the nature of the particular game, this may be anything between fifty and one hundred times in a match. And each time the umpire takes the ball the play is evenly poised – barring a scrimmage or a knock-back over the boundary line, one side or the other is going to come away in possession and start to make the play.

All this theory assumes that the ruckman is trying to use the ball creatively if he gets to it first. There has always been the hit-and-hope school of ruck-play, which relies on the big fist thumping the ball from the centre down towards the half-forward line to gain territorial advantage if nothing else, with everyone taking their chances from there. But Graham 'Polly' Farmer was never a hit-and-hope man; that style was the very antithesis of his attitude to football.

Farmer had an instinctive understanding of the science and psychology of ruck-play, but he was never content to rely on instinct and raw talent. He single-mindedly honed his natural abilities to maximise his effectiveness in the art of the ruck contest, to ensure that it would be his hand that reached the ball first as it floated back down from the apex of the umpire's bounce, or arced back into play from the boundary throw. He developed his powers of endurance and concentration to ensure that this effectiveness would last all day every day. And most importantly – the feature that made his contribution to football unique – he single-handedly developed strategies and techniques to use the ball better than any ruckman had before him.

Beating his opponent, to the ball was not enough in its own right. Palming the ball towards his rover was good, but he could do better. He wanted the man that received the ball from him to be in the clear, and on the move in the direction of goal. This is the basic principle of attacking football in the modern era. It is a principle that only began to gain general acceptance in the 1970s. Farmer had worked it out as a twenty-year-old, fifty-game player back in 1955. He saw his role in a team as the playmaker; his job was to gain control of the ball under contest in the ruck or in a pack, and deliver it to a player moving forward.

It is one of the truisms of football that big men, and ruckmen in particular, tend to mature slowly. Twenty-five to twenty-seven is considered the prime age. Gleaning the experience that only years can bring is one reason for this. The other is one of physical maturity; for the ruckman the solid strength of a hardened adult's physique is worth more than youthful exuberance. But here was a fellow just out of his teens being promoted as Western Australia's best and most skilful ruckman. How did he get so far so fast?

Farmer's first year of league football had been nothing out of the ordinary. In the good games that brought him under some notice, the comments picked up on important facets of his style of play: 'clever knocking and good handball', 'with his quick thinking and clever hand-ball, escaped from many a difficult situation'. He exhibited natural foot-ball intelligence and a desire to use the ball effectively from the outset. But in that first year he lacked the experience to exploit this properly, and was unable to perform consistently.

One of the jokes that did the rounds at the time, and still receives some circulation among the old hands at East Perth, was that 'Pol was the best man on the ground – he was never off it.' The problem was largely one of size. With no weight on his lanky frame, Farmer was easily knocked off his feet. He was also still very much a learner; he had no hes-itation about leaping early and leaping high, but would often land on his back, or sprawled on the turf when nudged out of position by an oppo-nent. Teammate Kilmurray remembers: 'Even though he was fairly nimble, he was falling over a fair bit ... he lost his balance, sort of, but he always got rid of the ball, he never lost it.' It is the last half of the state-ment that is important – the Farmer style was developing. The prime objective was to get control of the ball, not just knock it on. Go to ground if you must, to get the ball, or keep control of it as you come under pressure, and look for a way to feed it out.

The other impediment in Farmer's early years was getting the chance to show his prowess. Opportunity in the shape of an opening in a side as other players come and go is a critical factor in a footballer's career. Farmer's class was such that he was bound to win through eventually, but none of his rivals were going to make it any easier for him. Initially he was contending with two other knock ruckmen at East Perth. Ray Perry had been playing since 1945. He had represented the State, and in his day was in the leading echelon of ruckmen in Perth. John 'Gus' Kikiros had made his debut in 1952. He was two years older than Farmer, more strongly built, and an eye catcher with a good leap.

There were other big men and followers who could fill in, but these three had the class or the potential to make the running, and Perry was top dog. Just as there is a battle on the field to establish supremacy over the opposing ruckman, there is intense rivalry within the club for the status of leading the first ruck.

When Farmer was in the team, he had to wait on Perry's whim to get a run on the ball. 'Every time he kicked a goal, if he'd been in the ruck for twenty minutes he'd go in for another five minutes because it picked him up.' He never knew how long he might get to stay on the ball either, for it was Perry's prerogative to call him back to the pocket. 'But that was the way it was. That wasn't a problem for me. I was only trying to make my way, so I had no rights.'

With Perry unavailable at the beginning of the 1954 season, Farmer's real opportunity came. At that point he and Kikiros were sharing the ruckwork, and vying for the leading role, which was very much up for grabs. But Farmer's early season performances, from his best on ground in the opener against South Fremantle, quickly put him ahead of Kikiros and marked him as the rising threat to Perry. One press report described his improvement in the space of a year as astonishing.

This observation is endorsed, and to some extent explained by his teammate Tommy Everett. The previous year, Everett says, he had no sense of Farmer as anything special, but 'he blossomed pretty quick,' and in 1954:

He just improved day by day, week by week. He used to sleep with a footy. If you were going out to lunch somewhere he'd have a footy with him. He just lived and breathed it, and realised that his life was going to be football, and more or less set about making sure that he was going to be the best – which he did.

There was method, or at the very least an objective, in what some tended to regard as the madness of the ever-present football.

Everyone who followed the Farmer career has heard the stories of him constantly handling the ball, practicing his handball through partly opened car windows, or any other available target. It is a habit he tried to instil in his players as a coach. The idea behind the habit went beyond the mere practicing of skills though. It was a matter of feeling the ball as an extension of himself, as something totally familiar and natural. He had seen and admired the ball skills of the Harlem Globetrotters, and wanted to be able to handle and control the oval footy with the same ease they showed with the more accommodating round basketball.

East Perth stalwart Gus Glendinning still remembers the pointed way in which Farmer explained it to him:

Now you drink Gus. Some mornings you wake up not feeling very well, yet you sit at the table with your knife and fork, and because you use them so often, you eat quite normally. You use your knife and fork as if they were part of you, even though you are ill from your night out. A football to me must feel like that at any time.

Farmer's absolute dedication remained a hallmark throughout his career, but in those early years when he was raw, still learning, still establishing himself, it seems to have had a special intensity. To Farmer himself it was simple; not only did he want to develop his game, he was in a hurry to do it, to compress the timetable as much as possible.

His intensity did set him apart, but evoked admiration, not scorn or jealousy from his young club-mates. The kick-to-kick sessions before training were regarded by many as a warm-up, and a chance for a bit of fun and lairising, but not by Farmer. Kevin McGill, who started roving with East Perth as a sixteen-year-old in 1954, remembers the sessions well:

Polly was building his game up in those years. He was lean. He could spring. At training, if we had a new football for kick to kick, Polly would claim that new ball every time. They'd be kicking for high marking, so there was no way the small fellows would have a chance, all the taller fellows would be trying to mark it. Polly would probably get eighty-five per cent of that – everybody else struggling around while Polly was taking his speccies.

But, although he delighted in them just like any other footballer, Farmer was not just taking speccies. He was consciously using these congested contests to practice new variations and techniques of the bodywork that was so important to his trade as a ruckman; how to time his leap, how to get the best ride, how to maximise the lift he could get from an opponent's own jump, how to evade a knock, or turn a clash of bodies to his own advantage.

He never trained just for training's sake, with the single-mindedness of a fitness fanatic. He was always observing, thinking, looking for something new, a technique or an idea he could adapt and use.

Nor did he confine his quest for useful knowledge to the football club, where his questioning would at times irritate the elder statesmen amongst the players:

I asked a lot – about life. Anyone. I thought people had the right to say no, and a lot of them did, but I think everything is available to everyone if you find the right people to see. But in those days secretness seemed to be paramount, about football, about everything in life. The people who had it didn't want other people to know ...

I didn't think anything was a secret [and] was not embarrassed about asking about everything. I was a very inquisitive person who wanted his questions answered in a positive way. It seemed easy for people to tell you to pull in your head and mind your own business, but that didn't stop me. Most things are available, and if no one tells you, you can go and find it in the books anyway. I loved reading ... I always worked on the basis that you should listen to everyone, not say 'Well he's not a footballer, how would he know.'

Farmer spent his spare hours watching other sportsmen in competition and training. He wanted to improve his leap, and from high jumpers and long jumpers he picked up that the keys to improvement were greater speed and power in the first few strides off the mark, and strength in the thigh muscles. So he undertook the exercises and practice that were nec-

Graham 'Polly' Farmer in the coaches box (he coached Geelong 1973–75).

essary. This might sound commonplace today. Football clubs employ teams of experts to devise such exercises and drill the players. But in the early 1950s the phrase 'sports science' was yet to be coined.

Walking the streets he would leap at anything that seemed slightly out of reach, striving for that extra inch. He would jump at walls to practise the art of pushing himself off, extracting the maximum lift, then hanging in the air before he landed. There are echoes of that ultimate sporting champion, Don Bradman, and the legend of the lonely boy, endlessly throwing a golf ball against a fence and hitting it on the rebound with a stick, honing his natural eye and his reflexes to razor sharpness.

He watched soccer, and noted the way the players ran and ran to make position, and back into defence to cover, whether they were near the ball or not. From them he learnt the value of endurance, and of reading and anticipating the play. He decided he needed to put extra miles in his legs and took up jogging. He loved to do this on the northern beaches and the dunes that backed them near his Scarborough home, because he could go for miles and work harder at it in the heavy sand, and there was always the option of a swim at the end. This was before Percy Cerrutty had become famous for his torture camps for elite athletes in the sand dunes of Portsea, and in an era when many players and some coaches still believed it was time to stop training when you raised a sweat.

Farmer was still far from fully matured in a physical sense. He was much lighter than most of the opposing ruckmen, and could still be out-bustled in a direct physical confrontation. But the training he did was putting the muscle on him, and he was fitter than any of his opponents. He developed the capacity to keep on running, keep on coming back for contest after contest. And the more time that passed, during the course of a particular game, and from week to week and month to month through the seasons, the more of the contests he won.

In 1955, with Perry retired and Kikiros falling by the wayside with a knee injury early in the season, the full burden of leading the East Perth ruck fell on Farmer's shoulders, and he thrived on the challenge, going from strength to strength. He was playing consistently well by now, making the East Perth best player lists in the *Budget* in sixteen of the nineteen games he played. The long series of classic encounters with Jack Clarke of East Fremantle began, and during the course of the season he overtook Jack Clarke as the inheritor of McIntosh's mantle of WA's premier ruckman.

91

The descriptions of Farmer's better games began to reach for superlatives beyond even the usual generous prose of sports writers. There was a growing sense that Farmer might be something more than the latest in the line of champion ruckmen; when his game clicked he might be capable of rising to a new level of excellence.

The mid-season game against West Perth that won him a five-pound award drew this praise from the *Sunday Times* reporter:

> His display against the strong West Perth ruck was one of the best ever seen from an individual player. From the first bounce he was opposed by the much taller Foley and the other West Perth rucks, and although he received little assistance from his teammates he seldom missed the knock ... [He] was brilliant in the air and out-marked all who flew against him. Apart from top scoring for his side, he gave one of the most courageous and determined exhibitions of purposeful football seen in this State for some time.

Farmer had developed the technique that enabled him to dominate and frustrate his opponents. Being able to leap high was one thing, but there were others who could leap just as high, some who had a natural height advantage that could counter his spring, and others again who had the bodyweight to muscle him away from the ball in mid air – the leap itself was not enough. It was just as important to eliminate or at least neutralise your opponent's attempt to get to the ball as well.

Farmer was always a master of bodywork. In his earliest days at Maddington he could always ride the bumps and land on his feet. But the science of bodywork requires not only that you maintain your own balance and position, but wherever possible you use leverage and strength to put your opponents off balance and out of position. Time and again in photographs of Farmer this is apparent. He is reaching to one side of his body for the ball, with a hip thrust in the other direction, and his opposite number hopelessly out of the contest. His mastery of the art came through a combination of instinct, theory and practice, practice, practice.

At a bounce Farmer's favoured technique was to position himself close in and opposite the umpire – at right angles to his opponent instead of head on – and to leap early, just a fraction before his opponent. And he jumped into his opponent. When he timed it correctly, as he learnt to do, he would land with a knee on the other ruckman's thigh or hip. He would gain lift from the other man's own jump, and simultaneously put him completely out of position, as Farmer himself rose to the ball.

Jack Clarke is as well qualified as anyone to describe what it was like on the receiving end:

> He brought a style into the game that no-one else had ever done. He developed a style where he jumped early and unbalanced his opponent. Just as you were going to prepare to jump, he'd hit you with his bum ... I played the old-fashioned style, I was more the McIntosh style I suppose. I liked a clear run at the ball, and he'd get between me and the ball and give me the backside ... He used to run more or less side on to you, he wouldn't run straight at you; he used to run at a bit of an angle to you, and then he'd turn his back.

Clarke felt that the style was unfair, because it deliberately impeded his run at the ball, and he would often appeal for free kicks. But as he concedes, Farmer's eyes never left the ball during these exchanges. Generally, the umpires let Farmer's style go.

There was much more to this technique, though, than merely putting the opponent out of position. Farmer's opponents would come off the field with more than their normal share of corked thighs, bruised torsos and raking stop marks. Keith Slater of Swan Districts – no shrinking violet – remembers well his first league game against Farmer in 1955. At half time, he says, he was in tears, with hardly any skin left intact from his chest to his knees.

The style evolved into a fluid movement that enabled Farmer to achieve all of his aims of winning the ball, and feeding it out to a team-mate on the move.

One possibility was that he would draw a free kick in his own favour. To quote Clarke again:

> He'd hit you with his bum. You'd put your hands up automatically to sort of stop him bumping into you, and he'd get a free kick for it. I remember Lenny Gardiner was the top umpire at the time. I'd say, 'Len, he's interfering with me and you're giving him a kick for it.' But to his credit, he was getting away with it.

As both Clarke and Farmer agree, the only real rules on the field are defined by what a particular umpire will let you get away with. Both used whatever tricks they could, and if they did not work on a particular day, they would adapt as necessary.

If, as was more common, there was no free kick, Farmer would be on top, with the choice according to the relative position of himself, the ball and his rovers, of palming with his left hand across his body, or flicking it back to the other side. But as time went by, he increasingly used another variation that devastated the opposition.

The secret of it lay in his half turn in mid air, which presented his back to Clarke and the others. He would grab the ball in mid air, and land facing away from his own goals. Quick as a flash, sometimes even before he had hit the ground, the handpass would be fed out. More often than not, it would go back across his body with the left hand, to Paul Seal dashing down the left wing. The whole technique was revolutionary, but one of the keys to it was this reversal of direction. The opposition would expect a left-handed ruckman to be knocking the ball forward and across his body towards the right flank. Suddenly the ball was in the hands of a man one hundred and eighty degrees away, racing towards goal. It was as if a cricketer had invented an entirely new stroke, or a completely original bowling variation, like Bosanquet and the googly. The opposition took a long time to even comprehend it, let alone develop counter strategies.

Of course, Paul Seal down the left wing was not the only option. Farmer had an uncanny ability to know where his men were positioned, whether they were in front of him or behind, and to assess whether they were in the clear or not. He would always pick the man with a clear path towards goal, and direct the ball his way, with the knock or handpass. With his constant practice he had developed a dozen different types of handball with either hand: short, flat and fast; long and low; long and looping; on the full; on the bounce. Always it was delivered out in front of the player, not directly to him. Farmer wanted the man to be on the move as he received the ball. This was yet another new concept at the time. Until then the receiver had been used to making position, waiting to receive, then taking off. Once they adapted, and knew what to expect, his teammates found that by the time they laid hands on the ball, they were three or four steps further away from their man than they used to be.

On top of this quality ruck-play, Farmer won the ball over and over in the air, taking strong and often spectacular marks. He won the hard balls, and won the admiration and respect of his teammates and his opponents for it.

During the break between the 1955 and 1956 seasons, East Perth had reason to be well pleased with their off-field work. Not only did they convince Farmer to stay, although he was being courted by Richmond, but they lured Jack Sheedy across from East Fremantle as their playing coach. In the six years to come, East Perth would be the dominant club in the competition, playing in all six Grand Finals and winning three. During these golden years for the Royals, the story of the club revolved around these two pre-eminent figures, Farmer and Sheedy, often described respectively as the greatest footballer and the greatest character ever to play football in Western Australia.

Steve Hawke is a lapsed Geelong fan, and an avid armchair expert. He is more used to working and writing in his specialist field of Aboriginal affairs and history. But researching the Polly Farmer biography, spending time with Farmer and his footballing contemporaries was a great experience.

'Graham "Polly" Farmer: Redefining the Ruck' is an edited extract from his *Polly Farmer*, published by Fremantle Arts Centre Press in 1994.

12

THE DOC

Greatest Ball-handler of Them All

by Paul Ormonde

Darrel Baldock, a $500,000 a year player by 21st century standards, was lured to St Kilda in 1962 with an offer of $1000 a year and a job as a car salesman with Reg Hunt Motors. He and his wife, Margaret, rented a house in suburban Cheltenham. 'Times have changed,' Baldock commented, when I interviewed him recently. 'Good luck to them,' he says, of today's affluent new-age superstars, and acknowledges that 21st-century footballers are athletes of a higher order than the footballers of his day. 'If I were a kid today, I'd do the same training as they do. But back then, if Yabby had kept asking me to do yet another sprint I'd have told him to jump in the lake.'

Yet it is well to remember what Darrel Baldock meant to the generation of St Kilda followers – and lovers of exciting football generally – in the 1960s. At the mention of the Doc, ageing St Kilda fans delve into their memories of great moments. Fred Day, archivist at the St Kilda Football Club Museum recalls:

> It was the mid '60s, we were playing Hawthorn at Glenferrie Oval. The whole ground was a mudbath. They were ankle deep in it. Baldock at centre half-forward was virtually on his own, and surrounded by Hawthorn defenders. They were all over him. Suddenly he emerged from the pack bouncing the ball, and broke clear. The Hawthorn stand could not believe it. They all stood up and gave him an ovation.

It was, as they used to say, 'vintage Baldock'.

Baldock was widely regarded as the best ball-handler ever. Former St
Kilda captain and Brownlow medallist Neil Roberts says Baldock was the
only player he had ever seen running akimbo and simultaneously bouncing two footballs, one with each hand. Baldock could also run crouching
low while bouncing the ball – 'like watching someone run under a low
roof', says Roberts. Essendon champions Dick Reynolds and Bill Hutchison could do that too.

Roberts played with Baldock in 1962 – Baldock's first year with St Kilda
and Roberts's last – but had played against him the year before, in the 1961
interstate carnival, when Baldock was centre half-forward for Tasmania and
Roberts was Victoria's centre half-back. According to Roberts, Baldock
was more difficult to play against in the wet than Ted Whitten:

> In wet grass the ball skids off faster than on dry ground, and
> Baldock taught himself to pick it up at half-volley. His fellow Tas-
> manian Ian Stewart could do it too. But in Victoria we tended to
> stand back, then play it. Baldock's way was better. That was one of
> his great contributions to the game.

How could a centre half-forward only 5'9" (175cm) and 13 stone (82.5kg)
perform so brilliantly in a role naturally suited to a tall high-marker? 'The
ball comes off the deck eighty per cent of the time,' says Roberts:

> Baldock had the lowest centre of gravity of any player I have seen.
> He lacked height but he had great strength, and he used it.
>
> He also had great football intelligence and literacy. He con-
> stantly showed brilliant leadership by breaking into the open and
> virtually demanding that the ball be sent to him. Every time
> someone got the ball upfield they would look for him. In this
> sense, there was a special understanding between Baldock and St
> Kilda's centreman, Ian Stewart. They were a great combination.

St Kilda club historian Russell Holmesby had this explanation: 'Baldock's
talents would have been enough on their own, but coupled with Ian
Stewart, they were irresistible.' There were no tactics, Baldock told
Holmesby, of the understanding between himself and Stewart:

> Timing was the most important thing, because of my height. The
> ball had to come down quickly. That was a speciality of Stewie's,

because he was such a magnificent kick of the ball. He'd look up and I'd be halfway there. The greatest asset I had was reading the field.

It's hard to find any football identity of the '60s who doesn't remember Darrel Baldock with awe. Richmond's Jack Dyer described him as 'the most freakish footballer I've seen', noting an unequalled amount of 'courage, absolute dedication and ball-handling control'. Speaking to the *Devonport Times* in early 2002, Dyer rated Baldock 'the greatest ground player the game has produced – wet or dry'.

His ground skills marked Baldock out but, given the opportunity, he also had the ability to climb over a pack to mark over taller men. Triple Brownlow medallist Bob Skilton recalled, in the same article: 'I was paired up with Darrel at a Victorian training session and for fifteen minutes I didn't touch the ball. If you don't get in front of him, he's gone, the ball's gone and you're gone.'

The high point of Baldock's football life – leading St Kilda in 1966 to its first and only Grand Final victory – was achieved the hard way. There were many moments in the match itself, and in the lead-up games, that could yet again have confirmed St Kilda's flair for failure. But St Kilda players and fans were desperate for a flag and for respect.

Three weeks before the last match of the home-and-away series, Baldock had sprained medial ligaments in his right knee. A doctor had told him the leg should be in plaster for six weeks. Baldock recalled: 'I told him "No way. If you do that I can't play in the finals."' Club president Ian Drake put Baldock in touch with Adrian Wright, the physiotherapist for Melbourne, Hawthorn and St Kilda, who ordered a gruelling three-times-a-day program of exercises and weight training. Two and a half weeks later, Baldock was still in doubt for the last home-and-away match, against Hawthorn at Moorabbin. With the Grand Final approaching and St Kilda in contention, Baldock's knee was big news.

The whole St Kilda community – players, club officials and fans – was depressed that a Grand Final was looking so near and yet so far, such was Baldock's importance to the side's morale. On the Thursday night before the Hawthorn match, Baldock was selected as twentieth man. The decision was kept secret. Baldock had told the selectors he felt he shouldn't play but would be happy to sit on the bench.

As the match proceeded, Baldock sat beside coach Allan 'Yabby' Jeans and the selectors. At half time, the match was not going well and when Hawthorn put on four quick goals in the third quarter, Jeans decided

Baldock should go on for the last quarter. Twenty-two minutes into the third quarter, Jeans could wait no longer, and asked Baldock if he could go on. Baldock had replied that he was 'not too sure' about it, but nevertheless obeyed. Jeans's decision almost certainly saved the Saints.

As Baldock ran on to the field, supporters screamed approval and team spirit lifted. Russell Holmesby described how Baldock, with apparent nonchalance, had told him:

> One of my horses was running at Sandown that day, and I had enough time to catch the train to Oakleigh, watch the race, then come back to the ground without anyone suspecting that I was in the team ...
>
> I was sitting there hoping I wouldn't have to go on, but within the first few minutes I kicked a goal.

St Kilda won the match, securing its place in its most famous finals series.

There was more drama to come, however, before that crowning Grand Final. On Thursday night's training before the big game, Baldock felt his knee go again, but he did not want the world to know. He didn't fall over, he didn't limp, and he tried not to wince. As he told Russell Holmesby: 'I yelled out to Jeansie straight away, and he called everyone in to the centre and told them that training was finished. We all ran off so no-one would know I had hurt it again.' Following a cortisone injection, Baldock was in what he called 'unbearable pain' for twenty-four hours, and on the Friday night was doubtful if he could play. In frustration, he went for a jog about ten o'clock: 'I thought it was starting to feel better.'

On Grand Final day, before a crowd of 101,655, Baldock, like a never-say-die soldier, had recovered sufficiently to lead his team onto the ground and play the full hundred minutes of one of the tightest, toughest Grand Finals ever played. It was goal-to-goal courage from both sides, with neither ever making a winning break. What nobody reported was that Baldock played, in his own terms, stiff legged. 'I was terrified throughout the match to bend that knee,' he told me.

Baldock had won the toss and chosen the breeze. Early in the first quarter he took a mark well out from goal: 'Stewie called out to me, "Have a shot," and I thought, OK, so I booted the ball through for full points.' In the circumstances, the goal was remarkable. Later Baldock told Russell Holmesby: 'It felt like my knee went further than the ball.' That early inspirational moment lifted a team playing with a wounded captain and without its 'outed' star ruckman, Carl Ditterich.

Baldock played a team game that day, without being a standout matchwinner. He ran hard, hit hard. But, as he recalled: 'I ran over the ball a thousand times in that match, when I would normally have grabbed it. I could not bend my knees. I was almost stiff legged.' Former Melbourne wingman Brian Dixon, writing in the *Age* the following Monday, nominated Baldock among many contributors, but was almost alone in noting Baldock's quieter than usual performance:

As Dixon summarised the game:

Brian Mynott's early success against Ray Gabelich, the controlled exuberance and vitality of Ian Cooper, the solidity of Daryl Griffiths, the tenacity of Ross Smith, the marking of Brian Sierakowski and Barry Breen, the handball of Darrel Baldock, and the exhausting gap-filling by Ian Stewart were telling factors in the Saints' success ... (Ted) Potter beat Baldock partly because of Baldock's reluctance to battle into the packs with his normal bullocking balance and strength.

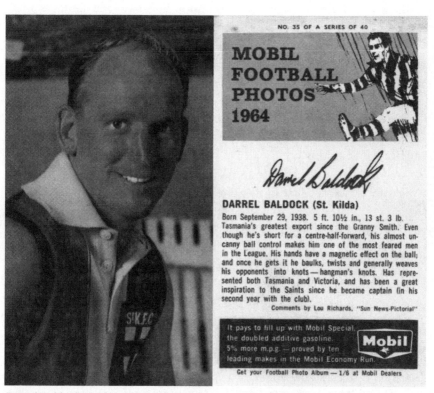

Darrel Baldock ties his opponents in knots, says Lou Richards.

Even people with only a passing interest in football can now recall how victory was delivered to the Saints with that famous wobbly punt from 18-year-old Barry Breen a minute into the final time-on for the never-to-be-forgotten 'point of it all'.

Against a setting of delirious joy from St Kilda fans at the MCG, Baldock could hardly contain his exhilaration. Teammates mobbed him as he headed for the group who were chairing Allan Jeans. After hugs all around, he stepped on to the presentation dais, where he and Des Tuddenham crossed arms over one another's shoulders.

Receiving the premiership trophy from VFL president Sir Kenneth Luke, Baldock immediately burst into 'When the Saints Go Marching In', waving the trophy over his head. The Channel 7 commentators were so astonished at the result, and at this unleashing of emotion by Baldock and his team, that they could not remember who kicked the winning point. In those days before instant replays, Mike Williamson thought it was probably Breen; co-commentators Alan Gale and Ted Whitten thought it was Jeff Moran.

Baldock followed Grand Final tradition and swapped jumpers with Tuddenham. Exhaustion was put on hold as he led his team on a lap of honour, all the way waving the trophy like a flag. In the dressing room, an emotional Baldock could remember little of 'the most exciting day of my life'. Searching for words to describe his feelings, he said:

> It's thrilling enough to win a premiership but doubly thrilling to see St Kilda win its first pennant ... I'm proud and honoured to have led St Kilda.
>
> I'd like to pay a tribute to Allan Jeans. He has done a wonderful job as coach. Most of us went out there to win it for him.

Off the field, memories of grateful fans stayed with him, particularly those ageing fans who would stop him in the street to say 'Now I can die happy.'

Baldock had started his VFL career relatively late, being recruited to St Kilda from Tasmania when he was 23. He was already a superstar, having distinguished himself in the North Tasmanian league, playing for Tasmania at age 18, and becoming state captain at 20.

There is no more distinguished St Kilda player than Baldock. He played 119 games from 1962 to 1968, scoring 236 goals, and such was his early impact that he was made captain in 1963. He was club Best and Fairest in 1962, 1963 and 1965, and in 2001 was named captain and centre half-forward in St Kilda's Team of the [20th] Century. Baldock had already been named a player-member of the AFL Hall of Fame during the league's centenary season.

Baldock returned to Tasmania in 1969 and captain-coached his old team, Latrobe, to four premierships. He was elected to State Parliament as Labor member for Wilmot in 1972, and held a number of ministerial portfolios, including Transport and Housing. Tasmania, with his wife Margaret, his tribal football and political constituency, and his thorough-bred horses and racing pigeons, was where his heart was. But perhaps, in another part of his make-up, Tasmania was not big enough for the man who 'had the ball on a string'. He never sought to be St Kilda's coach, but when the offer came, he was easily persuaded.

Baldock's coaching career at St Kilda began with a fiasco, somewhat of his own making. St Kilda was in the midst of one of its worst decades and approaching insolvency, and thought 'the Doc', with his enormous prestige, could give the team the spark to lift them back to glory. Baldock agreed, late in October 1984, to become coach of the Saints for 1985, even though he was still a member of parliament. The Labor Party leader in Tasmania, Ken Wreidt, angrily demanded Baldock's resignation from the Shadow Cabinet as spokesman for Sport and Recreation, Main Roads and Local Government, declaring that the job of a parliamentarian was a full-time one and that it was not appropriate for members to have a substantial outside interest. Baldock relented and resigned the coaching position before the 1985 pre-season training had even begun.

By 1987, Baldock's political career of fifteen years service was coming to an end. He was again coaxed back to St Kilda, this time without the political baggage, and with hopes high among Saints fans that Baldock could restore the team's dignity and self-belief. In his first season, he lifted the team from the bottom of the ladder, with nine wins, but later in that year he suffered a stroke. After that, his coaching career sagged. The Saints won another wooden spoon in 1988, with only four wins, and were lagging again in 1989 with seven wins.

Baldock returned to Tasmania at the end of 1989. He had a further stroke in the early 1990s. In retirement from football and politics, he has concentrated on training and breeding racehorses. He is particularly proud of his 6-year-old gelding Chardere, which in 2002 won the Newmarket and the Devonport Cup. In the previous three years, Baldock's horses have won about thirty races. He still keeps racing pigeons.

Baldock remembers his past with warmth, but has put it behind him. He has little contact now with his football or political friends – only an occasional chat with Ian Stewart. Yet this modest man retains a quiet pride in his past. The St Kilda motto, *Fortius quo Fidelius* (Strength through Loyalty), captured Baldock's commitment to football, to Tasmania and ultimately to St Kilda, where his illustrious playing career more than justifies his home state's pride in producing such a unique talent.

Paul Ormonde is a Melbourne journalist who lives in St Kilda and has followed the Saints from Moorabbin to Waverley to Docklands over thrity-five years.

'The Doc: Greatest Ball-handler of All Time' draws on interviews conducted with Darrel Baldock, Fred Day and Neil Roberts in February 2003.

13

KEVIN MURRAY
You Are Unreal

by Barry Dickins

I used to go with my father, Len, to watch Kevin Murray. 'He's different,' was what Dad said as he poked a ten-bob note through a filthy hole in dark bricks for a ticket or two to get into The Outer, as Hell was called. Fitzroy was violent, and you heard heads getting beat into dirt tins as you followed old Royboys to get somewhere to have a Bo Peep.

It was invariably raining or just about to get swirly. Drunkards swore with maximum rudeness at the umpies, who were called many things, such as *filth*, *scum*, even *Arabs*. Umpire Ron Brophy didn't really look like an Arab, but he was accused of being one as soon as he came on (which seemed a trifle harsh). The drunks hated the Seconds, and although the sober and respectable footy fans clapped the Seconds as they limped off when the siren went, the drunks sometimes chucked empty beer bottles or beer bottles full of mud.

St Georges Road, 1963, up against the Bombers, at home. Alan 'Butcher' Gale was our captain, Wally Clark was our rover, and there was a guy called Henderson at fullback. Henderson used to boot prodigious spiral torps into the gale that moaned into his indefatigable frame. I could see the homemade stops under his boots as he sunk the cowhide deep into the bladder.

The crowd screams scorn and adoration, and down the stone-cold concrete race the players run. Some already hobbledy Seagulls blaspheme. Men weep because it says in the *Footy Record* that Geoff Leek's going to retire. The ancient grandstand is full of grandfathers. Two thousand Turf are lit. One thousand cases of food poisoning are hatched from anthrax dimmies.

The umpire blows the shrill tin whistle and a blue breaks out. Due to what is called, these days, 'stress'. My dad pours me a cup of hot tea from our thermos and kisses me on the right cheek, and we prop on a ridge-thing made of concrete and bitumen. I cannot hear what he is whispering to me because a lovely old lady is calling Ron Brophy things I've never heard of before, at the top of her lungs. Dad sighs and blows his tea cooler until it's just right. He tells the old girl to watch her language.

Kevin Murray juggernauts after the ball like a tentacled tattoo. He seems more octopus than follower, for he follows the footy like the currents, like the eddying wind, like the unpredictable Bass Strait blow that makes men's sideboards quiver. But now Muzzah has the footy in the centre mud-patch, and although he is splay-footed and the very essence of awkwardness and completely without grace, he's got the Sherrin and that's what matters.

'He's all over the place like a mad dog's breakfast, that Murray,' mutters Dad, and puts the field-glasses on to watch him (Murray, or Muzzah, or Gummy Shark – because he chooses to play *sans* clackers, not even a gum-guard to protect that remarkable head that butts and brains) as he saws through legs and rams and speedily avoids and bites and snaps and corkscrews and pirouettes – even if the pirouetting is neither poetic nor balletic. It is courageous.

It is a style of stylessness, if there is such a thing. He runs like nobody else and breathes unlike the others and marks not frantically, no show-pony. He is writhing and all wriggly and always where the skew-whiff kick is. He realises wind. He *is* wind. He goes with the boundary breeze and collides with the grandstand in five o'clock shadow and seems concussed but isn't.

Our players do not pat one another on the bum. They did not praise each other in 1963. What they did was win or get done. Running on for the Lions was life's meaning. Being paid chickenfeed to play with Chicken Smallhorn. Doing a bit of circle work on training night. A few lopes around the oval then up to the corner of Johnson and Smith streets to drink with their beloved captain at the Birmingham.

That game I watched Geoff Leek kick the longest drop kick I ever saw, a little bit after three-quarter time it was. That gallant and gentle giant kicked a drop kick, left-footed, without a boot on, just in his Essendon footy sock. Right through the high-diddle-diddle at the gas-ometer end. The goal-umpie stared aghast and took a couple of seconds to organise the floppy white flags, but then he flapped them both, and Geoff Leek laughed at the fluke of it.

'Muzzah was all over the place like a mad dog's breakfast', said Barry Dickens' Dad.

I close my eyes and can remember every single thing in that game. I can see muddy men and bloodied centre half-backs cantering back towards grim orange-boys. I can see St John's Ambulance people attending to a child whose arse got impaled on something to do with wrought iron and her parents crying, the mum I think it was, and the father placing a tartan rug around his daughter, and I can see Kevin Murray having a breather.

My memory of Murray is as brilliant-hopeless and stupid-incredible and unorthodox-perfect and cretinous-genius and shambles-horror, but no matter how idiotic the manner, he got his hooks on the footy in times of need. Like all the time, let us say.

Was footy faster then? No, but it was different. Rough and spontaneous like a blood nose. The players had rocker hairdos and hands like shovels – they were conceived that way, and delivered by determination. Their mothers looked like them and kicked punt kicks like them when they went into labour five minutes into time-on.

Murray dived into the packs, got kicked and slagged on, got bit and thumped, got scragged and bashed and insulted and gouged and nose-bled and shirt-fronted and jobbed when he wasn't looking but every time I caught a glimpse of him he emerged with the ball. His was a homespun genius. He gave footy his heart and soul, both considerable arenas bathed with late-afternoon sunshine right on the mud and jade-green slushy grass.

His coach was Len Smith, who dreamt up the flick pass. You held the ball flat in your hand and hammered it sideways so it shot thirty yards or so at the speed of light. The friends of Fitzroy sighed at every flick pass. The flick pass was so incredible that Footscray copied it and Ted Whitten plagiarised it. These things cause loss of teeth in pubs after work.

Murray's teammates, well his teammates ran on with him, knowing, as he knew, that defeat means humiliation and having to shake hands with the Devil. We had Wally Clarke roving, a stocky little bloke with stand-up crewcut hair and very bold and nippy near the ball. He roved to Butch Gale, who palmed the leather off the ball-in from the snail-killer round the boundary. They were great together, Wal and Butch. Both gone now. I think of them sometimes in the middle of the night, which is when I miss them, miss Fitzroy.

Ten years back I used to turn up at the Brandon Hotel in Station Street in Carlton and over a lemon squash or a pot or a not-so-bad-thank-you counter lunch of salmon rissoles and so on, I'd listen to rememberers of battles long ago. When we were called the Gorillas and beat Richmond down at the Junction Oval in 1944. Really gusty stinking hot day it was. And skinny old Royboys dressed in moth-devoured blazers with the old Gorilla sewn on their proud breast-pockets recalled supporters driving to that Grand Final in modified bombs of cars that ran on coal-gas. Eddie Hart and his twin brother, Alby, relived that hallowed occasion and whacked four two-bob coins in the old pool table and, as loving Royboys, defeated each other.

I turned to our front window one day and saw the friendly countenance of Alby Hart again. He had come to see me and to let me look at sacred 1944 Grand Final tickets and embroidered tablecloths and altar-like raiments with the victorious players' names on them and old footy-boot stops with a single dark tack bent in, and in the old man's eyes were Royboy tears from the 1944 Grand Final victory day.

Somehow in my memory this little moment is araldited to memories of Kevin Murray, who won the Brownlow at last in 1969. I saw his inimitableness in the *Herald*, emblazoned and smiling, an enormous beaming grin. That's the only time I remember him smiling.

In the early '60s Murray and his son Glen used to run in bare feet up Banff Street, Keon Park, not far from where my parents lived. Up past the Keon Park Primary School on a wet and foggy morning they would jog, their similar frames trotting like mild-mannered centaurs over pebbly slush and tadpole ponds where little kids used to capture the wriggly things in discarded cream bottles you could rinse out after and cash in at an unlit milk bar for fourpence, a fortune.

I can see them still, running peacefully together along the footpath, moving out onto the road when a car came up on their path because a couple of men had managed to bumpstart it. Kevin and Glen Murray, with bare arms swinging along. And schoolkids chucking yonnies, stones really, at the magpies stuffing around in newly planted gum saplings.

Forty years back isn't much in the scheme of things, but in my insomniac slumbers I keep on waking up back there, in 1963, and I see simpler times and the old bloke who used to sell the 'fresh roasted peanuts' that were at least a hundred years old. No signage on men's guernseys then. They weren't playing for Omo washing powder or Kit Kat chocolates. And even though a lot of them worked as commentators for Channel 7, and got a few bob on the side, or bought a pub, there was an innocence about footy in the days of black-and-white TV. I remember being amazed in the early '70s when hot girls at 'Pie Park tried to dack Peter McKenna, who tried to look like one of the Beatles.

I listen to Rex Hunt do the footy on radio today and wish for people of panache, like Butch Gale and Mike Williamson, and I remember Smoke Rings Hickey inserting rum in his 7-ounce televised glass of Pura Milk on *Football Inquest* and shyly telling the mums and dads and children that milk was his go.

In St Georges Road, Northcote, in mothballs, is a barber shop with swivelling barbershop chairs, and on its wall are hundreds of 1960s hairdresser footy hero pin-ups in grinning cheshire cat black-and-white. Fred Swift who got murdered. Kevin Murray in crew cut and sideboards. Dear old Paddy Guinane of Richmond in the half-dark, looking like Errol Flynn. This is a time capsule of footy as I know it, with the aroma of thirty-year-old Soap On A Rope kits and plastic, tortoise-shell-patterned gent's combs, a shilling each. Verdun Howell and Dessie Tuddenham and a bloke named Sleep who played in his unconsciousness for Fitzroy back then. Melbourne's Bluey Adams with a big red wave combed up at the front, fronting the camera for the Victorian Hairdressers' Association.

Heroism and hero-worship are as ridiculous as they are crucial in the midst of global uncertainty; you dive back into history and find lost urban souls struggling for gods that seem, at least temporarily, credible. In the old days players lived and died for the colours they were born into, and nobody swapped jumpers except after a Grand Final. Today's footballer plays as much for the Commonwealth Bank as for his brain-damaged fans or one-season-at-a-time coach or smartly-stood-down president (who is a CEO in disguise). Once-holy guernseys are adorned with pictures of Chocolate Frogs or Jex Steel Wool Pads or similar products with no bearing whatever on footy.

Dad didn't drink, he had fun just watching the footy with me. He used to run a light HB pencil line in his copy of the *Footy Record* against the names of players picked for that Saturday's game. There were advertisements for Mentholatum Deep Heat and portraits of Qualcast lawnmowers in it, as well as crossword puzzles to fill in at half time with clues to the names of deceased ruckmen or photographs of Des Tuddenham or Russell Crow, our Warracknabeal ruck.

Muzzah never swore at the umpies and never swore at me and Dad in the Outer. He must be sixty or more now, and I don't know what he does for a quid these days. I can't remember him describing the action on the air or being amusing on the telly. Maybe he's uninteresting, like so many courageous heroes of the old times.

An old silent warrior now with backbrace and Drizabone stands in the rain looking up at the vandalised smoking tomb of Brunswick Street Oval Stadium, all prettied up now with gum saplings and hotdog vapour and criminals smoking in the centre-circle punching various mobile phone numbers and wearing sunglasses. I sit in perfect peace as an old Royboy myself, but don't bother interrupting Muzzah.

And forty years goes by like a vicious backhander.

Barry Dickins is a prolific writer, journalist and playwright. His plays include *Roy Boys*, and his books include *Ordinary Heroes, Personal Recollections of Australians at War* and *Black & Whiteley: Barry Dickins in Search of Brett.*

GONE But Not Forgotten

The champions of the,'80s and '90s loom large over today's football. They stamped their personalities on the game, playing with flair and spirit. They were sometimes reckless, sometimes ruthless, but always larger than life. Some came from formidable teams – the Carlton of Stephen Silvagni and Greg Williams, the Hawthorn of Dermott Brereton, the Essendon of Michael Long – others, like Tony Lockett at St Kilda, dragged workmanlike teams into the spotlight.

14

GARY ABLETT
Simply Spectacular

by John Button

In his retirement from football – a stage in his life that might have been private, had being a celebrity not made it so public – Gary Ablett showed feet of clay. Not so as a footballer, where his feet did spectacular things.

This is a story of Gary Ablett the footballer, whom I knew and watched between 1984 and 1996, as did thousands of others who love the game and admire its champions.

One of these people, football commentator Rex Hunt, has a special talent for nicknaming most of his favourite footballers. He called Gary Ablett 'YAABBLETTT' – not so much a nickname as a sound, like an excited cockatoo descending on a wheat crop. Ablett made Rex Hunt's adrenalin run. He thought him the best footballer he had ever seen.

Other commentators and gurus of the game couldn't match Rex Hunt for noise, but shared his opinion of Ablett's ability. They included Robert Walls, Mike Sheahan, Kevin Sheedy, Leigh Matthews, Dermott Brereton and Tim Watson. In their descriptions, the same adjectives keep cropping up: exciting, magical, sensational, freakish. They are not just the words of 'experts' but are etched in the popular imagination of the fans who watched football in the Ablett era.

Football champions turn into legends, some more powerful than others. Even supporters of the weakest teams can find comfort in the past. The legends are fortified by player statistics, video clips and press reports, and spread by word of mouth. Memories sometimes enlarge events in the retelling and can lead to arguments – one book of statistics is described on the cover as 'the greatest argument settler, a must for all

Aussie Rules fans' – but without football's folklore it's likely that some cosy corners in publics, dinner tables and coffee breaks would be as quiet as Trappist monasteries.

Footballers of earlier years are mainly judged by the written records. Triple Brownlow medallists have to be champions. The first of them, Haydn Bunton '1931, '32 and '35', won his first Brownlow aged 19 and the second a year later. In his 119-game career with Fitzroy, he averaged twenty-eight kicks a game and kicked 207 career goals playing as a rover. Later, at Subiaco, he won three Sandover medals. But there are not many alive today to tell his story.

But player statistics are one-dimensional. They only give part of the picture, providing support in arguments, but not much illumination. Some who know them too well can sound like audio versions of a football almanac, when what is needed are pictures, films and, best of all, eye-witness accounts to fill out the story.

Ablett's player statistics are dramatic and somewhat different from those of other champions. In his case they have been supplemented by books, films and the vivid testimony of those who saw him play. Most fans have an Ablett football story, sometimes exaggerated, usually colourful.

His achievements included many of football's less-remembered prizes: Geelong Best and Fairest in 1984 and runner-up in four other seasons; mark of the year; most games in a final series; most goals (nine) in a Grand Final (equalling the record of Gordon Coventry); eleven games for Victoria with an average of four goals a match; stints as captain of Victoria and Geelong; and all-Australian team membership seven times. Ablett kicked a total of 1030 goals in 248 games, making him fifth in total career goals, behind Gordon Coventry, Jason Dunstall, Doug Wade and Tony Lockett. As Geelong full-forward he won three Coleman medals, with tallies of 124 in 1993, 129 in 1994 and 122 in 1995. His performance in the 1989 Grand Final resulted in the Norm Smith medal. On three occasions he kicked fourteen goals in a game.

The most remarkable feature of his player record is that nearly two-thirds of his goals were kicked when he was playing in positions other than full-forward, usually as a midfielder or half-forward flanker. Coventry, Wade, Dunstall and Lockett were all career full-forwards. Ablett was not, with only four years in that position. In nine sometimes interrupted years at Geelong, before he became a permanent full-forward, he averaged sixty-two goals a season. This is a record unsurpassed for consistency and numbers. Leigh Mathews, Ablett's boyhood hero, came closest.

There are no Brownlow medals in the Ablett record book. In seven of his fourteen years at Geelong he managed to render himself ineligible as a result of decisions of the tribunal. In the years he *was* eligible, his Brownlow chances were often compromised by other factors: in 1986 he missed seven games through injury; in 1990 injury cost him five games; in 1991, a 'Clayton's' retirement meant that he played for only half the season. He still managed to notch up a hundred Brownlow votes during his career.

There have been many attempts to define Gary Ablett's talents. Mostly people give up and use words like 'magical'. Dwayne Russell, who played fifty games with Ablett at Geelong, took more time to think about it and explained it as:

> a combination of skill, strength, balance, and ability to read the play. His overall package – a one-off gift. He can out-leap, out-mark and out-sprint any one, as well as out-kick the best from a distance, an angle, with either foot or any style of kick you wish to nominate. There have been footballers his equal in individual areas, but no player has been able to do it all like Ablett.

His skills and athleticism were made more formidable because of his unusual physique, which Kevin Sheedy called 'this magnificent structure'. Dermott Brereton described it colourfully as like 'the old-fashioned fire hydrants – nuggetty, round-shouldered and concreted at the base'.

As a schoolboy footballer playing in under-age competitions, it was his natural ability at running, jumping and reading the game that attracted attention. But then he was a skinny kid with long blond hair. The physical strength, co-ordination and toughness came later. Ablett himself made it all sound simple. 'What you have to do', he said, 'is watch and practise,' advice reiterated by countless hopeful fathers at Auskick sessions.

He was a tough footballer. He handed out shuddering hip-and-shoulder bumps with superb timing. A 'fire hydrant' travelling at high speed is something to watch out for. It caused opponents some anxiety and many of them remember this.

Sometimes he was on the receiving end, caught temporarily off balance and upended, landing heavily on his back or his head. Ablett was matter of fact about this. It was part of the game, the give and take, about which there could be no complaints. In the dressing room after a match at the MCG I found him sitting in a corner, obviously in some pain, with his leg packed in ice. I said something like 'Not too bad, I hope.' 'No worries,' he said, 'just a mild corkage,' which somehow made him sound more like a laidback wine buff than a troubled footballer.

Ultimately it was Ablett's uncanny judgement and ability to do the totally unexpected that made the crowds gasp, though there were times, of course, when he had bad days and the crowd was disappointed. His record in finals, other than 1989, was not great. Sometimes, on the day, he was just beaten, perhaps most often by Carlton's Steven Silvagni, a strong spoiler with good judgement.

It all began with country football, the nursery of many of the league's best players, including a number of its champions. Like Tony Lockett, Gary Ablett came reluctantly to the city: Lockett from Ballarat, Ablett from the small Gippsland town of Drouin. The young Lockett wondered why he would want to play football with 'all these big heads' in the city. The young Ablett clung to the simplicity of country life where he had the choice of football, cricket, fishing or rabbiting. In the 1970s country football was in better shape than it is today. For the players it was very competitive. The games were often rough rather than smooth.

Gary was the youngest of a family of eight. His parents and other relatives of their generation were good at sport. So were his siblings. Four older brothers played football, two in country teams and two (Geoff and Kevin) in the VFL/AFL, mostly at Hawthorn. His three sisters played netball with distinction. It seemed they could all jump.

Gary won the first of a number of school high-jump competitions as a 9-year-old. At the same age he was playing football for Drouin under-12s in the West Gippsland league and won his first Best and Fairest competition. Aged 11 he was Best and Fairest in the under-14s and at 16 he was the youngest player in the Drouin premiership side. By this time he was much in demand as a cricketer and footballer. But he didn't always turn up for games, preferring to go fishing instead.

In these formative years many influences came together. Ablett had an inherited athleticism and a supportive family. When he was 5, his father taught him to kick with his left foot. His older brothers were all experienced footballers and he learnt a few things from them. In kids matches after school they did their own umpiring. 'Decapitation,' according to Ablett, 'was the only ground for a free kick.'

Sports writer Garry Linnell observed that at 16, 'with a body still growing', Ablett had 'earned his place in a world of older, tougher men'.

Linnell described a photo of the Drouin Grand Final side:

> He looks skinny and a little out of place. Around him are the thick arms and whiskered faces of the victors of Drouin, the local farmers, tradesmen and truck drivers, tough men who could cop a knock and keep on going.

He was 12 when the talent scouts of the city clubs first noticed him. In 1977 his father Alf Ablett told Hawthorn officials 'He'll be the best of the lot of them.' The following year, at 16, he played four games with Hawthorn reserves and in 1980 six games. He made his senior football debut in 1982 with six games at Hawthorn. In 1979 and 1981 he had gone back to country football. In 1983 he turned up at Myrtleford in the Ovens Valley league. He seemed to like it, and had a spectacular year. In 1984 he started at Geelong, played his first game for Victoria against Western Australia, kicked eight goals and won the Best and Fairest. It was the end of country football, the beginning of a career in the bright lights.

Geelong had chased Ablett to Myrtleford. Had they not done so he may never have returned to the ranks of major league football. Geelong provided an attractive compromise between the big city and the bush. Sometimes called Sleepy Hollow, Geelong had a sense of community, and in the 1980s the pressures were less. With Corio Bay at the front door and the surf coast at the back, an outdoor lifestyle was more accessible. The football club always had a strong contingent of former country players. At work and play there was less hassle.

Ablett's prior flirtation with Hawthorn is a story of misunderstanding and frustration on both sides. Ablett disliked living in Melbourne and resented the club's disciplined approach to football. Hawthorn made valiant attempts to accommodate him. At one stage he was even allowed to live at Drouin and be picked up for training sessions. The story familiar to country football and cricket clubs – that the teenage star was unavailable for training because he'd gone fishing – didn't sit well with the culture of Hawthorn. On another occasion, he failed to turn up for a reserves game. He'd gone rabbit shooting.

His behaviour was said to be 'wild', and in photos taken at the time he looked it. A few brushes with the law didn't go down well with the worthy burghers of the Hawthorn club. He was an enigma, hard to handle, which had led, in 1983, to his clearance to Myrtleford.

At Geelong the call of the wild, beckoning him back to the country lifestyle, was somewhat muted. But there were still occasions when coaches and officials were driven to despair when told that Ablett had gone fishing when he should have been at a training session. Once, on a Monday holiday, having spent the morning fishing, he arrived at the MCG twenty minutes before the start of a game.

This laidback approach created a dilemma for coaches. Other players couldn't miss training sessions and be late for games. Professional football is a serious business simply because it is a business. Perhaps it's become too serious, certainly it's more serious than it was before money and ambition dictated the rules of professionalism. On the day he was late at the MCG, Ablett kicked five goals in the first quarter. All was forgiven, at least until the next time.

In the story of Gary Ablett as a league footballer there is something reminiscent of Crocodile Dundee. In both cases the boy from the bush who comes to the big smoke has a rustic innocence and disdain for city life that is disarming, and, at the same time, has a toughness and a bag of tricks learnt in a hard school that eases but never quite solves the problem of adjustment.

When he started at Geelong in 1984 Ablett found it 'a happy club': 'If there was any trouble about, I didn't always know about it. I minded my own business.' It took him a long time to appreciate that other people didn't do the same thing, that a highly talented footballer is big media business. He disliked publicity and refused interviews. He was uncomfortable with the lavish praise of commentators and fans. On the field he was undemonstrative. A spectacular goal produced little more than a grin: a bad miss, a dissatisfied shake of the head.

The shyness, the reticence, the 'no comment' gave him an air of mystery in a world of media hype and star gazing. There was some suspicion that Ablett was a contemplative man. A yearning for the solitude of fishing, like pipe smoking, suggests this. Clearly he meant it when he said 'There must be more to life than what I'm doing.' Hence the conversion to Christianity in the mid '80s, which, according to former Geelong captain Michael Turner, changed him to 'a happy, well-organised fella'. Fortunately for football fans, there were no doctrinal dilemmas. 'As soon as I cross that line on Saturday,' Ablett once said, 'my aggression for the ball is there and I realise that once you're out there playing football, Christianity is irrelevant.'

Ablett was liked by his teammates, but made few close friends. They say he had a good sense of humour, they enjoyed his company, and he often offered words of encouragement. Bill Brownless has spoken of Ablett's affection for kids and his visits to sick children in hospital.

Geelong gave Gary Ablett a football home, and despite some hiccups he was good to them. When he was playing, the turnstiles clocked over more than ever before or since. It was the same at the MCG. Officials estimated that he would attract ten thousand extra spectators to a game. Geelong supporters had a good bargain, with two spectacles for the price of one. They went to see the team play, and they went to see Ablett. They got, as it were, the double chance.

Ablett was also good for the AFL, which gained in attendance and publicity for the game. In the '90s when Geelong played in finals, the song 'Ablett's in the Air' was a theme on radio and television promoting football.

In the memories there are some special highlights. A spectacular leap over Collingwood fullback Gary Pert at the MCG was one. Having taken the grab, Ablett fell heavily on his back and lay still. The crowd fell silent. One spectator shouted, 'He's just taken the greatest mark ever, but he's dead!' He wasn't, of course. He was on his feet in a minute and went on to take many more extraordinary marks, including his characteristic one-handers.

At times I chatted with him and found myself, a sceptical, middle-aged man, taking it very seriously. Afterwards, my sons would ask, 'What did he say … ? What did he say?' as if I'd been talking to William Shakespeare. I almost began to believe it myself. Other highlights were kicking fourteen goals against Essendon in a losing side at the MCG, bags of goals against other teams, and of course the 1989 Grand Final, memorable for many reasons, but mostly for him.

The reminiscences still go on; legendary tales are recycled and elaborated. Not long ago in a pub I found myself standing beside a man sitting in the corner of the bar waiting, like a trapdoor spider, with football stories for his next victim. The conversation turned to Ablett. 'You know,' he said, 'I saw him once in a game against the Eagles. He was running towards an open goal bouncing the ball. He spotted Worsfold on the boundary line thirty metres away. Do you know what he did? He veered to the left, accelerated and gave Worsfold an incredible bump. Then he ran on and kicked the goal.'

'Really?' I said, 'did you see that?'

'Mate,' he said, 'I tell you I saw it with my own eyes.'

When Ablett retired temporarily in 1991, a disconsolate former

Geelong champion, Neal Tresize, said 'The game's just not the same without Ablett. I don't enjoy it as much.' There's a bit of truth in that. Spectators and fans can be spoilt.

John Button was Senate Leader of the Hawke and Keating Labor governments from 1983 until his retirement from politics in 1993. His books include *Flying the Kite, On the Loose* and *As It Happened*.

15

PETER DAICOS
The Macedonian Marvel

by Stephen Downes

Peter Daicos, Collingwood's Macedonian Marvel, is proof that genius is the product of obsession. Dumbfounded by the centreman-forward's wizardry throughout a 250-game league career, spectators called his skills freakish. Not a bit of it – they were well learned. Daicos's brilliant slipperiness under pressure from opposing backmen could be explained by a long trunk and low centre of gravity, said commentators – it was hard to knock him off the ball. Again, not the full story. Although one of Collingwood's slowest players in a straight line, Daicos had learned to be evasive in the tiny backyard at his mum's. He could twist and turn like Houdini because he'd done it for years between a clothesline and a backyard lavatory. He knew tight spaces.

When Peter Stanley Daicos was growing up in North Fitzroy in the 1960s, many of the suburb's single-fronted weatherboard cottages were owned by migrants. Stanley and Phyllis Daicos eventually owned two, a couple of doors apart. They had come to Australia independently, as teenagers, from small villages in Macedonia, northern Greece, where, they'd lived simple lives – bread and cheese and village socialising. Now he was a butcher and she was staining furniture in a local factory. Their little house was perfect for a growing family. Their first child, Peter, was born in September 1961 and was later joined by sister Ellen and brother Victor. But with a younger sister and a much younger brother, the Lilliputian backyard space was for many years Peter's alone.

As a child, Daicos was never without his plastic football, bouncing it down the narrow path beside the house, aiming shots for goal through the just-opened lavatory door. Sometimes he'd bind up a toilet roll with tape and kick it around. And what had got into him, his mother asked, that he would guzzle plastic juice grenades so quickly then kick the empty containers around? Their son was by himself, Stanley and Phyllis observed, but never alone; he'd play matches between his beloved Swans and some other league team for hours on end. He'd have player lists – ins and outs. He'd be all positions on both sides. He was obsessed with football. Something resembling one was always in his hands.

It was Stanley's fault, of course. He'd gone to live with relatives in South Melbourne when he arrived in Australia. They took him to Hellas soccer matches, just to be together in their adopted country. But Stanley was intrigued by the awesome roars of the crowds watching another type of footy at the Lake Oval, a few hundred metres away from Hellas's home ground. One day he decided to find out what all the fuss was about, and was let in for free at three-quarter time along with hundreds of others. Despite South Melbourne's position as one of the lowliest clubs, Stanley was hooked immediately, a one-eyed Swans supporter.

Not so many years later, he began taking little Peter to matches. And not long after that the boy was as fixed on footy as his father. On Saturdays before the match, Peter would be in his Swans jumper by 10 o'clock in the morning, the famous number 21 of John Pitura spread across his narrow back. After the game, Stanley would pick up a *Sporting Globe* and Peter would replay the match in the backyard. He'd play and play, until he drove his parents mad or it was too dark to see. Peter was in a world of his own.

These days, Peter Daicos says he 'learned to love the game by actually going to the football'. But he gives equal importance to the solitary matches he played against himself at home. Even though he was picked for a few games with his primary school team, his backyard 'dreamland' footy, as he calls it, continued into his early teenage years. In fact, he didn't get his first full-size leather football – a Christmas gift from the big butchery where Stanley worked – until he was around 9 years old.

Peter and a few of his cousins, including the future playwright and novelist Tom Petsinis, lived near Fitzroy's Edinburgh Gardens. Peter would wait for hours while Tom did his homework so that they could go to the park together for a kick. One night the Clifton Hill under-11s, who were practising in the gardens, saw Peter and invited him to join the team. 'They were battling,' says Peter, but he decided to accept the invitation. In his first match he kicked seven goals. Within a few weeks he was captain.

When the Daicos family moved to Preston a few years later, Peter joined the Preston RSL under-14s. Astute coaching there allowed him to develop the left side of his play comprehensively, and by his mid teens he was patrolling the midfield for Preston and holding down centre half-back when asked. Every night, without fail, Daicos and a few teammates would practise man-on-man, kicking and goaling drills at a vacant ground. Without fail. Even in the rain. (One of those mates, Noel Lovell, played sixteen games for the Magpies in the early '80s.)

SCANLENS 52 of 168

COLLINGWOOD

Peter Daicos, magic man, the Macedonian Marvel.

Invited to train with Collingwood's under-19s, Peter was 'petrified of being a failure' and declined the invitation. This was the big league, and he didn't want to make a fool of himself. A little while later Paul Hepburn, a Preston RSL teammate, was also invited to try out. He went. 'Daics' thought it through. If Paul was there, the two of them could make fools of themselves and it wouldn't hurt so much. So he joined Paul and, to his surprise, was selected. The 15-year-old Daicos played in the last half dozen under-19s games of 1977, playing on the wing. Making minimal impression on club notables, he was listed under an inadvertent alias in Collingwood's annual report, which gave his name as 'Daccos'. (Hepburn played in the seconds but never made the seniors.)

The next year, football appeared to be less of a prospect. After being injured at the beginning of the season and unable to play in the first two matches, Daicos was not picked for the third round. He asked to be cleared to his beloved South Melbourne. Not on, said the Magpies, who were by then convinced of his sublime skills. Peter toyed with the idea of going back to Preston RSL, from where he could more easily move to South. Staying with Collingwood was the smartest decision of his life, he says now. He played ten games with the seconds in 1978, and in round 4 of the following season he was picked for the seniors for the first time. He was 17. He managed six games that season with the firsts, but also won the reserves Best and Fairest.

From 1980 onwards, Daicos was a regular in Collingwood's senior side. It took few matches for him to acquire star status – his ball-handling feats astounded the Magpie faithful, and his long, curly blond locks, strong short legs and surprisingly resilient upper body helped him stand out in the packs. Once near the ball, he charmed it. The fans might talk of spells and bawl 'Magic!', incredulously, from the outer, but they were watching the man grown from the child who could control erratic toilet rolls, plastic footies and soft-drink containers.

With the speed of a cartoon character on uppers, Daicos could scoop a bouncing ball. He would hold off defenders, spreading his legs, bending his knees and anchoring his low frame, while the ball was in flight. And while most of his body kept an opponent from the contest, he would mark the ball with one hand, using trademark touch to reduce its momentum with a backward swing of his arm. He would goal from impossible positions and angles, often dribbling the ball through on the bounce from twenty or thirty metres out. (Even this was a learned skill, he told me: if you kicked the ball low and forcefully enough, it tended to go straight.) He could get away an accurate kick – often resulting in a goal – in mid air, while seemingly off-balance. He was the only footballer ever to learn to make a ball rebound vertically with one hand, the ball oriented as it is for centre bounces. In his best playing days, he says, this skill had become instinctive.

Some of Daicos's feats have lodged more firmly in memory than others. In the 1980 preliminary final, he marked spectacularly in the last quarter over Geelong's Malcolm Reed. The following year he kicked nine goals against Richmond, and a goal against Geelong in that year's Preliminary Final that is among those he remembers most fondly. Collingwood hadn't scored for about twenty minutes and Daicos had marked a long way out from goal, with Ian Nankervis standing the mark. Then Peter played on. Ask him why, and he doesn't know. But he decided, instinctively, to handball over Nankervis's head. He believes it might have been because players had gone back to the goal square, leaving a lot of empty space behind Nankervis. He ran around the Geelong player and quickly retrieved the bouncing ball. He ran another ten metres and goaled from about thirty-five metres out, putting the Magpies in front.

He seemed to make a habit of goaling from twenty-five to thirty-five metres out on the boundary. Another favorite goal came in the 1990 qualifying final against the West Coast Eagles. It was instinct again, Daicos says, that had him hugging the boundary line in the left pocket and jabbing a banana kick with his right foot to score a major. That was perhaps his best season, and he finished it with some astonishing goals in Collingwood's Grand Final win.

Daicos concedes, modestly, that these were 'bonus' goals, the ones that make a difference in a game. He never trained specifically to score them. The ball went between the big sticks only because he was playing the 'percentages', as he puts it. His scoring ability was 'instinctive', he says, and he always ran towards the goalmouth with an open mind, trying 'not to confuse myself too much'. He knew pretty much what he wanted to do each time he got his hands on the ball. People would ask him how he conjured his miracles and he'd reply that he was on 'auto-pilot'. He simply did not hesitate. What he wanted to do and whatever it was that compelled him instinctively to do it were never in conflict. (Long before Anthony Rocca was urged to torp six points from beyond the 50-metre line, Peter would occasionally roost an enormous torpedo punt from a similar distance, just for good measure.) His ninety-seven goals in 1990 are a record for a non-full-forward, and he was Collingwood's leading goalkicker in 1981, 1982, 1990, 1991 and 1992, his last full season. His career tally was 549.

Daicos was subjected to very close attention throughout his career, and was tagged as a matter of course. Looking back, he wishes he'd had even a handful of games in which he could have played wide of his opponent and crumbed and goaled at will. What stats we would have seen then! Tagging and persistent tackles took a physical – but never psychological – toll, and Daicos has the dubious honour of being among the Magpies' most injured players. Without injuries, he believes he might have played another seventy games.

In all, Daicos had eleven knee operations, including a complete reconstruction of his left knee, an ankle reconstruction, three groin operations and a tendon graft from his forearm to save the fourth finger of his left hand. (Amputation had been an alternative.) He has had teeth knocked out and his nose broken. But his worst injury produced feet like 'eggshells' in 1987. He thought his career was over.

Towards the end of the 1986 season he had developed stress fractures in both feet, and had also torn a tendon off the bone in his left. At first, Collingwood's football department put him on the retired list. But some at the club argued for Daicos to continue. Coach Leigh Matthews had doubts. Eventually, it was decided that Daicos, who could scarcely walk, could play but would do only half an hour of training on Thursdays. Before each match painkillers were injected into the sides of his feet, and sometimes into the backs of the ankles. At half time he'd be injected again. He managed nine games, Collingwood declined to honour his full contract, and one of the game's greats made just $27,000 that year from his profession. The following season, he won one of his two Copeland trophies for being Collingwood's best player (the other was in 1982) and was nominated the best player in the finals.

Despite his early obsession with the Swans, Peter Daicos stuck by Collingwood to the end. Yet the temptations to leave were huge. In 1982, when the Magpies were paying him only $40,000 a year, he was offered $120,000 a year by Richmond. And in his last year of football, 1993, he earned a relatively meagre $80,000 – admittedly he only played five games.

The end, when it came, was far from satisfying. By that time Daicos was a life member of the club. He had been vice-captain for 1990 and 1991, having been deputy vice-captain in 1988 and 1989, and having earned a special award for services to the club in 1985. He had also represented Victoria in 1981, 1984, 1988 and 1990. But in 1994 Daicos, Michael Gayfer and Shane Morwood were simply dropped from the playing list by Colling-wood, who needed to stay within their salary cap while accommodating payments to star recruit Nathan Buckley. Peter says he would have loved to have continued into 1994. Collingwood, he believes, should have told him in 1993 that he was playing his last year; he would have appreciated playing all the more knowing the curtain was coming down, instead of suffering to recover from injuries so as to play on.

Daicos didn't need to play football for the money. He had successfully owned pubs and other real estate through most of his playing days. (Although the late-1980s crash and high interest rates saw him lose free-holdings and very large amounts of money.) But even now, he occasion-ally dreams of playing 'one last game'. He is well aware it is beyond him. He would do it simply for the pleasure. Paradoxically, perhaps, he says that he has learned to live without footy. Nowadays, his only professional contact with the game that gave him fame and huge satisfaction is through broadcasting matches for the Ten network and 3AW.

Daicos wouldn't consider coaching, even though he is one of the game's most perceptive analysts. (He regards football as all about learn-ing how to play when you haven't got possession; 'reading' a football match, analysing it, is what makes the best players, he says.) Coaching would absorb too much of his time, taking him from his adored wife, Colleen, and his children, Madison, Joshua and baby Nicholas.

Peter Daicos's skills burnt your retinas, and no-one who has seen him play needs an expert to say why he was so good. His skills were transpar-ent. Leigh Matthews, his 1990 coach and someone whom Daicos himself admires tremendously, says that the great goaling opportunist was a player who could do special things at the right time. 'That's what the people want to see, that's what captures their imagination … That is how Daicos will be remembered.'

Stephen Downes writes about food for the *Herald Sun* and the *Australian*, and is author of the award-winning book *Advanced Australian Fare*. His profile of Jock McHale appeared in *Footy's Greatest Coaches*.

16

DERMOTT BRERETON
The Kid Takes His Final Bow

by Martin Flanagan

Perhaps I saw later than most how complete a footballer Dermott Brereton was, but it was hard to assess the full stature of the individuals in the great Hawthorn side of the '80s because it was such an excellent team.

I never doubted his importance to the side, nor the sense of menace he was capable of engendering, which followed him around the field like a dark marauding spell. In 1989, I saw him single-handedly destroy Essendon in a final at Waverley.

That was the year he took the shirt-front to a new and terrifying level of efficiency, leaving victims with whiplash and other injuries consistent with car crashes. Greg Champion sang 'Dermott Brereton is a Hood', but in the commentary box, Mr Football, E.J. Whitten, said it brought him tears of joy to see the Kid with the blond perm in action.

In the Grand Final of that year, Dermott famously met with retribution, and retribution is a principle he has never argued with. Like most people that day, I was dazzled by the performance of Geelong's Gary Ablett, but when I watched a replay of the match a few years later what struck me, to my surprise, was not Ablett's peerless performance but the sheer ferocity with which Brereton played for a sustained period of thirty minutes or so after he was wounded. Legend has it that he passed blood in the toilet at half time and, by the end of the match, his injuries were such that his body had seized and he was standing immobile in a forward pocket. I was behind him when the final siren sounded. He immediately threw an arm around Geelong's Michael Schultz and embraced him. That was the Kid, the devil with the angelic grin, and if he was capable of being positively dangerous, there was also a sense that he possessed his own code of right and wrong.

In 1992, leaving the field after a reserves match against Essendon when he was attempting to come back from the hip injury that curtailed his career, Brereton removed the spectacles from the face of an Essendon supporter, crushed them and threw them ten rows back. The incident was widely reported in more or less those terms, but the real story was a whole lot better than that. True, the supporter had abused Dermott, telling him he belonged in a cripples home, but that had not caused him to take offence. The Essendon supporter had gone on to say that he belonged in the cripples home with two Essendon players, Terry Daniher and Simon Madden.

Anyone who saw the 1985 Grand Final will recall that Dermott and Terry Daniher spent the best part of one whole quarter attempting to strangle one another while a goal umpire circled them ineffectually, demanding they release each other. Dermott's attitude on match day towards his opponents was one of unholy aggression, but it is also the case that there is no game without them and, in his view, Daniher and Madden had been magnificent opponents. There is a bond, Dermott has written, that unites those who play in Grand Finals, victors and losers alike. He broke the Essendon supporter's glasses not because of what was said about him, Dermott Brereton, but because of what was said about the two former Essendon greats.

Over the past two years, I have come to follow Dermott's weekly writings in the *Age*. His pieces are thoughtful, and periodically they display a compelling candour. The most fully realised of them was about the 1977 Grand Final, which he watched as a committed 13-year-old Collingwood supporter behind the goal at the northern end of the ground, sitting on his folded-up lumber jacket to get a better view.

Ultimately, what Dermott saw was Phil 'The Snake' Baker kicking the goal that put North Melbourne seven points ahead late in the final quarter. It was, he wrote, a horrifying moment (and when he uses the word horrifying, I think he means it):

Snake turned and ran up the field to thank the previous ball disposer. He had two thumbs upright to indicate a goal.

He lifted his arms and his six-point signal began to look like Rocky Balboa's world champion victory pose. I wanted the ground to open up and consume him. I marvel at his finals performances now, but back then he was evil to me.

Snake Baker had made him feel despair.

But travelling home to Frankston on the train, listening to the chatter, seeing the excitement and animation around him, the 13-year-old had another perception. One person had created all this. One person had this effect on thousands of people. He wrote: 'I knew my life had a target from that moment.'

Dermott had two footballing heroes as a kid. The first was 'Fabulous' Phil Carman. (Remember Phil's white boots? Remember Dermott's luminous green ones?) His other hero was Collingwood's dour craftsman and captain, Max Richardson. In an interview before the '77 Grand Final, Richardson said Collingwood would approach the game like any other. The rules were the same; the ground and the teams were the same – why do anything differently? The young Dermott took this as a public guarantee that his beloved Pies would not get stage fright on the big day and was fortified.

Dermott Brereton, celebrates one of his five Premierships, *courtesy of Sport the Library*

Seventeen years later, however, he wrote that Richardson was wrong. Finals aren't like other games. You have to know that and be excited by the fact:

> You have to accept that your actions and moves control the emotions of 100,000 people.
>
> You have to realise you can make them yell, cry, admire or despise you. It is a very powerful feeling and very few people in this world ever feel it. I loved it. Snake Baker loved it.

So did E.J. Whitten. Like Whitten, one has the impression that Brereton would happily have played football with a minimum of rules, entrusting the maintenance of law and order to the ancient principle of payback. But, also like Whitten, he had a sense of the sport as theatre and of his own central place on the stage. You don't have to know a lot about Celtic mythology to suspect that Dermott has lived before. Did the legendary warrior of Irish mythology, Cuchulain, not say that he would happily live for only one day if his fame were to live forever?

The name by which Dermott first became known was the Kid.

When he kicked eight recklessly courageous goals and stood alone against the all-conquering might of Kevin Sheedy's Essendon side in the 1985 Grand Final, sportswriters wrote reams in his praise, but I thought Garry Linnell expressed it best in five words: 'The Kid has no respect.' No respect for the fact that his team was beaten, that his cause was lost, that defeat was inevitable.

You don't have to know a lot of Australian history to realise that there was a surplus of youths with the Kid's attitude to life languishing around the colony a hundred or so years ago when football was beginning to acquire some real social momentum. They may not have tinted their hair like Dermott, but in the case of the Greta mob they wore their hatbands under their noses and expressed their determination to be 'bold, fearless and free'. It was the determination of the authorities to take 'the flashness' out of them that contributed to what is known as the Kelly outbreak.

Only occasionally nowadays do I hear anyone call Dermott the Kid. More often he's 'Dermie'. Dermie's still flash and a bit of a lair, but he's a financially successful one.

But, unlike the Kid, Dermie knows the price of fame. Last year, he warned North Melbourne's Wayne Carey, his successor as the next great centre half-forward in the history of the game, that being famous means that a certain proportion of people will dislike you, possibly intensely, without even knowing you.

And in announcing his retirement this week he alluded in the most restrained way (Dermie is calculating in his use of the media) to a far greater cost. His father committed suicide in 1993 on the day he was to appear in court on sex-related charges. He said: 'I think it's fair to say that my father would still be alive if his son had not been a famous sportsman.'

My view of Dermott Brereton altered perceptibly one day at the Western Oval in 1994 when Footscray played the Swans. Dermott was soundly beaten, but that is an inadequate summary of his performance. When he left the field with a hamstring injury in the third quarter, the Swans promptly lost their shape and competitiveness. Even kickless, he could hold a team together around him.

He had lost the edge in pace necessary to play centre half-forward, but it was only seeing him thoroughly beaten, and seeing in a naked way the strategies he employed to get into the match – the shrewd positioning, the hard running, the patience, the tenacity – that I fully understood the element of craft in his game.

Dermott has strutted the football stage, arms oiled and chest inflated, but inside the performer was a very thoughtful footballer. When he returned in 1994 after a three-year absence, he immediately knew the game had changed. How did he know? The new centre half-backs were taller and quicker than their predecessors, and more adept at running off him, but they didn't lead him to the ball as Bruce Doull and Paul Roos might have done. They were better athletes, but not better footballers.

It is in the logic of his thinking that one sees Hawthorn.

The great Hawthorn side of which he was part trained for short periods but at maximum intensity and with the emphasis on faultless execution. They knew the degree of football proficiency they could achieve was higher than anyone else's, and they knew they could sustain it for longer. That knowledge was the source of their confidence or, to use Dermott's word, arrogance. That is Dermott's prescription for the correct approach to the contest: arrogant, but not overconfident.

Brereton's temperament meant that he fitted in at Collingwood like a hand in a black-and-white glove, and Magpie supporters can only wonder what might have been had he played with them in his prime, particularly in those years when the Magpie midfielders were running themselves ragged banging the ball forward and there was no-one to catch it or even hold it in.

But even an ageing Dermie had something to offer the Pies.

Against Essendon on Anzac Day at the MCG, he held back whole packs (illegally, of course) and allowed big Sav Rocca a clear run at the ball and the chance to begin fulfilling his awesome potential. Against North, he and Micky Martyn grappled like two pink sumo wrestlers in tight shorts before the ball had even been bounced. They made the vast stadium come roaring to life in a way that no video display or pre-match promotion ever will. (The AFL's response to the incident demonstrated a confusion between show violence, which is a legitimate part of the game, and real violence, which is not.) The last time I saw Dermott Brereton play football was against Fitzroy at Victoria Park. He still had the same theatrical muscularity, but he looked stiff, fragile almost, as if he was liable to break if dropped at the wrong angle, and I thought of the elastic-limbed youth I had seen in the '85 Grand Final.

Like Whitten, Brereton was not that big a man for the role he played on the football field or the impact that he had.

I thought of something else he had written: 'Once I thought I was indestructible because I was the aggressor. That aggression has not taken away my fitness abruptly, but methodically removed it in gradual stages like cancer ...'

Dermie was now like the old boxer in Jack London's great short story, 'The Fight', who knows he has only a couple of punches to throw and the art is in knowing when to throw them.

The Roys led all day, relying on erratic skills and wayward inspiration, but late in the third term their nerve faltered.

Dermott was in. A flurry of elbows in a pack served to discourage the opposition from competing too eagerly; minutes later, he followed it with a big mark and a goal. It is too much to say that he won the match for Collingwood, but there is no doubt he was part of the win.

But, as of this week, the show is over. I, for one, am pleased Dermott Brereton played the extra year with Collingwood; there is a sense of completion, for a spectator of the game, in seeing the whole of a player's career. But Yabby Jeans, one of the wise old men of football, was also right when he told Dermott he ran the risk of being remembered as the player he had become and not the magnificent player he once had been.

For me, Dermott Brereton's departure from the game is the most significant since Peter Daicos's, and possibly more meaningful.

If E.J. Whitten truly was Mr Football, I don't see anyone in the modern era who resembled him more, both as a player and a performer, than Brereton. And, in the end, as with E.J. Whitten, it has to be said of Dermott Brereton that he loved the game.

Martin Flanagan writes for the *Age*. His books include *Southern Sky, Western Oval, The Call* and his recent memoir *In Sunshine and in Shadow*.

'**The Kid Takes His Final Bow**' first appeared in the *Age* in 1995.

17

Dermott Brereton is a Hood

by Greg Champion

verse 1:

Robbie Flower is a champion,
　　Rioli is a star,
but they don't break legs
　　like big Paul Van Der Haar.
Tommy Alvin is a beauty,
　　Mark Arceri is reasonably good.
Jimmy Jess is Jimmy Jess.
　　But Dermott Brereton is a hood.

chorus:

Dermott Brereton is a hood,
　　Dermott Brereton is a hood.
A bloke that comes from Frankston
　　could never be any good.
I wouldn't try to tell ya
　　if I didn't think I should,
but he's your classic Aussie knucklehead,
　　Dermott Brereton is a hood.

verse 2:

Now some folks catch the umpy's eye,
    some just do their jobs.
Some are trim and fit
    and some are slobs.
Some are quite intelligent,
    some misunderstood,
some are well brought up,
    but Dermott Brereton is a hood.

repeat chorus

Greg Champion is an award-winning songwriter, and a longstanding member of radio team the Coodabeen Champions, for whom this song was written. His songs, *That's the Thing About Football* and *Cricket's on the Radio* are classics.

18

GREG WILLIAMS
Too Old, Too Slow, Two Brownlows

by Garrie Hutchinson

Greg 'Diesel' Williams is one of the greatest players ever to pull on a boot, and also one of the most controversial. He was one of the footballers most admired for their skill with the ball, but he attracted jeers from those who barracked for the clubs he wasn't playing for at the time. He hardly gave an interview in his thirteen-year career, which stretched from 1984 to 1997, but he chatted like a kookaburra to his teammates, directing traffic on the field.

Williams was twice rejected by Carlton before playing thirty-four games for Geelong, 107 for Sydney and then, finally, 109 for Carlton. He's a proud footballer who can let his record speak for itself: 250 games, two Brownlow medals, a Norm Smith medal for best on the ground in a Grand Final. But there are also thirty-four matches lost through suspension for offences including striking, kneeing and attempting to strike opposition players, and abusing and 'interfering with' an umpire.

Williams plied his trade as a professional footballer, seeking 'promotion' by moving from Geelong to Sydney and then to Carlton, and expected a pay rise with each move. Football was a job to him; it offered a determined Bendigo boy a means to make his way in the world, to set up himself and his family. He expected to be paid what the market would bear for his skills, and occasionally a bit more. Certainly Williams shifted clubs to better himself, but it mustn't be forgotten just how much he was wanted by those clubs.

From his first game, it was plain to all opposing coaches and players that Williams was a rare genius, one who would have to be tagged and scragged. They would try to suck him in to get his mind off the job. They would try to exploit his slow legs by hammering at his quick brain.

Williams expected to be treated that way. He didn't like it – thought he wasn't given the protection of the rules – but played on, his determination and belief in his ability sufficient to keep him going. Occasionally he did see red: once, famously, when Williams evened up after David Rhys-Jones, literally, broke his back; once when Sean Denham aggravated him sufficiently for Williams to shove a nearby umpire. When wronged, Williams sometimes tried, in word or deed, to put things right.

A measure of Williams's importance as a player is that his clubs defended him beyond what might have been sensible, especially Carlton in what became his final season – perhaps they were compensating for rejecting him at the start of his career. Williams repaid their loyalty. He could still be seen at Optus Oval in the dark days of 2002, when he served as a club director and part-time assistant coach, and occasionally jogged onto the field at quarter time, still looking fit enough to park in a forward pocket. Caught up in the battle over regime change, he retired as a director before Carlton's 2002 Annual General Meeting.

Cruelled from the age of 18 by the idea that he was too slow and too small to make it in league football, Williams, at 86 kilograms and 175 centimetres, was helped by two of the most significant laws of football physics. The first footy law is that the ball travels faster than any player can run. The second is that the ball spends ninety per cent of its time on the ground. Add to this that Greg Williams was an ambidextrous freak, perhaps the first footballer to be equally, perfectly good on both sides of his body. And he had eyes in the back of his head.

He averaged near thirty possessions over 250 games. More importantly, he did things with those possessions that tempted the aficionado to sit high enough in the grandstand to see the pattern of play and delight in the way he delivered the ball.

How do I describe what Williams could do with a footy? He could make it talk, he could play it like a yo-yo, he could direct it through a moving mass of players, spotting gaps as bodies kaleidoscoped in front of him and rocketing the ball through them to just the point he wanted it to reach. Anyone who thinks handpassing a footy twenty metres through a pack to a player timed to be in a specific space at the precise moment the footy arrives should try it while playing kick to kick on the 'G after a game (and the second siren). The calculations are immense; there's only a split second to think, and only the most skilful players can execute such a pass.

Williams used handball more effectively than other, bigger players had ever done. He had to; he is perhaps the first player to build a career by handballing more often than he kicked. As he wrote:

If you are slow in the legs, as I am, but quick in the head, handballing makes all the difference. It is so much quicker than kicking. You can do it from low down, where the ball is most of the time. You can do it while off balance. And you can develop pin-point accuracy up to 30 metres – further than that, I admit you have to kick!

Handball is the assault weapon to set up plays with your team-mates; it's the great initiator. And if you have peripheral vision – the ability to see mates who are out of the immediate vicinity – you can use handball in all directions.

Williams's equal skill on left and right, and ability to execute the pass at a distance, meant he could use handball as a first option. The technique has been handed down at Carlton to Brett Ratten. Supporters still peer into mauling packs and shake their heads in amazement as a footy rockets out to someone running past – 'Just like Diesel.'

With the passing of time, which is accelerated in the football universe – where a couple of premierships is an 'era' and a handful of good games makes a champion – Williams's remembered genius has just about overcome the passing controversies of his career. He was a touchstone in professional football because he was so good, and his reactive indiscretions – such as with Rhys-Jones and that ump – have to be seen in that light. That football is a physical game is one of football's clichés, and robust champions who are not angels – Jack Dyer, say – are forgiven their indiscretions in retirement.

How many players have scored three Brownlow votes in their first league game? Diesel did, on his debut for Geelong, against Fitzroy on 31 March 1984. His first game also happened to be the first for two of football's other controversial players, Gary Ablett and Mark 'Wacko' Jackson. That 1984 game saw Ablett gather twenty kicks, two handballs, eight marks and three goals, Jacko boot 9.2, and Williams rack up an astonishing twenty kicks and seventeen handpasses, and kick a goal. With talent like that, it's difficult to understand, in retrospect, why Geelong didn't do better in the Hafey years of 1983–1985.

In that first game, Williams also received eight free kicks – something that wasn't likely to happen again – and made his first trip to the tribunal.

He was there as a victim, because a Fitzroy player had been reported for biffing him. The case was thrown out. Ablett also appeared at the tribunal that night – and was given three weeks for whacking Garry Wilson.

Diesel's third game, at Princes Park, was a chance to show the powers-that-remained at Carlton what they'd missed out on. Williams had had a run with Carlton over the 1981–82 summer as an 18-year-old, when Parkin was in his first coaching stint with the Blues, but he was rejected as being too short, too slow. Williams had gone back for another tremendous season with Golden Square in the Bendigo league, winning the Michelson medal for the league's best player for the season, securing twice as many votes as the runner up. After that, he had had another run with Carlton, with the same result: back to Golden Square and another Michelson medal.

At Princes Park, that day, against direct opponent Wayne 'Dominator' Johnston, Williams gained eighteen kicks and sixteen handpasses, gathering two Brownlow votes, and Geelong won by twenty-nine points. Carlton coach David Parkin acknowledged: 'Everyone in football makes mistakes, and I'm pleased for Greg's sake that he is doing well.'

In Williams's first season for Geelong, 1984, coach Tom Hafey organised a motivational movie before a game at Waverley, then still called VFL Park. It was an American football game of biff and tackle, featuring the fearsome New York Jets / Washington Redskins running back John Riggins, known as Diesel. Mick Turner, the speedy Geelong winger, suggested that 'Diesel' would be a good moniker for the young Williams, and it stuck.

But where did Riggins get the name? After all, he was a 6'2", 240-pound frightening running machine who, once he got wound up, was as unstoppable as the old Melbourne–Sydney train, the *Spirit of Progress*. Riggins had scored the winning touchdown in 1984's Superbowl XVII with a tackle-breaking, forty-three-yard run, but it was in an earlier play-off game that a fan draped Riggins's car with a banner that said 'Riggins runs on diesel power, high octane.'

Williams reckoned the name was OK, because diesel has a low ignition point compared to petrol. Most of us, however, probably associate diesel with unstoppable engines that aren't too fast, start in any weather, and are completely steady and reliable. When David Parkin started talking about a team's 'engine room' in the early 1980s, he was referring to players like Williams, who would set up play by going in and getting the footy.

Geelong finished sixth in Williams's two seasons with them, and he was Best and Fairest in the second of them. Coach Tom Hafey liked him, called him 'uncanny' and, in a rare compliment from Kick It Long Tommy, praised a handballer who couldn't.

Football and Geelong being what they are, Hafey was sacked at the end of Williams's second season, and was snapped up by Sydney, then under the chequebook of Dr Geoffrey Edelsten. Williams would have preferred to stay at Geelong, but he wanted more money for 1986, requesting a raise from $45,000 to $50,000. Edelsten had already offered him around $100,000. When Geelong refused Williams's terms, he was off to Sydney, along with Gerard Healy, Merv Neagle, Paul Morwood, Jim Edmond and Glenn Coleman – not a bad bag of players.

Williams had a terrific 1986 season for Sydney, winning the Brownlow (sharing it with another robust centreline player, Hawthorn's Robert Dipierdomenico), and the Swans finished second on the ladder before exiting the finals in straight sets. In 1987, coming off a season as Brownlow medallist in a finals-playing side, Diesel was set up for tagging, and the attention would dog him for the rest of his career, prompting the occasional outburst. 'Sam' Newman asked him about it later that year:

'Do taggers ever make you lose your cool?'

'It's frustrating, it is for everyone who is tagged. I tell them straight, "If you hang on to me, be ready."'

'For what?'

'A hard day.'

Edelsten's assocation with Sydney ended, and the team, owing money to players, was taken over by a group called Powerplay, then by the VFL and then by Mike Willessee. Hafey left at the end of 1988, and Col Kinnear took over as coach. Williams wanted to leave too. After some legal and contractual acrimony, he ended up at Carlton in 1992, but not before he'd been fined $25,000 by the VFL and deregistered for eleven weeks (which included the first six games of the season). He had been punished for Sydney's breach of the salary cap, because the team had allowed a portion of his payment to be paid by a team sponsor in an attempt to place it outside the cap. Not for the first time, a player was scapegoated for faults of the system.

Greg Williams, a kookaburra on the paddock, *courtesy of Carlton Football Club*.

In 1993, Williams gave the only extensive on-the-record interview he seems to have given, speaking to Peter Wilmoth of the *Age*. It began like this:

Age: The public perception of you is that you are an extremely shy, retiring bloke.

Diesel: It is true. I am very shy. I don't like talking.

Age: Why don't you?

Diesel: I don't know. I'd rather listen. I talk to people I know, but I talk on the ground, probably more than anyone else on the ground … I just let it all out.

It continued in similar vein.

Age: What's your background?

Diesel: Spanish, Dad's grandmother.

Age: Has being a football superstar changed you?

Diesel: I don't think about it that way. I just train and play and go home. I don't think I'm someone special. Most players are like that. Supporters can get carried away with players. They think they're someone special … but they're not, they're just lucky that they have a gift. I'm lucky enough to be able to do it.

Age: Who's the real Greg Williams?

Diesel: I can play football. That's about it really.

Age: That's all? There must be more to you than that.

Diesel: That's all I've done so far. Football and brought up three kids.

Williams acknowledged in his 1994 autobiography that 'I appear to behave like two different people. On the field, whether it's at training or in a match, I am something of an extrovert. I talk all the time, getting my teammates to do things as I read the play.' Rod Carter, the great Fitzroy and Sydney fullback, described the same quality:

> Williams gives the impression that talking gives him pain. When he does speak, people strain to hear. But on match days things are different – a loud voice erupts from deep within his stocky frame. He is thoughtful and precise. These qualities combine and one feels his intensity in every word. When he speaks his teammates listen.

In 1995 Carlton made the Grand Final. Watching Diesel in that match was like watching a craftsman at work creating something perfect, a chair or a watch perhaps. All the elements were finely honed and perfectly balanced, the end result almost beautiful.

Having been caught from time to time during his Carlton career by young pups running off him, coach David Parkin and Williams's joint plan was to reinvent Williams as a visionary forward. Although the plan was hardly a secret, there wasn't much the opposing team, Geelong, could do about it. Diesel ended up with thirty-one possessions, five goals and the Norm Smith medal. He also provided the footy for three Stephen Kernahan goals. No-one noticed how fast Williams's legs had to be in this game because his footy brain was so quick. In this dominating Carlton team he seemed to reinvent himself as a centre-man/forward before our eyes – so much so that he sometimes seemed to reappear in the forward line on the end of his own passes out of the centre action.

Diesel reached his 250th game, his last, in a round 16 demolition of Essendon on 19 July 1997. As with his first game, he was named best on the ground by most scribes. Although neither Essendon nor Carlton would trouble the scorers in the finals, any win against Essendon was satisfying for the Blues. No-one knew for sure that it would be Williams's last game, but he was chaired off the field after a top class performance: twenty kicks, nine handballs, seven marks and a goal.

The win had special meaning for Williams, as it allowed him to confront Sean Denham, the pestiferous opponent who in round 1 had called him a 'fat ...' after the game, provoking the enraged Blue to push at field umpire Andrew Coates in a reflex action, for which he was reported. Denham had form as far as Diesel was concerned, having been reported for striking Williams early in the 1993 Grand Final, for which he was duly suspended, but in his 250th game Diesel, as in most of his games, had simply got on with the business of demonstrating his football skills.

Coach David Parkin was especially delighted by a demonstration of Williams's quick thinking that day, as he paused before giving a handball to Luke O'Sullivan for a goal. 'Most blokes would have just hit it,' Parkin said after the match. 'Luke wasn't sure whether to go or stay, but once Greg helped him just by hanging on to the ball a bit longer, it gave him a bit more space ... it's a very special ability.' O'Sullivan repaid the favour by being one of the players to chair the champ off the MCG.

The legal drama that followed Williams's round 1 report and subsequent nine-week suspension had its final act on 25 July, when the Court of Appeal upheld the tribunal's original order, after the AFL had appealed against a Supreme Court of Victoria decision earlier in the season to set aside Williams's suspension. Most observers, even those enamoured of neither Williams nor Carlton, had considered this an excessive sentence. Williams, who had been picked to play against North Melbourne in the following round, had to begin serving his sentence, and fulfilled his promise to the footy world to retire immediately. This meant that Carlton President John Elliott's desire to appeal to the High Court of Australia became redundant. So Diesel's 250th game became his last. A week later Carlton, without Williams, lost to North Melbourne, and with that result they lost any chance of playing in the 1997 finals.

Parkin reflected ruefully on Williams's career:

He's been a wonderful player who we've all sucked on, all of us, you journalists as well ... a most harshly done-by player ... From the time I gave him the arse here [at Carlton in the 1980s] everybody, every opponent, coach, player, umpire and now the competition itself has tried to stop him plying his trade in a reasonable fashion.

Greg's had to play the way he's had to play because of the treatment he has incurred, and I put my hand up – I was a coach who put people out to do the same sort of job, and it shouldn't be allowed to happen.

Justin Madden, who had recently retired himself, wrote:

Through all these months of uncertainty, Greg has gone about his life in a workmanlike manner he is known for on the field, and has displayed not one ounce of the bitterness or frustration that might be expected in such circumstances.

Diesel is uncompromising in his expectation of his own performance and the performance of others. On his arrival at the club it took little time for all to notice the intensity with which he trained and the direct relationship to his performance. [This intensity] was soon being practised by probably all his playing colleagues and hence the vastly improved performance on the field by the team ...

Relentlessly tagged throughout his career, there have been occasions when the lack of protection delivered to him by the umpires and the game have justifiably failed to live up to his and his colleagues' expectations.

Greg Williams was selected an all-Australian eight times and was named the AFL Players Association's most valuable player in two seasons. He won the Norm Smith medal once and the Brownlow twice. Williams has been named in the AFL Team of the [20th] Century. He is one of football's greatest.

Garrie Hutchinson has written and edited many books about football, and other Australian matters. He co-edited *Footy's Greatest Coaches*, which included his essay on Carlton's great early coach Jack Worrall.

'Too Old, Too Slow, Two Brownlows' appeared in an earlier version in the 2001 AFL Hall of Fame program.

19

STEPHEN SILVAGNI
Number One in Any Language

by Tony de Bolfo

When football historians reflect on the seventeen seasons of the game's greatest fullback in a hundred years, they will cite the aftermath of an otherwise forgettable home-and-away fixture as the pivotal moment of Stephen Silvagni's career.

The moment came late on the afternoon of Saturday, 15 May 1993, after Footscray had comfortably accounted for Carlton by 28 points at the ground then known as Princes Park. As the final siren blared, Silvagni trudged from the field knowing he had just turned in probably his worst ever showing in the famed no. 1 navy blue guernsey.

At the time, the 1991 club Best and Fairest had come off two injury-interrupted seasons. A torn anterior cruciate ligament in his right knee had put paid to the latter half of his '91 season, while '92 was a virtual write-off after he dislocated tendons and damaged a lateral ligament in his left ankle.

Now, a third of the way into season '93, Silvagni was suffering from a vastly different, but no less disruptive complaint: a leaky eye. Despite impaired vision, he had opted to make himself available for the Bulldogs match. He had miscalculated. In the Monday papers, members of the fourth estate were justifiably scathing of Silvagni's showing, and to this day he wishes the match could be wiped from the record books. But he didn't wait for the Monday morning fallout. In the dressing rooms immediately after the match, out of self-annoyance and anger, Silvagni took control of the situation, determined to avert the very real prospect of being a non-contributor for a third successive season.

Silvagni opted to alter radically his pre-match preparation. From mid-May 1993 through to his retirement in September 2001, Silvagni willed himself through a three-and-a-half-kilometre run before each training session, and would sometimes run another three-and-a-half-kilometres afterwards. He would never again take to the field under-prepared. The results were dramatic. Fate placed Silvagni in an era of great full-forwards – Tony Lockett, Jason Dunstall, Gary Ablett – but with his body honed and his self-belief bouyed, he more than held his own.

Of course, Silvagni was blessed with a football pedigree. His father, Sergio, made his name under difficult circumstances for both himself and Carlton. When Serge first turned out for the Carlton seniors – against the Swans in round 7, 1958 (co-incidentally, Stephen debuted against the Swans in round 7, 1985) – more than a decade had elapsed since the club's last premiership. Two hundred and thirty-eight games, two premierships and two club Best and Fairests later, the name Silvagni was as much a part of the Carlton vernacular as Lygon Street. And to think that Serge's father, 'Jack' Silvagni, had disembarked from an Italian passenger ship in Melbourne in September 1924 and spent his first night on a park bench in the Exhibition Gardens.

Five years after his retirement as a Carlton player at the end of 1971, Serge Silvagni returned to Carlton as an assistant coach and member of the match committee. Stephen, who had not yet turned 10, took his father's hand and followed him there, and has been there ever since.

Fortuitously for the boy, the team was on the verge of a spectacularly successful era, from 1979, when the players took out the flag under captain-coach Alex Jesaulenko, through 1980, when they completed the home-and-away season in second position, under Peter 'Percy' Jones, and on to back-to-back premierships in 1981 and '82 under David Parkin.

The players at Parkin's disposal were unquestionably talented, but they also played hard – on and off the field. Silvagni was shielded from the off-field goings-on by his father, but he learned plenty about football from the likes of Mark Maclure, Wayne Harmes and Wayne Johnston. It was Ken Sheldon, however, who took the boy Silvagni under his wing.

Silvagni was rapidly winning a handsome reputation at his school, Marcellin College, for his undoubted ability as a schoolboy footballer, and in mid 1984 he signed on for Carlton – putting pen to paper at his parents' North Balwyn home under the watchful gaze of club director Ian Collins.

Not long after signing with Carlton, Silvagni participated in a Saturday-morning training session at Burwood State College, which involved the entire Carlton senior squad. The players ran five kilometres from the college to a local oval and then completed a series of interval runs over 100, 200, 400 and 800 metres. Silvagni, believing he was not really a part of the senior squad, pulled the pin halfway through. At a skills session the following Monday, Parkin quizzed the kid in no uncertain terms, reminding him that he was very much in the mix for senior selection in season '85. Parko's revelation took Silvagni by surprise, and his spirits were lifted no end.

In 1985, Silvagni embarked on the first of his seventeen seasons, alongside hopefuls including Jamie Dunlop and Milham Hanna. Though he'd hung around the rooms with his dad for years, Silvagni found it a tad disconcerting to suddenly be turning out with luminaries such as Rod Ashman, Mark Maclure, Bruce Doull, Jim Buckley, Rod Austin, Des English and Ken Hunter. He learnt from all of them, and it's unlikely any other player has served a greater apprenticeship.

Silvagni's first appearance for the Carlton Football Club at senior level came in an intra-club match at VFL Park, Waverley. Not surprisingly, he wore the famed no.1 guernsey, which had been worn with such distinction by his father. Silvagni got a lift to the ground with Wayne Johnston and Mark Maclure for an impending appointment with one B. Doull. Thankfully, Silvagni wasn't aware Doull was to be his opponent, which, as he later declared, certainly made for a far more pleasant journey.

Season '85 finally dawned and Silvagni turned out for the Carlton reserves. This was a significant achievement, as he firmly believed senior football was still twelve months away. He lined up in defence for the opening four rounds of the reserve-grade season, before being thrown into the centre in the fifth round, against Essendon. Though the team got hammered that day at Windy Hill, Silvagni fared brilliantly against Peter Banfield and was promoted to the seniors for the Swans game the following week at the SCG. With his father in the coach's box as a match committee member, his mother, Rita, lending support from the grandstand, and his grandfather, Jack, watching on TV from his hospital bed, Silvagni stood Mark Bayes on a half-back flank and fared well.

Having been judged the VFL's recruit of the year for 1985, Silvagni could look to 1986 with optimism, however, he contracted glandular fever and was sidelined for eight matches at the start of the 1986 season. To his great credit, he turned out for the remaining thirteen matches of the season, which included two finals, in what were extremely difficult circumstances. Despite this, he was overlooked in favour of Ken Hunter for Carlton's 1986 Grand Final team. Coach Robert Walls imparted the bad news face to face. Although Silvagni still expresses some unease about the events of September '86 (which had prompted him to talk to

Stephen Silvagni, fullback of the century, *courtesy of Carlton Football Club*.

Parkin about the pros and cons of leaving the club), he had learnt – in the harshest possible way – not to take anything in footy for granted.

Silvagni returned in '87 with his own need to atone; Carlton's vanquished '86 Grand Final team came back hungry too. The absence from the team of Des English and Peter Motley, through serious illness and a road accident injury, respectively, strengthened the collective resolve. Silvagni also suffered a setback when he strained a lateral ligament in his right knee after a marking contest in round 7, against Geelong. Initially fearing a twelve-month layoff, he gladly accepted an eight-week respite, which gave him plenty of time to get back in form for the business end of the season.

As the 1987 season progressed, Hawthorn, Carlton and Melbourne emerged as the three standout teams. Coach Robert Walls had been hell-bent on building a Carlton outfit capable of defeating the Hawks, having recruited Stephen Kernahan, Craig Bradley, Jon Dorotich, Mark Naley and Peter Sartori to add to Carlton's seasoned competitors such as Hunter, Johnston and David Rhys-Jones. Walls also placed his faith in such new players as Shane Robertson, Mick Kennedy and Ian Aitken, the latter judged the league's 1987 rookie of the year.

Carlton emerged as minor premiers. A post-siren match-winning goal from Kernahan in round 22, against North, secured them top spot and a week's break before their first appearance in the finals. They then overwhelmed Hawthorn at VFL Park to take out the Second Semi-final by fifteen points, with Silvagni's direct opponent, Jason Dunstall, succumbing to serious damage to his ankle ligaments. When Hawthorn overcame Melbourne in a dramatic Preliminary Final the following week, Silvagni steeled himself for a Grand Final-day appointment with Dunstall, but it never materialised, as the Hawthorn full-forward gave in to his ankle injury.

Silvagni recently offered a player's insight into Grand Final day: 'You turn out in the biggest stadium in Australia in front of 100,000 spectators and a worldwide television audience of millions – as much as you want to enjoy the day, it's quite a stressful time.'

Silvagni knew that, given Dunstall's absence, he would stand either Peter Curran or Dermott Brereton at full-forward. In the end, Curran was selected at full-forward, and Brereton lined up at centre half-forward, earning Rhys-Jones as his unlikely opponent (Rhys-Jones went on to earn the Norm Smith medal for best on ground). At 20 Silvagni was Carlton's youngest player, and while a number of his teammates ended up dehydrated in the 33-degree heat, he pulled up fine. With most of the team, he dedicated his game to Motley, English and the suspended Bernie Evans. At the same time, the player known as 'Sos' – for 'Son of Serge' – was playing for himself and for his family. Unlike Serge's experience in the nip-and-tuck Grand Finals of 1968 and '70, Stephen was able to savour his first Grand Final, for Carlton's victory was secure some time before the final siren blared.

Silvagni would play in three more Grand Finals, all following his acknowledged turning point in May 1993. He was able to confront his demons in the wake of that dire home-and-away performance, but the Grand Final losses of '93 and '99 would be terrible disappointments for him. Yet sandwiched between them was quite probably Silvagni's crowning glory – the 1995 finals series.

Much has been made of Silvagni's efforts in managing to keep his opponents in that series – Daryl White, Wayne Carey and Gary Ablett – to a collective return of one goal. Silvagni continues to trot out the line that the players around him made this possible, but others integral to the Blues' record-breaking 1995 premiership will tell you otherwise.

David Parkin, one of four men to have coached Silvagni, tells of turning to the match committee ten minutes into the third quarter of the 1995 Grand Final and saying: 'We can't lose this game. Let's just sit back and enjoy this. Let's sit back and watch a fantastic team working together.' By then, a number of Carlton players were, like Parkin, savouring the moment. Not Silvagni. Ever mindful that his direct opponent, Ablett, was the one Geelong player capable of turning the game on its ear, Silvagni stuck resolutely to his task. When the final siren sounded, his overriding emotion was relief.

No doubt Silvagni slept especially well that night, for as surgeon David Young revealed at the player's testimonial dinner, years later, Silvagni laboured with injury through the second half of the '95 season. Halfway through the season, Silvagni had dislocated his left shoulder, taking a huge fragment of bone off the socket so that the shoulder was grossly unstable. This left him unable to raise both hands above his head without dislocating the shoulder. As a consequence, he was forced to complete the second half of the season under stringent instructions to keep his left arm by his side and use only his right arm over his head.

Reflecting on the Grand Final victories of 1987 and 1995, Silvagni has said that in '87 he was a young kid who almost went along for the ride, whereas in '95 he was part of the old firm who helped lead the way.

The events of '95 are fresher in his mind, so it's perhaps natural for that Grand Final to sit above the 1987 Grand Final for Silvagni, although he points out that both were special for their own reasons.

There would be no more premierships for Silvagni's Carlton after '95, but there was a crowning individual honour still to come: Stephen Silvagni was declared football's fullback of the century.

In September 1996, Silvagni accepted an invitation to attend the naming of the AFL's Team of the [20th] Century at Melbourne's Princess Theatre. By the end of the evening he was sharing centre stage with childhood heroes John Nicholls, Alex Jesaulenko and Bruce Doull, all members of this illustrious combination. David Parkin, Percy Beames and Bill Jacobs were among those who cast votes in the selection of the team. Parkin has since described asking Beames and Jacobs a question along the lines of 'You saw the likes of Jack Regan play – where does Sos rate in the overall scheme of things?' To which the pair responded that Silvagni rated as an equal, or even ahead, because of his longevity in an era of tougher opponents.

By 2000, the rigours of combat were beginning to take their toll on this most decorated of league footballers. Silvagni had endured hamstring surgery in the 2000–2001 pre-season period and underwent a significant groin operation following the round 4 match, against Adelaide, in April 2001. As he lay in his hospital bed, he had time to reflect. On top of these recent setbacks, a hip ache had been giving him grief after heavy training sessions, so much so that it began to interrupt his sleeping patterns.

Midway through the 2001 season, Silvagni sought advice from orthopaedic surgeon David Young. It was left to Young to advise, in the strongest possible terms, that the player had had enough. Silvagni was reasonably content with Young's prognosis. This was, after all, the man who had performed more than a dozen operations on Silvagni's battlescarred body. Silvagni played on, and his on-field form didn't waver through the course of the 2001 season, but he was doing it hard. At 34 he knew that if he wasn't able to complete necessary extras on the training track, his form would desert him. In the end, there was no alternative. Silvagni accepted Young's opinion and conveyed the news to the club's doctor, Phillip Pearlstein, and to his coach, Wayne Brittain.

On 12 October, 2001, less than a month after Silvagni's most recent on-field appearance in a navy blue guernsey, his management, Elite Sports Properties, released the following media statement on his behalf:

I have been advised by the medical staff associated with the Carlton Football Club that I am required to have an operation on my hip to repair damage sustained during my career.

Once the operation has been performed there is a real threat of permanent damage if I was to continue playing and that I should therefore cease my career as a footballer.

It is with great sadness that I accept this advice and will therefore not be playing in season 2002.

I would like to take this opportunity to thank all the people who have supported me throughout my career.

Firstly, I'd like to thank my wife Jo and sons Jack and Ben who have been a fantastic support. Sharing the experience of my 300th game with my sons was one of the highlights of my career.

Thanks also to my Mum and Dad who have supported me throughout my career from the early days when they took me to my junior footy games every Sunday morning through to my final year of football.

I would also like to thank the four coaches who I played under during my senior career, particularly Wayne Brittain who gave me every opportunity to play this year despite my injury problems and continued to maintain my enthusiasm and hunger for the game.

Finally, thanks to my teammates, who have made me the player I am and of course the fans who have inspired me throughout my career.

I am terribly disappointed that I will miss the 2002 season due to injury but I am lucky to have been able to play football for 17 years.

Obviously the highlights of my career would be the 1987 and 1995 Grand Finals, but I also enjoyed going through the rebuilding process with my captain Craig Bradley after 1998 when we had won just one out of the first nine games to reach the position we are at now, with a fiercely competitive team.

I look forward to pursuing some of my business interests as well as some opportunities in the media, together with an assistant coaching role at Carlton.

Some people may be surprised that I have not chosen to do a media conference to announce that I will not be playing next year. However, I feel that my career has already been celebrated enough through my 300th game and also my testimonial and I would like to make a quiet exit from football.

Once again I would like to reiterate my thanks to all of those who have supported me throughout my career and I look forward to this next phase of my life.

Stephen Silvagni well and truly fulfilled a dream – harboured since he was a kid – to succeed at the game at the highest level. By his own admission, football afforded him wonderful lifelong friendships and taught him how to deal with people in a team environment, how to deal with disappointments and successes, and how to handle pressure.

And for those of us who watched on, there's no doubting Sos was quite simply 'Numero Uno'.

Tony de Bolfo is a Melbourne journalist and author. His biography of Stephen Silvagni and his family memoir *In Search of Kings* were published in 2002.

20

TONY LOCKETT
No Ifs and Buts and Maybes

by Graeme Blundell

When Tony Lockett was controversially recruited to the Swans in 1995, it was still possible to find a seat close to the boundary fence at either end of the Sydney Cricket Ground, the Swan's home. Somewhere in what novelist Barry Oakley calls 'the deserted visitors dressing room of the Melburnian mind', being close to the game gave the Sydney version more authenticity for refugees like me.

The crowds were still small, but slightly larger than the early days of the Sydney experiment, when a team called South Melbourne was dropped out of the sky and fewer people were said to turn up to a home game than attended a Carlton training run at Melbourne's Princes Park.

There were always free tickets available to see this arcane transported Melbourne game at the Sydney Cricket Ground, and to watch dancing girls called the Swanettes – who looked as if they'd sashayed down from a Surry Hills transsexual bordello – and a pretty blond full-forward in hot pants, who was the Swans' front man in the early days. For a while a squad of gay boys who wore rouge and fetching wigs, and dresses over their jeans, and called themselves the Titettes would leap to their pretty feet each time a goal was scored and perform their own Oxford Street routine behind the girls. It was all a joke.

When Tony Lockett arrived, few Sydneysiders knew who he was. They didn't care that he wore a Brownlow medal around his neck, had kicked 898 goals for St Kilda (wasn't that a beach resort like Manly?) and, super-stitious, had carried his boots and jumper in the same Adidas bag throughout his career. They didn't know that even as a 17-year-old

Plugger could intimidate experienced, tough fullbacks such as Tilt Carter, Kelvin Moore and Gary Malarkey.

Those who did know were horrified. 'We don't want that thug,' was a common response in the Sydney circles that professed interest in the Swans. The St Kilda champion had made offensive gestures to the crowd while playing against Sydney, and had been suspended for using a brutish elbow to bloodily expose the nose cartilage of a Sydney player. Only the previous year, on his way to a haul of sixteen goals against Fitzroy, Lockett had trapped Mark Zanotti in an illegal 'choker hold' and even umpire Tom Pfeiffer, a full-time police prosecutor and part-time umpire from Adelaide, could not make him let go. Luckily Lockett could not keep the Fitzroy player trapped in his vice-like grip forever, and finally released him.

But the game would come to owe Lockett an enormous debt, as football became synonymous in Sydney with Plugger Lockett's boot, aggression and tricky groin. Ron Barassi saved the team from going down the gurgler when he became coach in the early '90s, but it was the sex appeal of Anthony Howard Lockett that saved the club from extinction. Plugger – they liked to call him 'Ayers Rock on legs' – knew how to win. And Sydney loved that. And as they contemptuously said in Melbourne, Lockett's roguish behaviour allowed the locals to believe that when they were cheering on the team, they were in fact followers of football and not of ballet.

How it changed. Sydney's hero Tony Lockett kicked his record-breaking 1300th goal at 12:40pm on Sunday 6 June 1999 at the Sydney Cricket Ground in front of 41,264 fans, to break Gordon Coventry's all-time goal-kicking record. Even the rugby-league-loving *Daily Telegraph* put Plugger on the front page. Radio stations played the tribute song 'There's Only One Tony Lockett' repeatedly, until it was eventually drained of meaning. By the end of his career, any appearance by Lockett seemed to be accompanied by a battalion of yellow-shirted security guards, ringing the boundary to stop the crowd clawing at their idol. When scientist Peter Doherty returned to Sydney having just won the Nobel prize, he recalls, the newspapers were full of Plugger's pelvic injury and Doherty was lucky to get a mention on page five. One journalist suggested it was as though the scientist had been tapped on the shoulder, like a Roman general during a triumph told by a slave 'Remember you too are mortal.'

In less than a decade, the Swans' fickle Sydney supporters had become barrackers, issuing their judgements in the cocksure, irrefutable tones of

TONY'S TRAINING TIPS:

From the pages of Lockett tribute comic *Plugger, courtesy of John Spud.*

loyalists who understand that they are watching something truly fine, something that only comes with years of toil and sacrifice, and able to believe that, in some magical way, they are instruments of the team's success and failure.

From depressed Moorabbin in Melbourne's suburban south, Lockett brought the Southern city's notion of football as ritual, social enactment and sacrifice. 'I don't want to dwell on "ifs" and "buts" and "maybes",' he once said. 'I'm not that kind of a bloke.' Archaic and intuitive, Lockett at his most imperious suggested a renaissance of ancient styles. Each performance was a voyage into the unknown of his ability. Football was a way of life that used his energy, his imagination and his bursting heart.

Lockett was an almost unprecedented act, because opposition barrackers never waste time watching another team unless it is playing their own. But you could understand why people had followed Lockett around for years, the way they had traipsed after John Coleman, to watch him play. Watching Tony Lockett was like seeing a full-forward's coaching manual come to life: the way he could hip an opponent out of the way while the ball was still ten or fifteen metres away (he knew umpires rarely penalised this move); the small push with both hands to the small of the opponent's back, forcing the lower part of their body forward; the accelerated lead that allowed the fullback to gain front position, only to run backwards into the outstretched arms of the stock still full-forward while following the ball's flight backwards and fall haplessly away from the contest. Sometimes Lockett would lead the wrong way and change direction suddenly, putting just enough space between his body and his opponents so that he could mark.

From up close in those seats near the fence, Plugger appeared like the hero of a hardbitten detective story. He had big square hands, probably calloused along the heel and index finger, and when he smiled (it wasn't often) his face was bold, the eyes like shotgun pellets, the jaw rectangular and hard. Wet nicotine seemed to have been rubbed into his guernsey along with a faint hint of testosterone, anger and dark blood. At the end of his career, his thinning hair (he could be seen on TV endorsing a hair restorer's salon without shame) was cut close to the scalp above his large ears, and he always seemed to be biting softly on his molars, flexing the lumps of cartilage behind his jaw line, a faint grin on his face.

No matter what the situation on the ground, Lockett always gave the impression he was about to step up two inches from the face of his opponent. If he was beaten – a rare occurrence – the blood seemed to drain from his cheeks, and a strange transformation took place. The skin grew taut against the bone, and there was a flat, green-yellow, venomous glaze over his eyes, the kind you only see in people who have worked success-fully for years to hide their propensity for cruelty. (You see it these days in the eyes of Denis Pagan as he leaves the coach's box after a Carlton loss.) You knew Lockett was never going to be a good loser. He would make sure he never received the one thing a good loser needs: practice.

Lockett was a source of fascination for those of us who wondered what it would be like to trade our routine and predictable lives for a real fling out on the ragged edge. To us, this burly 112-kilo no. 23 repre-sented a resurgence of the independent spirit among footballers, just as a corporative game was beginning to turn them into role models, terrific citizens and on-the-field automatons, eager slaves to the game plan and the machinations of the coach's box. Football was becoming a brand of burglary, in which the souls of players were taken and the coach's busi-ness card was left in their place.

Plugger was a bruising creator who knew that imitators belong to the second rank and would never be remembered. Watching him play through the late '90s I would think of my own profession and of how actors might find little room with a new generation of directors whose idea of drama was often preconceived and rigid. Most liked to use the actors only as shapes and ciphers to do their bidding. (One, who I had thankfully avoided working with, liked to organise his rehearsals with a conductor's baton, hissing and tapping impatiently if the performers lost the timing he heard in his head.) Plugger might burn inside with banked fires, but in front of an audience he was a tragedian actor, a protean figure who could create an emanation of himself out of willpower alone and become as benign, photogenic and seemingly anointed by history as a great film star.

As a performer Tony Lockett possessed a number of stock characters. For a start, there was Sullen Plugger, his leads ignored or not synchro-nised with the run of play, frustrated and increasingly angry, violently elbowing aside the bruisers with bare arms trying to get between him and another run at the ball, gazing sullenly down the ground as Paul Kelly kicked a rainmaker over his head again or midfielders Schwass and Stevens formed a deep emotional attachment to the ball and became reluctant to part with it. Sullen Plugger fumbled marks, missed straight-forward set shots when he did get the ball, and clipped the top of the posts with wayward kicks.

Then there was Violent Plugger, who was always about to emerge when this uneasy situation became boring, bumping Sullen Lockett over the boundary line and into the pickets. This was Lockett the Crasher, charging into packs, leaping high from the sides and shattering the group with sheer brute force. (It's little wonder that Lockett, a breeder of racing greyhounds, named his budding champion dog Collision.)

When Dale Lewis was on a run, kicking into a space that only he could see, Fast Plugger would appear on a lead, suddenly twenty metres in front of a struggling Mick Martyn or a foolishly loping and embarrassed Stephen Silvagni. Imperturbable Plugger, with Clint Eastwood-thin lips, stood between the posts surrounded by pesky defenders and simply outmarked them with the strength of his arms and legs. Spectacular Lockett, gladiator-like, flew over their heads with upraised outstretched arms to mark on his chest.

When Lockett launched the autobiography of his former captain, Paul Kelly, in 2003, he spoke about the newly imported Barry Hall, another full-forward, and he could have been talking of himself:

> He has got unlimited ability, Barry Hall. He probably doesn't realise himself how good he could be. His whole game is terrific, he's got presence. There wouldn't be a backman in the league that would want to play on him. They might say they do, but deep down I don't reckon they do. So all of a sudden he's always got an advantage over his opponent. He just needs to make that a positive not a negative, don't get sucked in by them, by the tactics. The way he plays, he's going to get decisions against him as far as umpires, I was the same myself.

Toning it down and learning 'how to put energy into the right areas' was the name of the game, Lockett said.

Plugger's exploits forced the Swans to rise to his sense of occasion; he lifted lesser players and brought them into the game with lightning handpasses, vignettes of surprising sensibility. Maybe only Carlton's Anthony Koutoufides could use shoulder strength and hand speed to create such miraculous passes from inside a pack of players to a running forward.

In his final game at the SCG – or the last before an ill-advised but predictably short comeback – Lockett was sprinting towards a loose ball with Adelaide fullback Nathan Bassett on his tail. Another Adelaide player was running towards him, but suddenly Lockett picked the ball up and flicked off a handpass. Effortlessly, and at preposterous speed. He was a master of the blind turn, too, a characteristic combination of strength and gall, especially when pinned in the pocket close to the white line with a further line of opposition players running at him.

'I will remember it as a Lockett day,' said Adelaide coach Malcolm Blight, of that last game against his team.

There were many Lockett days. The one I remember best was actually a night, the time he kicked a behind after the siren on a beautiful still, star-filled Sydney evening to give the Swans a one-point win over Essendon in the Preliminary Final of 1996. It was the night Sydney finally fell in love with the red and white. It was 'the moment of the city embracing us as one of their own and not an alien force', said coach Rodney Eade of Lockett's insolent low kick that sailed between goal and point posts like an old-time sloop entering Sydney Heads.

I was sitting in the front row of the stand just to the right of the goals that night and there was an electrical turbulence in all that sky above the ground as if the air was unstable. The next day friends told me that the exultant cry of 'Syyyyydddney!' screamed out by forty thousand fans, was heard all over the inner city.

It was a Tony Lockett night.

Graeme Blundell is a director, actor and author who moved to Sydney with South Melbourne, although his heart remained in Carlton. *King*, his biography of Graham Kennedy, was released in 2003. He contributed a profile of Rodney Eade to *Footy's Greatest Coaches*.

21

the day i stole the limelight off Tony Lockett

alicia sometimes

final quarter.
North Melbourne vs St Kilda.
early nineties.
Arctic Park.
Tony Lockett
still wearing black, white & red
the number 4 jumper half torn
mercilessly teasing the opposition.

St Kilda.
5 points down
twenty seconds left.
the big man marks
with those big tickling hands
straight
in front of goal.

i'm directly in his view.
i grab my friend's arm
& breathe in the crowd.
mum told me this morning
'make today important.
you never know
when you'll meet your next boyfriend.
this day could end up a conversation piece.'

with the smell of March
& the gumption of September
i remember exactly the way it happened
how Tony sent the ball, flying
express post to me
right in front of the scoreboard.

bang.
siren goes.
he kicks clean, torpedo punt.
6 points.
my nails leave the grip
of my friend's duffle coat
& reach for the heavens.

i see it coming.
i jump over the yellow seats
knocking my brother
treading on dad's hair.
one step, two step.

now climbing over old ladies
kids with 7-year-old's smiles
boys clutching flags
girls shouting their hero's name.
mothers cradling hope
fathers owning victory.
i was ruthless
leaving a wake of bodies
& a sea of white knuckles.

i leapt.
i had wings.
i was an angel

the ball impacted, directly
slap on my breasts.
all the boys went
'oooh,
that's gotta hurt.'
but the adrenalin killed the pain
i held the Sherrin
firmly in my glorious hand.

Lockett
may have been the highlight in that game
but in my family's loyal Sainter eyes
& those of boyfriends to come
this Hawthorn supporter
(for a day at least)

stole the limelight off Tony Lockett.

alicia sometimes is a Melbourne poet, writer and 'spoken word' performer, and
a co-editor of *Going Down Swinging* magazine.

22

MICHAEL LONG
Running with the Ball

by Martin Blake

Bill Kelty, the one-time ACTU secretary who currently serves as an Australian Football League commissioner, gave a speech in Melbourne a few years ago in which he posed the question: How do you put a dollar value on Michael Long sprinting through the middle of the MCG on Grand Final day, 1993?

Kelty's point was that football need not just be about profit and loss and television rights and tribunals, even in the professional era. He should have declared his bias, of course, for he is a lifelong Essendon man, and as an extension of that, a devotee of Long, the champion Bomber midfielder of the 1990s. But admiration for Long transcends all sorts of boundaries, and certainly is not restricted to the red and black brigade.

Michael Long is more than a great footballer. He is one of the most significant people in the history of the Australian game. His performance in Essendon's Grand Final win over Carlton in September 1993 left thousands of Australians with indelible memories as he danced and snaked his way through the hands of his opponents and taunted them with his artistry. When he took a stand against racial vilification two years later, he changed the game forever. Thus his contribution to the indigenous code of football was twofold.

He has paid a heavy price on both counts. He had to leave behind family in Darwin to make the break to the then-VFL in 1989, and this has never been easy for him. Twice his right knee has had to be reconstructed under the surgeon's knife, and he has spent long periods on the sidelines. When he spoke out about racism in football and set himself up as a crusader for the Aboriginal people, he was criticised in some quarters as being thin-skinned and politically motivated.

But wherever he went, he made things happen. It was always the same.

He had started playing for Northern Territory club St Mary's with coach John Taylor and was playing for West Torrens in South Australia when he stepped out as a skinny teenager for Northern Territory in the 1988 bicentennial championships in Adelaide. It was the last of the national carnivals, where all the states used to turn up and play for a so-called national title, and it was a disaster. The crowds were so poor that the organisers could not even pay the prize money they had promised.

But those titles did have the Northern Territory and they did have Long. He was exceptional. The territory won the second division with a team that played spectacular football, and Long was named an all-Australian. He ran half the length of Football Park bouncing the ball; he kicked check-side goals on the run from the deep pockets. He was a revelation.

Yet when the clubs of the VFL sat down for the national draft later that year, a string of them overlooked Long. He was chosen by Essendon at no. 23. Some years later it emerged that at least one club recruiter, Bill McMaster of Geelong, had wanted to pick Long. But McMaster was told not to go ahead because Long was Aboriginal, and Aboriginal players were too much trouble.

Too much trouble. It is a familiar refrain, yet it is changing thanks to people like Long and Kevin Sheedy, the Essendon coach. Sheedy liked the idea of collecting people from a variety of backgrounds at Essendon; in a sense, it was a challenge for a brilliant football mind to draw them all together and point them in the one direction.

Michael Long made an immediate impact in Melbourne, and not just because his shorts were so outrageously big, fashionable before their time. Peter Schwab, then playing with Hawthorn and now their coach, wondered aloud whether the guy ever wasted a kick. Long had speed or – more importantly in the football sense – acceleration, he had peripheral vision, and he had the ability to deliver the ball to teammates with precision.

But he had his troubles. Like so many players who made the trip down to Melbourne from Darwin, he froze. Noel Judkins, who recruited him to Windy Hill, recalled seeing Long sitting, fully clothed, in the club's sauna as he waited to begin training.

Then there was the isolation. Long came from a big family. He had six brothers and two sisters. He missed his family and he missed fishing for barramundi and hanging out in Darwin. Back then, there were far fewer Aboriginal players in the game and only one other at Essendon. Long wrote in 1997:

> Most Aboriginal players come from big families, but small and often isolated communities where family is so much a part of life, it is the core. Without the reassuring noise of kids and brothers and sisters about, without the closeness that is just a natural part of everyday living back home, longing can eat away at your heart.
>
> It did me, in the early years, even though I had my brother Chris living with me in the two-bedroom flat Essendon provided in 1989. Chris is one of six brothers I have.

But everyone loved the way Long played the game, with flair and panache as well as courage. By the time 1993 came around he was ready to scale a new peak. It was the Year of Indigenous People in Australia and Essendon, with Long and Gavin Wanganeen among its number, duly made the Grand Final.

Carlton's most significant player was centreman Greg Williams, a genius whose work with a handball was incomparable with any player in the history of the game. Customarily teams used a strictly defensive player on Williams in the hope he might niggle him and reduce his output. Williams hated taggers; he had a habit of punching them. The former Collingwood coach Leigh Matthews once said that Tony Shaw, his preferred opponent for Williams, always expected to get a broken nose when he played against Carlton.

But Sheedy reasoned that Williams was always going to get plenty of ball regardless of who took him on. He knew that Williams was almost entirely offensive in the way he played, for he never needed to chase a man. His opponent was always in his jock strap. Sheedy put Long on Williams to see what transpired.

Great players thrive in the sort of physical and emotional pressure that Grand Finals produce. It's not a trial for them, as it is for ordinary players. It's what they are born for. Gary Ablett did it in 1989 with his nine goals for Geelong. Pull out a videotape of that game and you will see him at one stage kicking a dinky, left-footed goal and you would swear he is in the middle of a training drill. In 1992 Peter Matera kicked five goals off the wing for the West Coast Eagles. Now it would be Michael Long's moment.

Two images of that game spring to mind. One is of Long charging through midfield, bouncing the ball a couple of times, and leaping in the air as his kick sailed through for a goal. The other is of his incomprehensible taunting of Carlton under the Olympic stand, when he simply held the ball and waited for an opponent to approach him, then sprinted off unbridled. It was outrageous football, the sort of sport that made you laugh out loud. In the Channel 7 commentary box, Ian Robertson was screaming: 'Long just backs away ... have a look at this ... "Take me on. Take me on. Take me on!" he says, and still gets away with it.'

At the end of the game Maurice Rioli, Long's childhood hero and a man he considered 'more or less like a brother', presented the Norm Smith medal to Michael Long for best player afield in that game.

That night, Essendon celebrated its triumph across the way from the MCG at the Hilton hotel. Here, Long would show the other side to his character – the joker. Brought up to the stage to rapturous applause, an interviewer inquired whether he had been seriously hurt when he lay motionless on the turf for a period in the final quarter. 'Just lookin' for worms,' he said, bringing the proverbial house down. Footballers are drilled in the art of the cliché and they know all about false modesty, but Long is a mickey-taker from way back. 'Jeez I played well,' he told the audience with a smirk. Quietly spoken, Long was earning a reputation as Essendon's stand-up comic. Sheedy took to calling him 'the Bill Cosby of Australia'.

Later that evening he privately dedicated the game to his late mother, Agnes, who had died ten years earlier. Agnes Long had been part of the Stolen Generation of Aboriginal people. Born near Daly River, she had been removed from her parents as a young girl and taken to a Catholic mission on the Tiwi Islands. It was there that she had met Michael's father, Jack, who also had been removed from his parents near Alice Springs.

Long is proud of his heritage, and the pain he felt over racial abuse did not kick in until 1995, when his complaint at a comment passed by Collingwood ruckman Damian Monkhorst began a series of events that would change the way the AFL thought about Aboriginal players. It had been going on forever. The Aboriginal players put up with it because they did not want to make a fuss. Maybe they lashed out occasionally, but they did not complain to any authority.

The difference with Michael Long was that he knew it would never change unless someone stood up. He drew other Aboriginal players alongside him, inspiring them:

In 1995, as the racism debate first raged, I asked 'Mag' McLean for a bit of help. I needn't have requested anything. He was there for me throughout the ordeal and beside me as we walked from Optus Oval a week later.

Long and Monkhorst came together for a press conference and within two years the AFL had in place a set of rules outlawing racial vilification, with heavy fines attached. Nicky Winmar, the St Kilda champion, had ignited the issue when he lifted his jumper at Victoria Park the same year, pointing to his skin. But it was Long who took the ball and ran with it, so to speak. The birth of his first son, Jake, may well have played a part in this, for Long wanted his son to grow up in a different world from the one he had been raised in. He knew he couldn't eliminate racism, but he could put a dent in it, however small.

But back to 1993 for a moment. This was a time of triumph and football must have seemed so perfect to Long right then. He might have known better. In the very next pre-season, a few short months later, he injured his knee for the first time, forcing a reconstruction and his absence for the entire 1994 season. He would return with a vengeance in 1995, almost winning the Brownlow medal. His game had changed slightly, for he had spent time in the gymnasium getting the extra bulk he believed was required to survive at the game's highest level. Previously he had mostly operated in space on the wing. Now he would move into the centre, seeing more of the ball, directing the traffic.

Then in 1996 Long's knee buckled again. Returning to the side in the AFL's centenary reenactment game at the MCG, his foot went from beneath him as he kicked for goal. The patella tendon had snapped. Watching, it was hard to escape the feeling that we might have seen him play for the last time. Long felt that, too.

But he came back in 1997, and the knee went again, this time requiring a second reconstruction and another twelve months of rehabilitation. In the four seasons following his virtuoso performance in the 1993 Grand Final, he managed only twenty-nine games. When Essendon cobbled together another great side in 1999, he was a diminished force, but still managed a second premiership in 2000, fading peacefully from the game the following year.

Michael Long's career at Essendon had been honoured in 1998 with his inclusion in their Hall of Fame. Bill Kelty had it right. Michael Long is priceless.

Martin Blake is a senior sportswriter with the *Age*.

'Michael Long: Running with the Ball' was published in an earlier version in 1998, in *AFL's Black Stars*.

FAN
Favourites

Fans choose their favourites for all sorts of reasons – in fact, there are probably as many reasons as there are supporters. But certain players seem to inspire a special kind of affection. They are unlikely heroes and colourful characters, unconventional champions and resolute matchwinners. These are the players who remind us why we love the game so much.

23

REMEMBERING DON MCKENZIE

by Richard Holt

Some careers in football are short but so brilliant they become woven into the fabric of the game's history. Some careers in football are long and distinguished but fade fast with the passing of the years. Perhaps the distinction between champions and legends, so popular among today's football spin doctors, is well made.

In his Fletcher Street flat, barely two decent drop kicks from Windy Hill, my grandfather would regale me with stories of one of the best: John Coleman. His voice would lower in reverence as he began, usually starting with the observation that precedes most tales of the great spearhead, of crowds gravitating en masse from one end of the ground to the other between quarters so they could keep a close eye on their idol. All the elements of tragedy and triumph were there in these stories. Coleman had grace, skill and aggression and his achievements reflected the rarity of his talent. His fans adored him. Thousands lined the local streets on the day of his wedding. Hundreds protested in disbelief when the tribunal, acting on a report still regarded at Essendon as pure vindictiveness, rubbed him out of the 1951 finals series. And untold numbers, including many who had admired him grudgingly as he split the defences of their own proud teams, were shocked and humbled when, at just 25 years of age, a crumpled knee cut his stellar career short.

Alongside the great Dick Reynolds, Coleman stands as a towering figure at a club that has had its share of greatness. Pa would talk about Bill Hutchison too, and the rugged Doug Bigelow, and Norm McDonald. But it was the pathos of the Coleman stories that struck a chord. As a boy just starting out on the lifelong journey that is barracking, I hoped to find an equivalent figure upon whom to construct my own Essendon story. My timing was bad, but with the optimism of childhood I was sure I would find the champion for my era.

By the early '70s, when I was old enough to appreciate football and make the crosstown journey to Essendon for home matches, the team was in decline. Thwarted by four points from winning the flag in '68, by a more disciplined Carlton, the club entered a period of stagnation. Among the plodders, show ponies, tryers and hacks who wore the red and black, there remained one great name. One player, above others in that team, carried the somewhat tattered mantle of champion into the lacklustre '70s.

Don McKenzie was a veteran by that time, having passed 200 games in round 1, 1971. He had been playing for the Dons since before I was born – that was reason enough to be in awe of him. During the '60s he played in two premierships. He captained the team in 1969, as he had on that afternoon the previous September when 116,000 watched another flag slip from their grasp. He was Best and Fairest in '66 in a team that boasted names like Jack Clarke, Alec Epis, Ken Fraser, John Birt, Hugh Mitchell and Barry Davis. By his retirement in 1974, his 266 games was the third highest of any Essendon player, behind only the great duo of Reynolds and Hutchison.

McKenzie played against some of football's truly great ruckmen, including Nicholls and Farmer, who between them redefined the craft. They're always mentioned in discussion of football's pivotal big-man position. Brownlow medallist Gary Dempsey was also a star during McKenzie's later years. As a kid I preferred Dempsey to Nicholls. I always thought the Carlton big man was a bit on the fat side (but in hindsight, of course, it was bulk he used to maximum effect). Though he could hold his own against them all, McKenzie's career achievements might seem modest against these great ruckmen. But fans can choose their own champions. Though an unlikely selection for an unassuming and shy boy, McKenzie was mine.

This was not how things had been planned. Mum, a god-fearing Magpie supporter, had picked out Johnny Birt as the appropriate footy role model (having given up on the Wayne Richardson dream, I suppose – the unseemly bidding war that the two sides of my family waged for my football affections is another story). So, on conceding the inevitable, Mum picked the Essendon player with the best spiritual credentials and the easiest number to sew on a guernsey (11, a number bequeathed to the bespectacled Blethyn in 1968). Secretly, however, it was the veteran tough man that I really wanted to watch from the old Social Club Stand that overlooked the bowling green.

The early '70s, I suspect, is an era history has largely misunderstood. The influences of the summer of love, of Vietnam and political change reached the suburbs in strange and perversely magical ways. On the field, long-haired kids were being picked alongside short-back-and-sides traditionalists. In the stands there was an anarchic element best represented by the outrageous floggers of the period, particularly those of the Collingwood cheer squad. They frequently dwarfed their owners and were carried reverently to and from the ground in huge plastic sheaths. These intimidatory weapons of tissue paper were eventually banned, after causing a series of potentially disastrous boundary fence fires. The bearers of these absurd, compelling artefacts were the glam rockers of the league: hedonistic and tribal.

Football in the '70s was one constant in an era of fragmentation – of skinheads, sharpies, surfies, hippies, straights. Mainstream Australia's uncertainty about what to do with the new social freedoms often manifested itself through reckless irresponsibility. Public drunkenness, in particular, became a way of life – in the summer months young men would arrive for a day at the cricket with bathtubs full of beer. Violence was never too far from the surface. Yet there was an endearing innocence that underpinned the social confusion of the era. As a kid growing up, it seemed there was much about adult life to wonder about.

And so, for all its inherent weirdness, I have fond memories of that period. Those memories coloured my early experience of football. Back then no amount of mediocrity could shake my belief that anyone who donned the club colours had achieved greatness of sorts. I think I understood that McKenzie represented a link with a passing era. Young tearaways like Johnny Cassin and Robbie Amos were representative of the changing times at the club. Even the older blokes grew those ridiculous short-long hair cuts so popular among the office workers of the time. Geoff Pryor returned to the Bombers from a stint overseas sporting a Kris Kristofferson beard. As if to emphasise the brave new world, Essendon surprised the football public when it selected a Magpie toughnut as playing coach in 1972; for Bomber fans, the early '70s are remembered, with perverse fondness, as the Tuddy years.

McKenzie, by comparison with all this, was strictly old school. He was nevertheless a great contributor. He played taller than he was. At barely more than six feet on the old scale, he was a small mobile ruckman who used a big leap and impeccable timing to overcome the greater height of his opponents. I chose these attributes over Barry Davis's silky skills, although I marvelled at Davis's abilities until the day he defected to North. (That afternoon I burned my newspaper clippings of him on the laundry floor.) I liked Ken Fletcher's dash and Allan 'Lurch' Noonan's unlikely capacity for goal-scoring. Blethyn, another forward, was a natural role model for a kid with glasses, but I never kidded myself he was one of the very best. When he became only the second Bomber (after Coleman) to reach the ton, it seemed that everyone was doing it. He'll always be among the second tier of 100-goal forwards, with players like Simon Beasley, Michael Roach and Alex Jesaulenko (who was great for so much more than just dobbing goals at will).

Don McKenzie could ruck all day. He could take a big grab and, either as a back pocket or ranging across the backline, would often repel opposition attacks. I remember his big-hearted performances in a team not noted (at the time) for theirs. He liked to take a clean swing and launch the ball from the centre bounce into the Essendon forward line. The effectiveness of these big clearances is captured in the grainy footage of the '65 premiership win. That day McKenzie and Brian Sampson dominated the ruck contests, setting up many of the team's forward moves.

McKenzie was a tough footballer and never one to take a backward step. But physicality was not his only weapon when there was a point to make or a score to settle. He would get under the skin of his opponents, to whom he would direct the unforgettable, comically mocking grin that he wore throughout his career. Part boyish bravura and part pure disdain, it was an expression designed to infuriate opposition players and delight fans and he used it to maximum effect. It was an invitation for suckers. On more than one occasion it led to free kicks being reversed in McKenzie's favour after opponents made futile attempts to wipe it from his face.

If I'm truthful about the way Don McKenzie impressed me, then I must be prepared to risk a degree of misinterpretation. It is of no consequence – I was 10 years old (and not even worldly as 10-year-olds go). Whenever I jumped the fence and sprinted out onto the churned up turf, the players that I'd scramble around for autographs or touches were giants. But McKenzie was (though small for his position) a giant among them. And I remember well the intimidating solidity of his physique. Others, like the mercurial Neville Fields, seemed to leave the field still in the refined trimmed and oiled state that they entered it. McKenzie left like a farmer leaving a newly ploughed paddock. His enormous arms swung lithely and sweat would flick from them across the circling throng of adoring kids. He had a stride that was lazy but meaningful and a grin that acknowledged the satisfaction of a job completed. Get close enough for an autograph and he smelled of hard work. He was fatherly in the way he responded to us kids, though not in a way that I could ever imagine my own scrawny father being, and masculine beyond the comprehension of a prepubescent lad.

Don McKenzie was the heroic ancient of the club. As far as I knew, and it is how I would have said it, I loved him – loved the skills and fighting qualities he still displayed, the arrogant good humour with which he presented himself and the history he represented. Such is the passion of a small boy for the great men of his team.

That passion was never matched by success. I'd longed, as a boy, for a side like the legendary teams of my grandfather's stories. I'd have to wait. Success would come, but not during that sorry decade of underperformance.

In 1974 Don McKenzie played his last senior game for the Dons. It was a year best remembered at Windy Hill for the all-in brawl against Richmond (a game McKenzie was no doubt disappointed to miss) and for the arrival of a young tall named Simon Madden. Madden had height, leap and stamina. He was a strong mark, an accurate kick in front of goal, and had a natural disposition for the ruckman's craft. He would play a pivotal role in back-to-back premierships ten years later, and became, without question, the Bomber's greatest ruckman. But to me he would always be the custodian of Don McKenzie's position, and the inheritor of a place in the club history that had been pencilled in for his smaller predecessor.

Richard Holt is a writer, visual artist and passionate Essendon supporter, who wrote about the 'coaches in the outer' for *Footy's Greatest Coaches*.

24

BRUCE DOULL
No Frills, No Fuss

by Ian Robinson

What makes a great footballer?

Some players, especially forwards, are remembered most of all for their great games – Garry Ablett for his nine goals in a losing Grand Final team in 1989, or 'Lightning' Ted Hopkins for the four goals that spearheaded Carlton's remarkable comeback in the 1970 Grand Final. If such stand-out performances are a frequent occurrence, as with Ablett, then the player becomes recognised as a 'great'; if they are rare, as in Hopkins's case, the game is remembered as a curiosity, a one-off.

Defenders have a more negative and therefore generally less flamboyant role in the game of football, but we can still remember and celebrate their triumphs, such as Stephen Silvagni keeping the great Gary Ablett goalless in the 1995 Grand Final, or the greatest performance by a backman I ever saw live, Glen Jakovich's display against Wayne Carey in the 1998 Second Semi-final, unrivalled for the comprehensive skill, intelligence, athleticism and concentration it displayed for 100-plus minutes.

No-one could doubt that Bruce Doull is in the company of the greats. He was beloved not only by Carlton fans; unless he was up against one of their own champions, supporters of all the other clubs held him in esteem and affection. In 1996 he was inducted into the Australian Football Hall of Fame and in the same year took his place on the half-back flank in the AFL Team of the [20th] Century, alongside the supreme Ted Whitten at centre half-back and Brownlow medallist Kevin Murray on the other flank.

Yet unlike for most of the other greats in that team, particular games of extraordinary Bruce Doull brilliance are singularly hard to recall.

Unlike the more spectacular Murray, Doull seldom troubled the umpires' notepads in the Brownlow medal voting. In an unusually long and distinguished career, Doull appeared in the top twenty Brownlow vote-getters only once – in 1977, when he was equal fourth with Leigh Matthews and Len Thompson.

Bruce Doull is happy to receive the Norm Smith Medal 1981, *courtesy of Carlton Football Club.*

Even Doull's performance in the 1981 Grand Final, for which he won the Norm Smith medal for best on the ground, is no more striking or sensational than most of the other games he played. His teammates, such as Mike Fitzpatrick in the ruck and Alex Marcou around the ball, were much more in the limelight during the course of play. Doull was just there in the background, punching the ball away when he was behind, marking surely when he was in front, maintaining his balance and focus once the ball hit the ground, tackling unrelentingly if his opponent got a break, and, once he had possession, effortlessly sidestepping pursuers and delivering the ball with military precision to a forward.

Oscar Wilde once claimed that a true artist doesn't change and develop but revolves in a cycle of masterpieces. If he were prescient, he may well have had Bruce Doull in mind. Because the greatness of Doull lies not in especially spectacular performances but in his consistency and reliability – week in, week out – over a then record 359 games for the Blues, during which time he was seldom beaten. A circle of perfection.

Doull's game had few frills and even fewer deficiencies. Coach David Parkin has said that he never knew a more competitive player than Doull, who applied himself to the task at hand with much more than due diligence. He was a self-starter and didn't need motivating. He just went out and did the job because he enjoyed doing it to the best of his ability, and if he made one of his rare mistakes, he didn't need to be told – he took a breath and got back into the game with even more application and concentration.

In the modern game, clubs employ football psychologists who analyse every player and work out, for the benefit of the coach, how best to address their mistakes. Some need a public rap on the knuckles delivered immediately by the runner, some respond better to a quiet word in private during the next break, others are best left alone to get on with it. Doull, of course, was one of the latter. Not long after coach David Parkin arrived at Carlton, Doull made one of his rare mistakes and Parkin immediately rang down to the runner and instructed him to tell Doull what he'd done wrong. The runner ran out onto the ground and headed straight towards his player, but before he could say a word, Doull yelled to him from about eight metres away, telling him to 'go back and tell that idiot to look up his player profiles' because '*I don't get the runner.*'

If Doull didn't like to be told, neither did he like to tell. He was the most reticent of champions. As his Team of the Century citation puts it: 'Both on and off the field, Bruce Doull was renowned for giving nothing away.' What added fuel to the Doull legend, if not to his greatness, was his absolute refusal to play the part of a famous footballer. He would not talk to the press, appear on football shows, or let himself be singled out for special attention or honours. On the field his presence was unmistakable, with his beard, his balding pate and his trademark headband restraining what remained of his flowing hair. Off the field he was anonymous.

After he retired from league football Doull was frequently able to use some of his spare time to give junior teams and coaches in his neighbouring northern suburbs the benefit of his experience, but it always had to be on a low-key basis – no-one was allowed to make a fuss about his presence or acknowledge that he was anything more than just another willing helper.

For those interested in numbers, the stark facts of Bruce Doull's football playing career are as follows: He was recruited by Carlton under-19s from Jacana in 1966. He played his first senior game on 3 May 1969. For two years he was in and out of the team and actually missed selection for the famous 1970 Grand Final. In 1971 he finally cemented his place in the Carlton line-up, playing in the record-breaking 1972 Grand Final team. Two years later, another Carlton great, John Nicholls, retired after chalking up a club record 331 games. Doull won the club's Best and Fairest that year, and again in '77, '80 and '84. He also played in the '79, '81 and '82 premiership teams and represented Victoria from 1976 to 1981 and again in 1984. In 1977 he was vice-captain, an uncharacteristic step at least some of the way into the glare of the spotlight, one which wasn't repeated the following year. Although plagued by injury towards the end of his career, in his middle years he was relatively injury-free, and at one stage played in 166 consecutive games. In 1985 he overhauled John Nicholls's club total, on the way to a total 359 games for his team, a record that finally fell in its turn to Craig Bradley. Doull played his last game for Carlton in a losing Grand Final team, on 27 September 1986. He refused to allow his teammates to chair him from the ground at the end of the match.

For those interested in aesthetics, the poetry of Bruce Doull's football may be set out as follows, chapter and verse:

He possessed superb judgement. He seemed to always know when to go for a mark and when to spoil his opponent – or if he hadn't always known, he soon learnt from experience. In the opening minutes of the 1979 Grand Final, Doull played in front and his opponent, Alan Edwards, took a couple of telling marks over him. From that point of the game on, Doull always played from the rear – every time Edwards went for a mark the unerring Doull fist appeared from behind him and thumped the ball away. Once the ball hit the ground, Edwards had little hope of beating Doull, and he scarcely got another kick. Doull's marking, when he deemed it appropriate to attempt a mark, was sure and safe – he seldom needed more than one grab at the ball.

Coupled with his judgement, he had sublime anticipation. He had an uncanny knack of knowing where and when the ball was going to arrive in the opposition forward-line and was able to get there before the opposing forwards.

Doull had wonderful balance and was usually the first to recover once the ball hit the ground. His attack on the ball was unwavering, unrelenting and fearless, and his tackling was fierce and uncompromising. Few players were able to extract themselves from a Doull tackle. If he was not the first Carlton player to the ball he would be there to back up his teammates with a protective shepherd or the receipt of a relieving handball.

Although not the fastest man on the field, Doull's superb balance, remarkable anticipation and sharp awareness of what was going on around him ensured him plenty of time to run with the ball, avoid being tackled by opponents, and deliver the ball further down field. His effortless disposal skills were legendary, as was his delivery to a leading forward. One story has it that Wayne Johnston and Peter Bosustow would fight in the dressing room before each game over who would play on the same flank as Doull – both wanted to be on the end of his precision passes, to say nothing of the probable large number of them.

Despite being hard at the ball and intensely competitive, Doull was scrupulously fair, and for this reason, and perhaps also because of his idiosyncratic appearance and unflappable demeanour, he found a place in the hearts of football lovers in general.

The only person who ever ruffled Doull's composure on the football field was a 17-year-old Adelaide stripper called Helen D'Amico. When Doull's famous headband was ripped off by Essendon's Cameron Clayton in 1983 and thrown into the crowd by Tony Buhagiar, Doull simply produced a spare from down his socks and got on with the game, but when D'Amico streaked onto the ground in the middle of the 1982 Grand Final wearing only a Carlton scarf, Doull was nonplussed and ran the other way. Wayne Johnston was made of sterner stuff, and dragged the naked lady off by her scarf.

Doull's natural position on the field was the half-back flank and he was undoubtedly one of the greatest to ever play in that position. However, like many other great half-back flankers, as the best defender in his team he was frequently required to play on the opposition's leading forward, which put him at either centre half-back or fullback. One thinks of the Demons' Don Williams, who played on the half-back flank in three premiership teams in a row but in his fourth consecutive Grand Final, in 1958, was asked to take over centre half-back, where he was out-muscled and overpowered by the awesome Collingwood Captain, Murray Weideman. When asked to relinquish the back flank for the centre half-back or, in his later years, fullback, Doull generally acquitted himself with his customary efficiency and effectiveness, even against taller and larger opponents. But it was playing at fullback in his last match that Doull finally met his nemesis.

The penultimate word on Bruce Doull should be left to the ever loquacious Lou Richards, writing in *The Sun* on the eve of Doull's last game:

> By keeping his mouth shut, his anger to himself and his mind on the game, Doull has made himself not only one of the best men ever to play the game, but one of the most popular. That title 'legend' is thrown around all too loosely these days, but if ever a bloke deserved the epitaph, it is the 'Flying Doormat' … I reckon it would be a fitting finale if Doull was to take a premiership cup home from his last match.

Unfortunately that wasn't to be. Just as the great Don Bradman made an inglorious duck in his much anticipated final innings, the great Bruce Doull was soundly beaten in his final game – a young full forward from Hawthorn called Jason Dunstall, in just his second league season, kicked six goals against him.

But such ignominious exits as Bradman's and Doull's are only remarkable because of the greatness of the careers leading up to them, and in Doull's case this last game fades into insignificance in comparison with the 350-odd games that preceded it, during which Doull stamped himself as probably the best half-back flanker the game has ever seen.

Ian Robinson is a Melbourne writer and teacher, following a distinguished career on the half-back flank with Ivanhoe Amateurs.

'**Bruce Doull: No Frills, No Fuss**' draws on the memories of many Blues fans. The writer would like to thank all those who shared their memories of Doull, in particular Neil Watson and Ian Gust, and also 14Big Tim, Robinson, whose love of the game overcame his love of Collingwood long enough for him to say some complimentary things about a Carlton player!

25

the days of
Trevor Barker

alicia sometimes

the days when you could run on the field & high-five Silvio Foschini on the bum & not get arrested. when Peter Landy was sporting the first signs of grey. when a moustache was worn as proudly as a heavily badged duffle coat. the days of high flying marks on the back of Scanlen cards. when you would call up a friend whose team had just lost to yours just to have them hang up at the first utterance of *suffer*. when Ray Card's hair was just too curly. when Billy Picken was plain cheeky. the days of the utility. the days of Trevor Barker.

when Ray Biffin grabbed Barks and kissed him to keep him from touching the ball. the long-sleeved shirts and photos of the scruff blond always falling to the ground clutching the Sherrin. his high jumping days as much ahead of him as behind. the era of twelve VFL clubs. the epoch of singing footballers. Barker crooning *I Can See Clearly Now* on a 1978 LP. my brother's friends all watching him warm up on the wing. boys tossing toys in the air and catching them in front of the mirror. girls with posters of the Saint spunk.

from number 25 to number 1. everyone from chilled pie boys to rugged-up grandmothers shouting *Carn Barks!* and pausing a moment as he goes for the ball. the brute of his tackling. scrambling at the bottom of the pack. the days of loyalty. when he bought tracksuits for new recruits from his own pocket. when he could have walked but didn't because of the roar of an audience and the love of a team. the days of club discos. before he was captain. before he'd reached that 231st game. before the hints of him becoming coach. before the cancer.

when you could look at your dad's face as he watched Barks take a screamer and know that this man must be important. the way kids would fight to get to him and then stand poised politely when he was talking. those hands. the taped knee or the injured thigh. the football a footy frank red. the anthem something to stand for. spanking your friends on the back of the calf with the wooden spoon they'd given you. the exhaustion of losing. the way Barker would give you glimpses of sitting high on the ladder. of winning finals. wearing the scarf proudly after the game. knowing there was always next week and *Barks would do it for us, wouldn't he?* the weight of fans' expectations. the Metro gum you would chew on anxiously. *for God's sake, pick up the ball.*

when footy stars were more talked about at recess than film stars. when knowing stats meant something. the days you would wear blue lips, frozen hands and happily get rained on. all in the name of St Kilda and its favourite son. all in the name of Trevor Barker.

alicia sometimes is a Melbourne poet, writer and 'spoken word' performer, and a co-editor of *Going Down Swinging* magazine.

26

MEMORIES OF THE '80S

Robert Flower, Leigh Matthews,
Garry Dempsey, Malcolm Blight,
Wayne Johnston & Brent Crosswell

by Garrie Hutchinson

Robert Flower 19 June 1982

Underneath the members' stand at the MCG, on the draughty wall outside
one of the bars, are more than forty stone tablets inscribed with the names
of the players who turned out for Victorian cricket teams from 1857
onwards. Among them, for 1857 and 1858, appears the name T.W. Wills.
He was captain of Victoria in 1858, and one of the great colonial cricketers.

In 1858 he also wrote a letter to *Bell's Life*, the leading sporting
journal of the day. Tradition has it that this missive kicked off Australian
football. Not a bad year's work, but one that is publicly remembered only
by the stone tablets beneath the members and a plaque in the wall outside.

Tom Wills's letter was published 125 years ago next month, and the
legendary 'first' game it caused was played on 7 August 1858, round
about where the Richmond ground now lies. Tom Wills was one of the
two umpires and luncheon was taken in the pavilion, on the site of the
present Members' stand. Tom Wills was the first captain of the Melbourne Football Club.

Wandering around the pavilion, and seeing again the trove of wonderful cricketing material on the walls, or the absence of it (the centenary
Test memorial bat seems to have disappeared), was a reminder of how
little concrete public value is placed on football traditions. Memories and

yarns and statistics and the occasional book, but we the football public who aren't MCC or VFL Park members can't (it seems) even keep our Grand Final at the birthplace of the game. Moving that ceremony will rank as one of the great acts of vandalism of our culture.

In this 125th anniversary year of the Australian game, perhaps a more public tribute to Tom Wills and the other father of the game, Henry Harrison, might be erected, say, outside the MCG near where the first game was played, to recall where it started and what it means or meant to our city. There must be a couple of trees still standing where Tom Wills roosted a footy, and one of them might be made into a kind of shrine, honouring the rise and fall of the relationship between a once great Victorian city which is losing its way as its institutions flee.

For the moment, the game played by the current captain of Melbourne, Robert Flower, will serve as a fitting memorial to celebrate the game Wills invented.

There can have been few better displays of football ever seen on the MCG, or anywhere else, for that matter, although captains of Melbourne have turned in some humdingers over the 124 years of the football club. Statistics (twenty-two kicks, fifteen marks and sixteen handballs, kicking 2.3), as usual, don't tell the whole story, although thirty-eight possessions and another dozen knock-ons and dive-ins do give an impression. What the numbers don't indicate is the intelligence, courage and grace that accompanied the work.

In the first quarter on Saturday against Richmond, for example, he kicked two goals of spellbinding elegance, running around the Southern stand flank. Both required the simple notion of giving the pass to a team-mate on the half-back line and continuing to run. A hundred metres down the ground Flower accepted the ball again, and having all the time in the world, and all the balance of Blondin, kicked two very complete goals.

It wasn't just the relatively easy business of passing the ball accurately to a teammate on his own and on the move, though that is difficult enough for many players, God knows, but the determination to keep running, leaving an opponent way behind (who didn't chase presumably because he didn't think any harm would come of it), believing that he would get the ball again. That conviction is the essence of creativity on the football field: it was Flower's continuation to run, which is presumably to have confidence in himself, that invented the play.

Flower was nearly always the target of kick-offs. Whether this tactic was divined on the spot by Flower and the fullback, or was invented by

Ron Barassi, it was a wonderful success, enabling the most creative player on the ground to set up moves right from the back pocket. Flower was able either to get a step away from his opponent or simply outmark him man to man six or eight times during the game, and then put the ball to advantage. It's only a tactic that can be used when the player kicked to is going to mark the ball no matter what. If he doesn't, it's a good way of letting the other side in for a score.

On a couple of occasions, Flower's use of the baulk left opponents dizzy trying to keep up. Seemingly trapped on the half-back flank in front of the scoreboard, Flower has the ball facing the 'wrong' way. He runs away from his goal, feints to his right with the ball, and turns in, towards the boundary line. Here another Tiger lurks. This time he dummies with the other hand, blind turns and is suddenly free, on the boundary side of the second opponent, heading for goal. Another dummy and a twitch of hips and two opponents crash into one another, after he's dashed through the opening.

Flower needs to have some special control over his body and the ball; he looks so frail on the field compared to the rosy, muscled appearances of many of his opponents. If they have 'muscles on muscles', Flower has skin on bones. Or so it seems from the boundary line. He also has the champion's ability – often called heart – to do the right thing in a crisis, to keep going when stopping is easier.

It's the beginning of the final quarter and scores are level. The Tigers have fought back in the third quarter, and most observers are of the opinion that the Demons are about to fall in a hole. Flower patrols the Olympic stand wing. In the first five minutes he has delivered a handball, taken a mark and kicked the ball into the goal square, scrabbled around on his knees, trying to extricate the ball from under a pack, and watched in some alarm as Michael Roach kicks a behind before shaking his arms and getting into position for the kick-off.

A little later, his opponent, David Palm, actually outmanoeuvres and outmarks him for the one and only time that afternoon, boots the ball into the Richmond goal square and Wall kicks a goal. A 'mistake!' that is soon made up for. Flower collects the ball from a pack in the centre, shoots out a handball to a free player. It ends up with Healy, and there's the goal back.

Twelve minutes gone, the footy is booted into the forward pocket and into the apparently inevitable clutches of the pack when Flower floats through the air, against the rush of the play, arriving at the precise piece of space where the ball is and the opposition isn't. After all that, he hit the post. Scores were level again.

For the other half of the quarter he magnetised the ball, took mark after mark in attack and defence, kicked another point, and kept putting the ball into the goal square. Kelvin Templeton scrambled a couple of goals and put the issue beyond doubt.

None of this quite describes the amount of time and space Flower manages to create, against (or is it in agreement with?) all principles of physics. The game looks easy played at this level. All you have to do is get by yourself a lot, escape predatory opponents, not be there for the tackle on you, appear invisible to opponents with the ball and grab them from nowhere, fly through the air, run rings, and have all day to think about what to do with the ball.

That's all there is to playing one of the more miraculous games seen in 125 years on the Melbourne Cricket Ground.

Leigh Matthews 15 May 1983

A great footballer is as much craftsman as genius. He operates on technique as much as on inspiration and achieves what his coach dreams every footballer might achieve: a good game every week and a great one every month. When age drains the spring from his creaky ankles and knees, and takes away the half a metre of speed that is the difference between a loose man and losing the ball, it is craft that provides the material for performance.

Craft is holding onto the ball when you're in position to mark, on those three or four occasions when this blessed event happens. Craft is getting where the ball is most likely to be after it hits the hands of a pack. Craft is using all dodges and lurks to gain the best advantage for your team, whether it means converting a half-push in the back to a swallow dive into the fence, or rabbiting a youthful opponent and getting one for round the neck. Craft means being able to kick straight from sixty metres out, when necessary and being able to drop a pass onto the full forward's chest when he needs a lift. Craft is doing four things a quarter, no matter what, every week.

Leigh Matthews is a great footballer because he is a great craftsman. Consider his game against Essendon last week. To say that he won the game for Hawthorn is perhaps putting it too highly, but not by much. Perhaps our measurement of what is important in a game is astray, and we do not give sufficient weight to, say, a player who prevents his opponent getting a smell, or to the player who makes the plays, unobtrusive though he may be.

Lethal is getting on in football years, and he looks, well, a bit thicker on the field these days. To say he was playing on one leg on Saturday may be an exaggeration. His hair has grey patches, and patches of absence. His run, caused by whatever injuries he currently carries, is a leisurely scoot, but it is still immensely strong. His momentum and fearlessness carry him almost inevitably through aspiring tacklers. On one, two or no

Leigh Matthews, already thinking about what to do next, *courtesy of Sport the Library.*

legs he aggravates opposing fans merely by standing still and makes matters worse for them by doing his four useful things every quarter.

More than that, he set up Hawthorn's win by being the motive force behind the goals in the first quarter that had Essendon on the back foot, always behind, chasing Hawthorn all day.

Lethal's game begins quietly enough. On the ball he jogs after the play between the half-forward lines, taking a handball and passing it on, standing under a pack and not getting a free (and why not?), ghosting in looking for a free, spinning out of one pair of clutching arms into another pair, and that's just the first seven minutes. A warm up. Then he's in the proper place at the proper time for a handball, a couple of paces and a pass drilled into Moncrieff's grateful mitts. A goal.

A few minutes later, now stationed in the forward pocket, Lethal leads out and suffers one of the innumerable blows to the head a variety of players cop this afternoon. Over he goes. He makes it look so painful there's no chance of a free. Someone says, 'Don't give that mongrel a kick. He's been staging all his life.' Such are the compliments of opposing fans. A Hawk says, 'The ump's put him under more pressure than David Combe!' Back on the ball, he's on his own on the half-back line, trundling upfield, in the proper place to receive a pass from a teammate, who doesn't give it to him. Lethal yaps at him.

Twenty-two minutes into the quarter he manoeuvres astutely in a loose pack and marks on the forward edge of the centre square. In retrospect it seemed he had his name on the ball, though at the moment he took it no one knew where he came from. The length required must be sixty metres, and he judges it to a centimetre, Rugged Ronnie Andrew's punch from just behind the goal line notwithstanding.

A minute later he collects the ball from the tap out and delivers it not quite perfectly to Moncrieff, who spills the mark under duress. Lethal seems annoyed. Moncrieff gets the free, and the goal, and happiness is restored. The quarter ends with a black look at Wallace, who failed to handball when he could have, and a burst through two packs of players, where in getting the ball he's accused of MAN! and in getting through the tackles with it of BALL!

The second quarter is notable for the first of the attempts by Essendon players to niggle Lethal. What they don't seem to realise is that, if they niggle him, firstly he'll exaggerate what they do into an incident and, secondly, they can't put him off his game at all. Nineteen minutes into the quarter and Lethal leads out from the forward pocket, collects the mark, kicks it into the air, and someone interferes with Moncrieff, who happily accepts one of his many goals from a free kick.

After half-time not much happened, except that when Hawthorn needed a goal to repel an Essendon fight-back, Matthews gave one to Tuck, and he copped one in the back of the head going for a mark in the forward pocket. This biff turned Lethal's legs to rubber, and he was unable to stand, even with a pair of trainers supporting him. He's groggy! He's only just conscious. Down he goes again! His feet won't work. Give someone else the kick! Moncrieff is handy, give it to him! The umpire does. What a showman! Moncrieff kicks yet another goal. Lethal shakes his head, looks at the sky which clears the brain and jogs off. No apparent ill effects, but a goal for Hawthorn.

During the last quarter Lethal gives Kennedy a goal, acts the goat by doing acrobatics with a niggling opponent, cops an elbow in the head from a shepherd, and accepts a handball from Peter Knights for the third goal from his own boot. That doesn't count the ones he gave away. I don't suppose anyone counted the ones he gave away. Hawthorn won. Another craftsmanlike performance from the captain.

Garry Dempsey 31 March 1981

I don't know how it was for Garry Dempsey, but it took half a game for me to get into it. That was when, in spite of the small crowd, I managed to score my first pie. Pies were cold before the game, then disappeared, and during the second quarter, every time a pie boy came within cooee, his entire stock was consumed by starving fans further down the terrace.

It was tough concentrating. You had to keep one eye on the play and the other out for the pie boy, and anyway it was plain North were going to win this one without too much effort. Not that Malcolm Blight wasn't trying to jolly the game along. One of the game's most expert nudgers, he put several players off balance, swooped on a few loose balls, ran to the most difficult spot to try and kick for goal, and lectured poor Kerry Good every time he did anything.

It's bad enough having a playing coach who inspects the troops on all fronts, but to have one standing next to you all day must be a pain in the neck. Maybe Malcolm should have gone up the other end where David Dench kept dropping off to sleep. Not that Dench's opponent, Roberts, had any importance in the game – he couldn't kick straight no matter how hard he concentrated.

By half time, however, Garry Dempsey's pattern for the year was beginning to move smoothly in the groove. He'll play better games, he'll get more marks and hitouts than he did on Saturday, but his game will always look much the same. The opposition will still kick it to where he goes, they'll still leave him alone jogging quietly between half-forward and half-back, and they'll still wonder what it is that gives North Melbourne the impetus to get the ball moving.

Watching him during the third quarter last Saturday was interesting because, although he wasn't a dominant player, he was working very hard and playing on technique. He was always in the play, he didn't flash in and out and he was always where the ball was or was going to. No wonder the new boys, Spencer, Kelly and Hodgeman, followed him around.

First he contests the bounce that begins the third quarter, and follows the ball down to the South Melbourne forward line. They get a free kick. He has a look and decides he'd better get down and cover the possible attempt at a big mark by full-forward Roberts. He does, and South scramble a point. Out he trots.

He diverts attention from where Dench kicks the ball; it travels at speed to the other end, by which time Dempsey has loped down towards North's half-forward line, where he patrols the perimeter.

Unfortunately, he loses his boot. And, of course, while doing it up, the ball arrives. He goes for a mark, laces flying, knocks it down, and does his boot up while North score a goal. He wanders back to the centre. Five minutes have gone in the third quarter.

A couple of indecisive centre bounces soon result in two South Melbourne goals, the ball going over the lurking Dempsey's head. This revival of South's fortunes plainly needs to be nipped in the bud, so Dempsey punches the ball thirty metres from the centre, for a North behind, which allows everyone to draw breath, see that South are within eight points, and get on with the game.

The coach kicks a goal, and from the fumbles at the next centre bounce, the play creeps towards South's goal. Dempsey lengthens stride to catch up to the ball. It tumbles along the ground towards him. He tries to gather it, and whacks it out of the way.

About eleven minutes have passed, and South are still in the game. They're the ones with the noise and aggression and determination. North are off the boil.

A few minutes later Roberts has a shot for goal that goes out of bounds on the full. It's kicked back in, but is marked by South's Barry

Round. His kick is aimed at someone who isn't Dempsey, but it still dives towards him. He grabs it while under siege from South players, kicks it wildly and it slams into Robert McGhie, of South.

For no apparent reason McGhie and Dempsey take exception to this sequence of events, and barge into each other, do a couple of ritualistic chest bangs, and then roll about on the grass, delivering tremendous haymakers to the air near each others heads. The earth doesn't move, but everyone else within thirty metres rushes in and has a good push and shout. No one knows why except Garry Dempsey, I reckon. Whether he was niggled into it (North do seem to be susceptible to the niggle) or he did it deliberately, it marks the end of the South Melbourne revival.

North raise the tempo of the game in time-on. Dempsey feeds the little blokes, and North kick five goals, which is enough to skate home in the last quarter.

Dempsey goes back to his solitary patrol, running the patterns, being where the ball is. He's going to make it mighty hard for any side to beat North because his game does not rely only on individual effort, motivation or touch.

Dempsey is one of the few players I have seen (Leigh Matthews is another) who has a system, a pattern, a technique that operates whether he's feeling wonderful or not. That means he's always in the game, always doing something, always playing well, always getting the ball, always has a high work rate.

And if the best ruckman in the league never puts in a bad game, his team is going to be mighty hard to beat … again.

Malcolm Blight 9 April 1980

Who will ever forget that sunlit afternoon at Princes Park when Carlton were goals in front, and Malcolm Blight still won the game for North, while most Carlton supporters were reaching for the celebratory can? The mark on the siren, the question to Keith Greig, and the answer: kick it. And the kick a seventy-metre torpedo that sank Carlton when they had one foot on the wharf and one arm around a friend.

Or the game against Hawthorn in 1977, when the mud was so thick that to tell one player from another required Superman's eyes? Blight was pushed in the back as he kicked the behind that drew the game, and his dilemma was leave it a draw or go for the win. He, of course, went for the win, and kicked it out of bounds, and North Melbourne lost.

Malcolm Blight is a footballing genius, a man whose anticipation, skill, reflexes, vision, concentration and lateral thinking make him one of the players we travel a long way to see. Even to the Arden Street Oval, where when the wind blows it's perhaps the most uncomfortable ground in the league. But, as always, we will put up with anything to see a good game, or even a bad game. And maybe Malcolm Blight will give us another moment, another example of the impossible come true. Because beyond commitment to a team (to a point of view) football is about being amazed by the miraculous performed in front of our eyes. The magic chain of handpasses, the giant mark, courage. It's like the circus used to be.

After a minute the ball is kicked down towards the North Melbourne goal. Blight has a look, leans forward, then takes a step or two back. Stewart, his opponent, doesn't mind. The ball comes quickly, pushed on by what seems to be a stiff breeze. Blight sticks a foot in Stewart's back, levers himself creakily into the air, and watches the ball bounce off hands in front of his own, some time after he has returned to earth. Blight shakes his head, purses his lips, and trots back towards the goal square. Stewart happily stays between him and the centre.

A few minutes later, the ball flies out of the centre towards Blight and Stewart. Stewart goes after the ball with a pack of players. Blight feints forward, drops back and waits. The ball does not come to him.

Collingwood goals, and Blight runs to the opposite flank to where the play appears to be heading after the bounce. The ball explodes out of a scrimmage, hits Blight on the chest and bounces off.

Now Blight marks on his chest standing in the forward pocket. He allows himself a smile, and seeing a colleague in the goal square gently hoofs it towards him. The colleague can't get near it. The ball swings and bounces through for a goal. Clarrie Grimmett would have been proud of the ball. Blight looks, smiles, does a little swooping movement with his hand. Still, maybe the tide's turned. He shrugs his shoulders. Seconds later, the ball bounces out of Blight's chest again. He goes after it, gets it, hand-balls out, has a look, makes position, gets it back, handballs again, muffs it.

He trots back towards the centre, eyes on the ground. He's not playing well. He goes to where the ball should be, and it isn't there. He pushes and prods the ball to where someone else ought to be, and he's not there either.

His opponent watches the play, and you can see his legs lead him to where he judges the ball will go. Blight, on the other hand, waits, especially when North is playing with the wind. He lurks behind and moves to where the ball ought to go. When it's flying through the air, the velocity ought to increase, and it ought to stay in the air a little longer. Blight goes for marks ... Too soon too often. Somehow his physics let him down, or maybe there's a problem with the person kicking it to him.

Blight's problem is North's problem. They seem to have only spasmodic interest in the game, whereas the fierce Collingwood players concentrate and say nasty things through clenched teeth. They just keep batting the ball forward more often than North can. Both teams are equally adept at kicking the ball over the boundary line on the full, and the umpires vie with each other for confusion. It's a grim struggle, North Melbourne playing from memory of better days, Collingwood content to play not well, but more interestedly.

It's obvious that Blight or Dempsey or Dench or Greig or someone is going to have to win it by himself. Maybe they could win it together. After a minute of the second quarter, Blight gets the ball. Two minutes later he gets it again, blind turns, sidesteps, handballs out, runs on, and on, waiting to get the ball back. It doesn't come. He kicks a divot, watches the ball pop up at the other end of the ground. He runs past the pack a couple of times, takes a mark, has a blind kick and then after twenty-three minutes of frustrating football, he gets a free kick at centre half-forward. This is nice, a big kick, and maybe ...

Then a strange thing happens. Ron Wearmouth decides that some extra height is required by the man on the mark, and he gets upon his shoulders. That's funny. Any other day, any other game, it would have been funny. But this game is a scraggy, skill-less sort of game, the kind of game we usually see on a muddy July Saturday. So it isn't funny, it's inappropriate, out of time, and Blight happily accepts fifteen metres, and another fifteen are granted to rub it in. He dobs it.

In other years, something peculiar like this incident might have changed the course of the game. North players would have cheered up at the sheer looniness of it, loosened up and played. Not this week.

The third quarter opens with Blight and Picken both wanting to stand on the same square metre of ground. A time-honoured wrestling match ensues while the game begins again. Picken stamps his foot, lets go a straight right that whistles past Blight's chin. Thus surprised, Blight slams Picken to the ground. The ball passes nearby, an umpire lets the boys know. They get up, look around and now that the particular square metre of soil has become irrelevant, jog after the ball.

Blight, running the wrong way, grabs the ball as it slides off the top of the pack, whacks it with his left foot and drills it through for a goal. But that's a forlorn hope. Blight misjudges the ball in the air again. A bit later, Blight's on his own, the ball comes to him, he fumbles, sidesteps, kicks it towards goal; it's not marked, no result. He wanders about again.

For a quarter Blight handballs to where he thinks someone might be, stages for free kicks, taps the ball forward and finally has a blind shot over his shoulder for an out of bounds on the full. His heart doesn't seem in it, and it's a great surprise to everyone that Collingwood only lead by five points at three-quarter time.

But it's one out. Or one at a time-out. You can almost see the light flick on and off in Blight's eyes as he realises he could almost win another game off his own boot. In this quarter he has four kicks and a handball, and each of them might have resulted in a goal. But the fates were unsympathetic. A handball went begging, the boot didn't connect sweetly with the ball, the ball bounced unkindly. And North Melbourne lost by five points.

Not Blight's fault, but still …

Wayne Johnston 15 August 1983

It's half-time at Princes Park on a balmy afternoon, and it could almost be spring, except for the scoreboard. Carlton are thirty-two points down and playing like they have sunstroke. Discussion about whether it's worth going to the pub to get out of the heat ensues. Someone remarks that it's already too late to spray the fruit trees. Mothballs seem imminent. Several of the crew on the press box wing are reminded that the last time a gathering such as this took place, Carlton were walloped by 111 points. Gloom.

Hardly anything can be worse than feeling the season is already over and being persecuted by chatty Hawthorn supporters. One passes by and offers to take the wager of a misguided and gullible optimist (me) that Carlton would not only win three premierships in a row but were also good things for four. Any money, he says, house, children, anything.

A moment's reflection and a glance at the half-time scoreboard reveals that most of Melbourne and a smidgen of Sydney are in the same boat. Pessimistic. Swan and South fans, in terminal depression. Tigers, eaten up alive, and Saints eaten up with nerves. Bulldogs, realistically pessimistic, Lions realistically relieved. Cats, not far enough in front, waiting for the storm from North, and vice versa. Demons and Bombers a sinking feeling between them. The only fans without a care in the world are the Magpies, and their fate is out of their talons, anyway. None of this was any kind of consolation.

Leigh Matthews was making a monkey of Carlton's backline and looked like he was in for a ten-goal afternoon. In the second quarter he got three goals in about three minutes. One he garnered from the foot of the pack in the goal square, the next came after he sauntered away from his dozing opponent and accepted a pass on his chest, and the other was a gift from Geoff Southby's kick-off.

SCANLENS   **33 of 168**

CARLTON

Wayne Johnston, The Grand Final Dominator.

Matthews demonstrated the kind of determination to make his own luck that makes him one of the footballers capable of winning a game all by himself. At Carlton no one seemed to have that sort of concentration in the first half, except for Southby and Fitzpatrick. The ball bounced cruelly and was rarely within reach. Elementary skills like kicking in the air and getting the distance with a handball were missing – tributes to both Hawthorn's tackling and Carlton's poor application. The whole game was being played at a slow pace and without much fervour or enthusiasm.

More than five goals down, it should have been ten, and even the most one-eyed supporter was saying that Carlton had had a wonderful run, that three flags out of four wasn't too bad, that Richmond had done a lot worse, that next year they'd give it a shake. A Fitzroy victory was going to be good for the game. Oh ye of little faith!

We reckoned without Wayne Johnston. He'd been referred to by a scornful humourist as the 'lowest common d ... d ... dominator' and had barely had a kick in half a game. We reckoned without fifteen minutes of the fiercest and most determined football ever seen at Princes Park, and that includes the 1945 Grand Final. If ever a game was turned, and a team regenerated by one player's example, this was it. It was reminiscent of the first five minutes of last year's Grand Final, the burst that set up the win.

It's obvious enough that the more goals that are kicked, the more times the ball is bounced in the middle. If you've got a winning ruck (Fitzpatrick didn't miss a hit-out all afternoon) and suddenly you get a bloke who is going to get the ball out of the centre from the taps, then you're going to attack more, score more and get more chances to score again. Johnston's move into the centre did that. And started a snowball effect.

Other moves of coach Parkin's came off too. Harmes put Matthews out of business and became a constant source of attack. Hunter at full-forward was able to run around and field anything that dropped short, Glascott and Marchesani on the wings defended, and linked up moves from the backline, and Marcou and Ashman found space to run into the flanks. And Bosustow took one of the more extraordinary marks of the season, a kind of spring upwards via Justin Madden's head, before he discovered that he was too high, descended, and twisted to take the ball in his hands facing away from its flight.

But it was Johnston's fierce attack on the footy that was the real inspiration. Of his fifteen touches – kicks, handballs, tap-ons – in fifteen minutes, there were a couple that sent the slightly flustered Hawks flying.

His tackling and recovery were what gained possession four or five times when perhaps in less charged-up circumstances he would have got away. One of these resulted in a goal via Ashman to Marcou, another he got himself after a passing exchange with Hunter, and another when he crashed through an attempted sandwich from a kick-off and had his shot taken by the telescopic fingertips of Hunter in the goal square for another major.

Another long passage of attacking possession football began when Johnston ran onto a long Southby handpass, wheeled and feinted, and kicked to Glascott. There was a dispute with some Hawks, Johnston came in and skittled the lot, gave the ball to Hunter whose shot at goal was cleared for a moment, but went to a Hawk with nowhere to go except into a Marchesani tackle. He kicked a goal.

In the end it was a ten-goal quarter, a whole-team effort inspired by the Dominator. He led the twin strategies of bottling the ball up on the forward line until a score resulted, and loose man attacking combinations from an open backline.

A game like Saturday's inspires manic-depressive behaviour in Carlton supporters. If only Carlton would play, say, two quarters a week including the first, like that one. Then they'd be a lay down misère for the flag. On the other hand, if they did that we wouldn't have such heights of ecstasy, after such pits of depression.

As for Wayne Johnston, I've seen Leigh Matthews and Robert Flower and Kevin Bartlett and Simon Madden and Ross Glendinning and Bernie Quinlan turn a game or two on their own, but generally they take a whole game, not just a quarter of an hour.

Brent Crosswell 2 May 1983

Brent Crosswell hasn't hung his boots over the mantelpiece. Modern boots are hardly worth preserving. They barely survive a season of kicking and jumping. But the old ankle coverers ... they were more like weapons, not slippers.

Seen close-up in a pack, the old boot was a frightening sight. Planted on a lumbering back it provided trampoline-like spring. Sunk into the footy, it sent it a hundred yards.

Now when there is talk of sinking the slipper, we really mean sinking the slipper, the soft-toed, light-footed, multicoloured runner that hardly deserves the attention of a craftsman bootstudder.

Doubtless, modern footwear doesn't become waterlogged and glued to the earth, and its feather weight is more comfortable, but it's hardly going to put the frighteners on anyone is it? It's not built for drop kicking, either, if such a thing were allowed. You need a bit of toe to perform a droppie, as well as a bit of cheek.

Football has changed since the day in 1968 when the young Tiger, besotted with the game, made the trip overseas from Tasmania to Carlton, from simple ambition to the complicated metropolis, and achieved nearly everything straightaway. A Grand Final first year in. He kicked a goal, and scored the last behind of the match to give Carlton a three-point win.

Tiger might have preserved those boots had he thought about it. He might have added them to the ones he wore in the 1970 Grand Final, the ones that kicked the winning goal in what was the most extraordinary Grand Final till then, or until the two 1977 Grand Finals he played with North Melbourne.

Tiger's had an extraordinary football career: 222 games, twenty-four finals matches, eight Grand Finals, and four flags. And three clubs.

Perhaps because Tiger and I are more or less the same age, and I came to watch football in a grown-up kind of way in the year he began playing, and because I used to see him around the streets and pubs of Carlton from time to time, I've always liked him. If you're allowed to have private heroes who nourish your appreciation of the great game, then Tiger's one of mine. He's there with some of the other magical players: Jezza, Ted Hopkins, Lethal, Huddo, Blighty ... Tiger not only accumulated a legend around his prowess on the football field, however, he also became a legend on the streets.

Footballers tend to be disappointingly normal if you happen to meet them. It'd be better if they were heroic in daily life somehow, as well as able to perform great deeds with the pigskin. Like actors who embody beauty and sexuality on the screen, but are ravaged by time and make-up off it, footballers who have lightning reactions, instant intelligence and do extraordinary things with their bodies in a game just aren't like that in the flesh. Well, they are like that potentially, but daily life doesn't offer the same opportunities.

Tiger's not different. He's not physically overbearing, but he is very conscious of what he was doing in football. Like an actor, he can talk about how he created the character that he played on the field. But in a way he talks about himself as dispassionately as he talks about other footballers, and much less than the way he talks about some, like Jacko.

Tiger was the one chosen by the mythmakers of the '60s to represent how it would be if they, now all with their haircut and often with a job, had had his opportunities, and played football. I've chosen him, too, I guess. To Tiger, however, the hard work and the increasing grind of footy day to day was hardly the stuff of legend.

As for the tall tales, well, who's going to confirm or deny them. Not Tiger. Take the hoary legend of the footballer who took a coke in the dressing room before the game at the old Glenferrie Oval and observed the trains passing by in a stoned daze, filled with the feeling that these beautiful sights were more important than the ball heading his direction. Ask Tiger about that one and his eyes glaze over. True or False? Take your pick.

He's more inclined to recall his first season with Carlton, living a tram ride up Sydney Road from the ground, in Coburg. A boarding house, with three other footballers. What a life it was. Playing with a successful team in your first year, training two nights a week and that, more or less, was it! It gave you a bit of money to spend, not much, but enough to drink and meet women. Admittedly you were owned by the club, and treated like a chattel, but the compensations were great. Football meant freedom, for fifteen years.

It's the players who play the game and provide the entertainment for the paying customers and the television viewers. When fans think of the football team, the football club, they don't think of administrators and officials. They think of the players. The players provide the real continuity, it seems to Tiger, whereas to many committeemen it's the other way around. Players can be bought and sold, gained and lost, but the club, in the form of the administration, goes on. Players are just like an annual supply of football boots. They are paid to perform. If that's the way it is, Tiger thinks they should be paid properly.

In the last half of his career, Tiger was conscious of creating a character on the footy ground. He purposely didn't shave from the Wednesday before a match, so that he would look fiercer. He looked a rough-head, and with a reputation that took the field before him, was equipped to gain physical superiority over his opponent. It's a bit like intimidation. Some players are known to be soft, known not to like being played so that your smelly breath is down their jumpers, known not to like the hard tackle. And others are out to get you, using boots and fists and fingers in the protection of the packs, giving you a whack at every opportunity. Tiger copped more cuts and bruises to the face in the last couple of seasons than in the thirteen before – a sign of growing old, of slowing up. He knew well enough that four umpires wouldn't be enough to keep up with all the villainy that goes on during a game. It goes on in front of upwards of a hundred thousand fans too, of course. We don't 'see' half of it.

Tiger sees players as gladiators out fighting in front of a crowd who love to see aggression and hurt, and who need to be catered for, played up to. Players like Tiger and Jacko (potentially) are the entertainers who put on a show. Tiger holds the ball aloft, ostentatiously chests a player, paces up and down to unnerve his opponent when the ball is at the other end of the ground, even waves his arms around to get something going, change the pattern, the feeling of the game for spectator and team-mates alike.

But it's an act. Tiger reckons Jacko might actually believe that what he's doing is real. Tiger could never quite believe in all the pre-match hullabalooo. He thinks football is a game of concentration, of determination, man to man, as well as the ability to run through a brick wall. Tiger got by on minimal training and on making the most of his natural ability. Which is where he got into differences of opinion with those who felt he could be a world-beater every game.

There is a feeling that he admires, as opponents, players not dissimilar to himself. He wasn't going to try and rough up anyone like Bruce Doull, for example. He liked him too much as a person as well as a player. He couldn't be intimidated anyway. He would beat you with skill alone. Perhaps Tiger was in trouble with the players he liked.

Take Malcolm Blight. He would just stand still, hands folded in front of him, loose and relaxed, flatfooted almost, when the ball was somewhere else. No matter what you did you couldn't stir him. You'd even think, Well, I've got him this time. He's not even watching the ball. He's looking at the ground. Suddenly the ball is nearby, and whoosh! Malcolm's taken a mark and kicked a goal. You hardly had time to applaud.

It's those sorts of moments when Tiger, last year, began to feel his ankles creak, and his knees groan. He reckons that he could nearly play today, he's probably in the top few over forty metres, but it takes two laps to even get the blood circulating. And perhaps he's too old to dominate an opponent in a key position as he once did, especially in the seasons at Melbourne.

There's another legend about that. Tiger has had a broken arm a couple of times from the collision of hard heads with it. To prevent mortal injury to it, he wore a soft leather brace on it. Purely as protection, naturally, inspected by the umpires. It seems that the yarn got around that inside Tiger's soft brace was something akin to a knuckle-duster. Pliable as it was, it caused opponents to steer clear. Even then, teammates at North eventually believed in the power of Tiger's arm. Soon the man himself believed it. It was like the shield of a crusader. Naturally, when he went to Melbourne, he always played well against North. And for some reason he seemed stronger than ever, even with the brace removed. Its power stayed with him.

Tiger tells a story of one thing he learnt from the coach he seemed to follow from Carlton to North to Melbourne (appearances can be deceptive in this matter), Ron Barassi. He always wondered why Barassi, whenever there was a need to give the team a sermon, would pick on poor old Tiger. When it came to establishing some discipline in the classroom, Tiger discovered the technique of talking straight at one individual, one incorrigible example. Just like Barassi.

He likes going to the football. It's a great game. He'd prefer it if it was like it was when he was a kid, when you could go to the footy and have a picnic as well, a kick at half time and a listen to the three-quarter-time address. But you can't get that in the VFL where the standard of the game is at its highest. Tiger thinks he might take a thermos and a sandwich along some time soon.

He ought to be able to put his feet up, now he's hung up his boots.

Garrie Hutchinson has written and edited many books about football, and other Australian matters. He co-edited *Footy's Greatest Coaches*, which included his essay on Carlton's great early coach Jack Worrall.

The stories in **'Memories of the '80s'** first appeared in the *Age* in the early 1980s, and were published in book form in *From The Outer* in 1984.

27

I ❤ JOHN PLATTEN

alicia sometimes

Dear Johnny Platten

I think you make all the difference at Hawthorn. You are
the star. Don't let anyone tell you any different. I really
want to see you at a social day at Glenferrie. I want to give
you chocolates - would that interfere with your game? I want
to ask you some questions. Do the other girls tease me
because I don't put photos of pretty Timmy Watson on my wall
but I have pictures of you on my pencil case and folders and
locker? Is that what's annoying them? Is it the I ❤ JOHNNY
badge that I pin on my yellow and brown parka on game day? Or
is it because you look like Tina Turner from the film clip
'What's Love Got To Do With It?'

Is everyone jealous?

Whenever you get near another player on the wing I always
shout DACK HIM, DACK HIM! so you get to have an edge over him.
When you look soaked in the rain and the crowd calls you a
rat, I squeal back LEAVE HIM ALONE. WHAT'S HE EVER DONE TO YOU?

Do the girls rib me just because you cried at the Brownlow?
I thought it was <u>mature</u> and <u>manly</u>, something Harrison Ford
would do. Even your shoulder hair can't keep me away, it's not
like you have a Gary Ayres mullet or anything. You're the
sweetest player in the VFL. It's those eyes and that <u>perm</u>. Is
it weird that I write in biro on my arm J PLATTEN IS BULK ACE and
write the number 44 over everything I can get my hands on?

You are so generous, always passing to Pritchard and Dear
and Buckenara and Condon. Dunstall would be nothing without
you. You're dangerous when you want to be - I saw you rush at
Fletcher's ankles. He was so confused. I laughed for days.

When one of my girlfriends took a sign to the last Essendon vs Hawthorn match saying FLATTEN PLATTEN! I just want you to know I stuck a sign that said I AM PAUL SALMON'S LOVE CHILD on the back of her beanie. I'd do anything for you. Will you come to my school and be my friend?

Yours 4 eva
Your greatest fan
1986

alicia sometimes is a Melbourne poet, writer and 'spoken word' performer, and a co-editor of *Going Down Swinging* magazine.

28

The Importance of Being Nicky

by Stephanie Holt

It was never going to seem real. Not the headlines on the back page. Not the awkwardly posed photo in the stiff new guernsey. Not the name buried in practice-match reports. Not until Nicky Winmar took the field in the Ansett Cup, in an unfamiliar strip with a strange number on his back, did it sink in that this most loved of players, a champion who through highs and lows – his own, as well as the team's – seemed to epitomise St Kilda, had gone. St Kilda without Winmar may well be a stronger, more disciplined, more successful team. It may yet achieve the elusive triumph that a core of champions with a talented supporting cast has been promising for years. Crowds will continue to cheer it on; the players will continue to respond to the exhortations of coach, teammates and fans. But Winmar's leaving leaves St Kilda profoundly diminished.

A few seasons ago I fronted up to St Kilda's first Ansett Cup game, light-headed with anticipation, and decided to take out a membership for my daughter, tucked up in bed at home. Undeterred by long queues or by the lack of financial soundness in signing up someone too young in any case to pay admission, I only began to doubt this course when faced with nominating her favourite player. This was something I had to get right; his signature (no scepticism permitted) would be appearing on a birthday card in a few months time. I agonised aloud for several minutes before finally offering 'Nicky Winmar'. The laugh in response was warm and quick: 'Oh, they all say that!' And it was true. Look around a St Kilda game three or four years ago, and small backs bearing number 7s peppered the crowd. Listen, and his name punctuated the barracking.

'Nicky, Nicky, Nicky': a war cry, an entreaty, a shriek of excitement. In the privacy of lounge rooms before small-screen games, a groan of exasperation or a gentle croon (speaking here from observation, not experience) to placate a fractious baby. Even through the years when Tony Lockett stole much of the limelight, crowds and commentators joined them in a blessed trinity: Winmar–Lockett–Goal. Others routinely describe his skills and talent: his deft ball-handling, strong tackling, soaring marks (he won Mark of the Year in 1992) and precision kicking (former coach Stan Alves once nominated Winmar as the player he'd most like to see with the ball if victory rested on a set shot after the siren from outside forty metres). This is all true, and unmistakable, but the quality of adoration Winmar evoked in St Kilda supporters drew on more than this. There was an intensity when they urged him on or applauded his game that was his alone. We were not spectators, we were there to bear witness.

If we could explain this, we might be closer to understanding the meaning of this game. Every team has its champions, the talented players who tip the odds towards a win. Them we admire. Then there are those who seem to exemplify not only the best qualities of the game but the particular character of their team. Them we adore, in all their strengths and failings. And then there are those, like Winmar, who offer all this and more, who seem to play as we in the outer barrack. Them we love, unreservedly.

Strange things happen to time in football. Match time is strange enough, the illusory precision of twenty-minute quarters played out as a succession of first and final moments, played so fast it's hard to acknowledge that each mark, each kick is a new beginning. A game's momentum can swing in seconds, a moment's hesitation or dominance increasing exponentially. The crowd responds to almost imperceptible cues, the team lifts, one player after another finds the form that's been eluding him. One kick can turn hopeless despair into a race towards victory. Which is why, however dire things are, each goal, each desperate tackle, demands of us a reaction.

Winmar, more than any of those around him, played in that moment. This is not to suggest that he was inconsistent or unreliable over the course of a match. Nor simply to note the versatility and quick reflexes that were the bedrock of his game. He was everywhere the ball was. He knew the frustration of the bench and the release of a return to the fray, the exhilaration of the wing, the steadfastness of a key position. His volatility was both blessing and curse, but swung into a new position, or urged to a greater effort, he could trigger seemingly miraculous changes of fortune. He dragged himself to training, just as we so often dragged ourselves to the scene of near-certain defeat; but once there, his tenacity was renowned. It was Winmar who got us into the 1991 finals, our first for eighteen years. It was Winmar who got us through the Ansett Cup in 1996, into our first 'Grand Final' for a generation.

Martin Flanagan once characterised St Kilda supporters as having, necessarily, 'a well-developed capacity for taking the long view'. They do. They've also had to develop the strong oral tradition of all down-trodden peoples. During the bleak years early in Winmar's career, as tel-evised highlights increasingly defined our collective memory of the game, St Kilda could get through a whole season without ever playing the Match of the Day. *If Winmar pulls down a screamer at Moorabbin and there are no television cameras there to record it,* we mused, *did it really happen?* To others, our ritual recitation of obscure moments, obscure names, may have sounded like some laughably misbegotten obsession. We were testifying.

If those fragments can be woven into some kind of cohesive narrative – if there is some way of making sense of their significance and the fine calibrations of greatness that took the place of accepted measures of success – it is as a hypothetical history. And Winmar has been uncannily central to the 'what ifs' that have propelled St Kilda's recent past; that are, in fact, the leitmotif of a century of passion and failure. What if he hadn't been wiped out in 1990 for half the season for what we now know, thanks to Dermott Brereton's belated honesty, was a response to racist abuse? What if he hadn't walked out early in '93 over a contract dispute, having put in four best-on-ground performances? What if he hadn't injured that knee in 1996, to put him out of a season begun with such promise? What if his father hadn't died on the eve of the 1997 Grand Final? Even last season's grotesque dénouement saw hopes flare, some Pavlovian response activated, as Winmar lunged towards a loose ball in front of goal in Sydney and threatened to give St Kilda one more undeserved week in a finals series in which they were clearly outclassed. Give us, the fans, the perfect ending that we longed for and never got. In that split second we were already dreaming of Winmar mobbed by his teammates and carried from the ground, reparation made, forgiveness granted. Already hearing the Marching Saints, sung as a hymn of tran-scendence and redemption. What if ...?

'The Worth of Winmar', from Marching In fanzine
courtesy of John Spud

220

JUST BEFORE THE '91 FINALS I WENT TO A SPORTSMANS NIGHT IN EMERALD STARRING WINMAR & LOCKETT. NICKY DISPLAYED HIS SELDOM SEEN ORATORY SKILLS...

WHETHER YOU'RE BLACK OR WHITE, YOU GO BLUE WHEN YOU'RE COLD, GREEN WHEN YOU'RE SICK AND PURPLE WHEN YOU'RE UNDERWATER

NICKY WAS GREAT IN OUR HEART-RENDING '91 ELIM. FINAL LOSS TO GEELONG. THERE'S A GREAT PHOTO OF HIS DETERMINATION IN THAT GAME

P.284 — 'THE POINT OF IT ALL'

UNUSUALLY FOR A PLAYER FROM DRY W.A., NICKY EXCELS IN WET CONDITIONS ALSO, AS SHOWN V. EAGLES IN DRIVING RAIN IN 1992.

WHAT HAS NUMBER 7 DONE?

HE'S KICKED A GOAL!

'CLASSIC DON SCOTT COMMENTARY

LATE IN '92 ESSENDON GAVE US A TOWELLING AT THE M.C.G., THOUGH THAT DIDN'T STOP NICKY TAKING MARK OF THE YEAR IN THE LAST QUARTER

I CAN SEE MY HOUSE

PROVING ONCE AGAIN THAT YOU SHOULD NEVER LEAVE EARLY, ESPECIALLY IF WINMAR'S PLAYING

NICKY'S SINGLE GREATEST MOMENT CAME IN '93 VS. COLLINGWOOD AT VIC. PARK WHEN ABUSED BY RACISTS...

I'M BLACK AND I'M PROUD TO BE BLACK

©John Saad 97

AS ALWAYS, HIS ACTIONS SPOKE LOUDER THAN WORDS

SOME SAY HIS WORST MOMENT CAME THE FOLLOWING WEEK WHEN HE STOOD OUT IN A BID FOR MORE MONEY. I WON'T PRETEND I WASN'T UPSET, BUT IT DID PROVE HE WAS WORTH IT.

THE WORST I'D ACCUSE HIM OF IS TRUSTING HIS MANAGER.

NICKY MISSED TRAINING EARLIER THIS YEAR AND WAS DROPPED. YET AGAIN, THOSE WITH SHORT MEMORIES BEGAN THEIR LITANY

HE'S NOT WORTH IT... WE SHOULD GET RID OF HIM

THAT'S THE PRICE YOU PAY FOR GENIUS...

...WAS MY WELL-WORN REPLY

THERE ARE THOSE WHO SAY NICKY'S BEST FOOTY IS BEHIND HIM, BUT AS RECENTLY AS THE SYDNEY GAME, HE PROVED HIS WORTH ONCE AGAIN...

SWOOP

KEPT US IN IT IN FIRST HALF...

THERE WAS A GREAT PHOTO ON THE FRONT OF THE MONDAY SPORT SECTION IN THE AGE AFTER NICKY'S 200TH GAME

AUSSIE

COULD HAVE POSSIBLY BEEN WEARING SOME OTHER JUMPER

HIS LOOK OF PEACEFUL CONTENTMENT BROUGHT A TEAR TO THE EYE

WHEN NICKY WAS INJURED VS. MELBOURNE IN '96, IT COST US NOT ONLY THAT GAME, BUT A SPOT IN THAT YEARS FINALS. (WE ONLY STARTED TO GET IT TOGETHER WHEN HE CAME BACK).

AT THE START OF THIS YEAR NICKY SAID HE OWED A LOT TO ST.KILDA AND INTENDED TO REPAY THE DEBT IN FULL...

I'LL DO EVERYTHING I CAN TO PAY ST.KILDA BACK!

THAT'S ALL VERY WELL, BUT THERE'S AN INHERENT FLAW WITHIN THIS STATEMENT...

NICKY WINMAR HAS REPAID US MANY TIMES OVER AND WILL CONTINUE TO DO SO. IF ANYTHING WE OWE HIM FOR ALL HE'S DONE. OF COURSE, IT WON'T BE UNTIL HE'S GONE THAT WE'LL REALISE WHAT WE HAD.

NICKY, WE HARDLY KNEW YE!

THANKS NICKY

Like all St Kilda fans, I longed to see a Saints premiership. But more than anything, I longed to see Nicky Winmar play in that premiership side. I knew, if I knew anything about my team, that he would rise to the occasion and play the game of his life. He would play a kind of football we'd only dared dream about. One premiership would only whet the appetite for another, but seeing Nicky shine like that would be a privilege never forgotten. When the opportunity came, his game was over before it began. He had steadied himself in the face of his father's illness all season; the shock and grief of death stacked the odds impossibly against him. No scriptwriter would get away with timing like that.

His team's lack of success both clouds Winmar's achievements and enhances his significance. He could play as if surrounded by champions, and sometimes that was enough to lift a mediocre team to great and unexpected victories. Illusion and belief, a brilliant defiance, characterised his game as much as they did the fervour of his team's supporters. In this, he epitomised the essential qualities of the club we loved. But if his team's story is one of missed opportunities and unfulfilled potential, of a much-noted propensity for self-inflicted sabotage, Winmar's own story could too easily be cast in the same mould. Greatness brought low by its inherent flaws, after all, provides one of our culture's archetypal stories. Winmar has often been portrayed as a victim of his own restless intensity. In a journalistic sleight of hand, his failings are retold as a story – albeit a regrettable, disappointing one – of failure. His record suggests otherwise.

Playing for most of his career alongside Brownlow medallists Tony Lockett and Robert Harvey, Winmar was twice club Best and Fairest, twice runner-up. A West Australian who could never wear the Big V, he was twice selected all-Australian. A big-game player in an often struggling team, the closest he came to ultimate victory was the 1996 Ansett Cup win – and in that game Winmar shone for four formidable quarters and took home the Michael Tuck medal for best on the ground. The ability to characterise such a career by its failings is facilitated by St Kilda's mythic place as the least successful side of all time. Less obviously, it draws on racial stereotypes, unavoidably evoked every time Winmar's absences are dwelt on, his free and spirited roaming of the field and 'uncanny' skills (self-centred and intuitive, rather than team-oriented and hard-earned) discussed, his 'unpredictability' (lack of discipline) noted. But Winmar's legacy for Aboriginal football is decisive. A player who shied away from the activism of many of his peers, he none the less gave football its most resonant image of black pride and proud defiance. Marked from his earliest days in WA as unreliable, he was the first Aboriginal player to earn life membership of a club for ten years' service, giving twelve seasons to those who ignored the local wisdom and recruited him to the big league back in 1986. In 1997 he became the first Aboriginal player to play 200 VFL/AFL games, an achievement, St Kilda fans can remind you, that was effectively and unjustifiably ignored by that week's *Football Record*.

Where Winmar is concerned, actions speak infinitely louder than words. Footballers are rarely beautiful, but Winmar is. His is a lithe, muscular beauty. He has the masculine grace of a classical David – with his finely turned limbs and sleek silhouette, more Donatello than Michelangelo (cast Stewart Loewe in that role). In photograph after photograph, Winmar is poised in contraposto. The play of angles and curves, tension and fluidity, says far more than a single spectacular leap or kick about the dynamism of the game he excels in. He handles the ball with a ferocity and tenderness we recognise, as fierce and protective as the liturgy of the outer.

Winmar's media appearances were awkward at best, embarrassingly contrived at worst: his gestures on the field were something else. His reflexes were as quick sprinting to a young teammate for a behind-the-scenes pat on the back as gathering a loose ball in defence and spiriting it away up the opposite flank. Walking off after a game, his victorious grasp of his teammates was as unyielding as his fiercest tackle. These rituals of giving and receiving acknowledgement were a constant of his on-field demeanour. His gestures of loyalty placed him at the heart of his team, even as they marked a strange separateness. It was as if his dedication existed essentially, and only, in a state of continuous affirmation. His was a passion enhanced, not diminished, by the effort and vigilance it required. All this, too, we saw in ourselves.

My daughter wore his number, chanted his name and received his birthday cards for several seasons. She worried about his injuries, advised all and sundry of his prowess, and put her dark brown pencil to good use as he starred in countless drawings of her team. Concerned by his absence from a St Kilda vs Dogs clash after he'd done his knee against Melbourne, she found her own explanation. That was the day word passed through a departing Waverley crowd of some kind of craziness down in Tasmania, and the traditional drive-home postmortem of dressing-room interviews, talk-back radio and best-on-ground deliberations was replaced by the horror of a broadcast body-count. Catching repeated TV footage that night of a stretchered body, Lydia deduced that 'the naughty doggies hurt Nicky.' I didn't correct her. Together we counted down the weeks to Nicky's reappearance and celebrated his eventual return, her eagerness matched my desperation to pretend we shared a world where bad things would come good.

Now we're getting ready for a season without him. We'll probably get a number 10 for her jumper, and the club's streamlining things their end, with a designated ready-to-wear hero for the young supporter, who now joins the Spider Club. I've got a feeling we'll be out of town when St Kilda meets the Bulldogs.

Like St Kilda, the Bulldogs are a proud club with a passionate following, a notoriously inhospitable suburban headquarters, and a single premiership to their name. Like St Kilda, they seem to be every second supporter's second team. The dream Grand Final that never was, in 1997, cemented these teams together in Victorian minds as the deserving underdogs whose time had come. St Kilda fans will remember how fixtures threw them together at intense moments. Think of the Footscray banner – a red, white and blue message of condolence – two days after the death of Trevor Barker. Think of the tears of Danny Frawley after his last game, the day the Western Oval was renamed in honour of his friend Teddy Whitten and the whole crowd urged him on – to no avail – as he skewed a backman's shot at goal late in the game. Under Terry Wallace, the Bulldogs have a good track record conjuring strong careers from second chances. There, Winmar has probably his best chance of consistently finding the game of a longstanding champion. And then, as would be fitting, he can leave football with pride and dignity. Like other greats who've changed teams late in their career, history will bring him home. Just as Dermott Brereton will always be a Hawk, Winmar can only endure as a Saint.

Go Nicky.

Stephanie Holt is a writer and editor specialising in art, football and other topics of vital cultural significance. She co-edited *Footy's Greatest Coaches* with Garrie Hutchinson in 2002.

'The Importance of Being Nicky' was commissioned by Philippa Hawker and originally published in the *Age* in 1999.

29

A FAN'S LAMENT
The Greatest Player Ever Isn't from My Team

by Gary Walters

Sometimes I wish I were an omniscient, omnipresent centenarian with the wisdom of Solomon and the impartiality of a United Nations Secretary-General. Because then I could answer the eternal and impossible question: Who is the greatest Australian Rules footballer of them all?

Instead, when people suggest 'What about Haydn Bunton, Dick Reynolds or Barrie Robran?' (for example) I have to answer 'Dunno, I never saw them play.' (Actually, on occasions this is bordering on a lie, because I may never even have heard of them.) Rather, I'm just like a lot of people who watch their team reasonably regularly and get to see other matches on the telly about as often, which means seeing rival teams very much less than my own team – though that can still add up to quite a few matches and a lot of players over thirty-eight years.

Having 'followed' with extreme prejudice for most of that time the team with the most premierships, it is tempting, when selecting *the* player, to succumb to the allure of a Terry Daniher (but wasn't Neale potentially the greater?) or a Simon Madden (definitely better than Justin, although we will never know how good a sports minister Simon might have been). And then there's the doyen of Dons, the essence of Essendon, the talented Tim Watson, who thrilled us for many years with his magical acts.

Who among the chosen followers could forget Timmy the teenager – having made his senior debut as a 15-year-old – blindturning, dancing and slipping away from rings of Hawthorn defenders in the '84 and '85 finals? Yet an even stronger memory remains of a match against the Hawks a decade earlier, in which a chunky Hawthorn rover demolished Tuddenham's Essendon, both physically and on the Mocopan scoreboard, with a crushing eleven goals. Over the years I saw a lot more of this mini-tank called Leigh Matthews (or Barney Rubble, by his teammates) than I would have liked. An excellent mark for his size, he showed great ball-handling and manoeuvrability combined with unwavering courage ... and more.

And there are a number of other players who must be considered, such as the classy Alex Jesaulenko, the gifted larrikin Ted Whitten and one Gary Ablett (although we at Windy Hill mistakenly thought the Geelong rabble were cheering for *our* God: **Gary O'D**onnell).

Jesaulenko's groundplay was skill personified, and he proved to be a highly successful goal scorer, the only Blue to score a century in a year. Then there was his inspiring mark followed by a match-winning goal in the 1970 mother of all Grand Finals.

Ted Whitten senior, during his 321 games, simply did everything better than anyone else of his time. I only saw him once, toward the end of his career in the late '60s, when in pouring rain on an MCG quagmire his shadowy figure hovered high above a huge pack and took one of the great marks, eventually gliding to his feet. With the kind of impartiality I yearn for, an umpire took the ball from him and awarded a free kick to the opposition, thus consigning the mark to history's dustbin. A brilliant exponent of the flick pass, Whitten was so highly regarded at Western Oval that at 23 he was appointed coach – before he had even been considered mature enough to captain his older teammates.

But has there ever been a more explosive or crowd-drawing player than Gary Ablett? He could kick a bag of goals in an important match, creating opportunities from nothing while leaving his (multiple) opponents lying on the ground. And, dare I admit it, he was Tim Watson's choice as the greatest footballer he ever saw play. Matthews's fellow spearhead Tony Lockett, by contrast, was immovable.

I have of course omitted many of those who could always be relied upon to win one-out contests, who, when tackled, always got an effective handpass away and who, near goal, were virtually unstoppable: Gary Lyon, Dougie Hawkins, Paul Roos and King Carey come immediately to mind.

But while Lethal was certainly never as classy as Jesaulenko, he was undeniably ruthlessly efficient, with enormous ability to amass kicks. He also possessed great stamina – those that claimed he played with a big heart weren't exaggerating: it was physically enlarged. And while Ablett's Geelong or Lockett's St Kilda could have trouble getting the ball to their champion in front of goal, leaving them cold and out of the play, Hawthorn, with Matthews, had a man who could dictate play from anywhere on the ground, pushing his side forward from the centre bounce or cutting a swathe on the backline through the opposition's forwards.

Certainly, Matthews wasn't one of the great kicks of the then-VFL – he was no Bernie 'Superboot' Quinlan – but he could kick the ball far and straight enough. He goaled with his first kick in senior footy, and by the end of his career had scored more goals than any player in VFL/AFL history with the exception of six of the Lockett, Dunstall and Ablett ilk. Twice Matthews booted eleven in a match, including on that fateful day in Round 3, 1973 against the Bombers. The Coleman medallist of 1975, he scored ninety-one majors in the 1977 season alone. In total, Matthews kicked 915 goals, second at Hawthorn only to their champion Jason Dunstall, and well ahead of the mercurial Peter Hudson.

Lethal may not have been the toughest, either, when you compare him with the likes of Jack Dyer (so I'm told), Tony Lockett and Dermott Brereton, and at 1.78 metres (5'10" in the old money) he was definitely not the biggest, but his 86 kilograms (13 stone) made him solid. He was indestructible, a machine among men, as many of his opponents found out. Although Matthews claimed that the ball was his object, those who got in his way found it was a bad place to be. The 'fairest' part of the Brownlow was never at risk: some have suggested that at least a few of Matthews's victims suffered chronic injuries or retired early as a result of his brick-shithouse tackles. Strongly built from teenage days, he once shirtfronted a behind post and came off best, snapping it in half. His five or six broken noses are testament to the fact that many of the opposition were out to square the ledger.

His record included players from most VFL clubs and the two great interstate rivals, SA and WA, among them the small but super Barry Cable, flattened by a 19-year-old Leigh. Footscray's Grant Simmons was left unconscious and with an epileptic fit after contact with Matthews, but his most infamous clash was undoubtedly with the Cats' little man Neville Bruns. Deregistered for four weeks by the VFL, Matthews was found guilty of assault after a police investigation and, until an appeal was upheld, had a recorded conviction. (To his credit, Matthews has expressed regrets about some of his onfield actions, and has been involved recently in a Queensland program to remove violence from footy and protect umpires by having parents of junior footballers sign 'good behaviour' contracts.)

When it came to finals toughness, few were better equipped than Lethal. This vigour, along with that of many of his teammates, including Dipierdomenico and Brereton, had much to do with the brown-and-gold's finals success, success that no other team has matched over the last forty-two years. Although there are numerous examples of one Grand Final side exerting 'physical pressure' to blow away the other early in a match (note the Magpies' destruction of the Bombers in 1990 and Essendon against Carlton in 1993), on few occasions has it been better illustrated than in the 1983 premiership match when the Hawks took out Timmy.

Matthews won eight club Best and Fairests – double his nearest Hawk competitor – during a period when his club was regularly in the finals, his first coming in a premiership year that saw Hawthorn full-forward Peter Hudson sneak 150 goals. He played in four premierships, dominating in those triumphs. In captaining the Hawks from 1981 to 1985, Matthews also became one of their longest serving leaders. In fact, Matthews epitomised longevity. He went on to notch up 332 games, second at Hawthorn only to the VFL/AFL record-holder, teammate Michael Tuck, and one of a select few players over more than a hundred years of the competition to play more than 320 games.

Most of Matthews's rivals in greatness fail to reach his standards in one or another department. Ted Whitten scored a mere 360 goals in his 321 games and effected only one flag. Neither Ablett nor Lockett played in a premiership. Some of Matthews's competitors for immortality suffered from 'temperament' problems: Matthews was in fact rarely suspended, unlike Lockett, Ablett and Carey. Tim Watson didn't have his physical presence. (Umpire Rohan Sawyers, a nice chap I once met at a cricket match, was pilloried as 'the man who shot Bambi' after booking the normally mild Baby Bomber.)

Without those qualities of perfect knowledge I crave, it is almost impossible to compare eras – I only ever saw eleven of the Same Old's Team of the [20th] Century and had not even heard of eight of the others. Thus we are stuck with what we know, glimpses from the past and a little of what we have read.

When I asked other fans for their best five, the names of players from their own teams would inevitably and parochially crop up: the Swans' Bob Skilton (and with three Brownlows, why not?), Ronald Dale Barassi, and North's super-aerialist and goal-after-siren specialist Malcolm Blight a few of the best. But the one name raised by nearly all supporters for the greatest ever was Leigh Matthews. Glenferrie Oval's ultimate player was the man that opposition supporters loved to hate but respected supremely. While we at Essendon always believed 'Is Don, is good,' it turned out, during Lethal Leigh's reign, and perhaps forever, that Hawk is better. Matthews was never the fairest, he was simply the best.

Gary Walters is an author of walking guides and travel articles, and is currently working on a book on Aussie Rules strategies. More importantly, he is an Essendon fan.

CHAMPIONS of Today

Today's champions play in an era of unprecedented media
and corporate involvement in footy. Their acts of courage
and skill will be endlessly analysed, photographed, replayed
and discussed: this is the stuff of Monday's experts. But
greatness can be a liability. The great are expected to show
skill, leadership and commitment off field as well as on.
Their disappointments and indiscretions will be front-page
news. And despite their many honours – the Brownlows,
the Norm Smiths, the captaincies, the all-Australian
selections – only time will tell if they will
pass into football legend.

30

ROBERT HARVEY

Poise, Perseverance, Humility

by Peter Weiniger

The 2003 season was to be a watershed for Robert Harvey. Plagued by a succession of injuries, the dual Brownlow medallist had managed only nineteen of a possible forty-four games in the previous two years, playing well below par in several of them due to interrupted preparation. At 31, many in the football community were wondering whether the St Kilda champion still had it in him to play 'good footy', or if the ravages of age and an ailing body had taken their toll.

Harvey wondered, too. On the eve of his 250th game, in 2002, he had publicly contemplated retirement. After another long layoff and a second knee arthroscopy during the off-season, he resolved to carry on. Time not only heals the body but can allow contemplation and reflection. Refreshed, in mind and body, he returned to the training track with renewed resolve.

Any lingering doubts were finally put to rest in round 7 of the 2003 season, when the Saints took on Carlton at Telstra Dome. In the dying minutes of the final quarter, with the Saints grimly hanging on to a narrow lead, Harvey ran into space deep inside St Kilda's 50-metre circle, signalling to young gun Brendon Goddard, who responded by sending a fifty-metre pass into Harvey's outstretched arms. Taking his time, Harvey lined up the goals and kicked truly, putting the game beyond Carlton's reach.

The win, St Kilda's fourth for the season, was a great start for the struggling Saints. But the symbolism of the moment perhaps meant even more than the four points. Goddard's pinpoint pass and Harvey's match-winning goal gave long-suffering Saints supporters renewed hope that the club had a future. In that flowing move, St Kilda's bright new star, Goddard – a 17-year-old high school student – had linked with the club's finest player of the decade to seal a morale-boosting win. Between them, Harvey and Goddard amassed around fifty possessions to share best on ground statistics. Surely, now, with the right blend of youth and maturity, the Saints had turned the corner and were poised to deliver the success that had for so long eluded the struggling club.

If Goddard arrived at St Kilda in a blaze of publicity, Harvey's ascendency was more muted. John Beveridge, St Kilda's longstanding talent scout, remembers Harvey's arrival at the club in 1987:

> Harvs had played in our schoolboy teams as a 15-year-old, but went back to Seaford later that year. He returned in 1988 and started in the under-19s. I had a battle to get him into the team, because the coaching staff were a bit reluctant to try a skinny kid who hadn't turned 17, so he sat on the bench in the first game but came on and kicked a couple of goals.

From then on he was a regular and caught the eye of senior coach Darrel Baldock, who was eager to give young players a chance in the seniors. After eight games in the under-19s and six reserve grade matches, Harvey was selected in the senior side to play Footscray at the Western Oval in August that year, at the age of 16. The future champion was on his way.

A quiet, unassuming, character who prefers to let his football do the talking, the young Harvey had to be convinced by others that his future lay on the footy field. Beveridge recalls sitting alongside Harvey's mum when the shy youngster was playing in junior state teams. Together, they would call out in frustration, 'For God's sake, Harvs, get a few kicks. We know you're a good player, but you've got to show others as well!'

It was Beveridge who convinced a dubious under-17s state coach, Ray Jordan, to select Harvey in a Teal Cup side that included Wayne Carey and Jose Romero. 'Is this Harvey any good?' Jordan asked.

'Even then, he was a very humble young fellow, and although he believed in his own ability, I don't think he appreciated how good he was in the context of the whole scene,' says Beveridge. By the time the carnival was over, Victoria was victorious and Harvey was selected in the all-Australian squad.

Unlike many AFL footballers, Harvey hadn't contemplated a career as a professional footballer. 'I never really thought about being a professional footballer until I *was* one,' he says:

> I just enjoyed playing footy, and came to St Kilda on the chance of getting a run. I was actually keener on cricket. I loved it as much as I did footy. It wasn't as if I made a conscious decision to play professional football.

That Harvey's first love was cricket shouldn't be all that surprising – he's the grandson of Merv Harvey, who played Test cricket for Australia, and the grandnephew of Neil Harvey, one of the nation's batting greats. In contrast to his famous cricketing forebears, Robert chose the cherry rather than the willow, and developed into a more than handy fast bowler. A left-arm fast-medium bowler and right-hand batsman, Harvey played district cricket with Fitzroy-Doncaster and Frankston Peninsula and, as a junior, gained selection in the Victorian under-19 squad. In his senior debut with Peninsula, he claimed 5/60.

But the fast bowler's curse – back problems – flared up, and any dreams Harvey may have had of wearing the 'baggy green' were quickly set aside. The pressure of football eventually forced Harvey to abandon cricket, though not without a twinge of regret, as something that had been an enjoyable way of keeping fit in summer began to threaten his blossoming football career. 'It's something I still really miss,' he says. 'Of all the things footy gives you, the biggest thing it's probably taken away was the chance to keep playing cricket and possibly one day play for my country.'

In its place, football gave Harvey an illustrious career spanning more than 250 games, two Brownlow medals, three E.J. Whitten medals, seven all-Australian selections, four club Best and Fairest awards, the captaincy of St Kilda, and the respect of the entire football community. All that's missing to date is playing in a premiership team. And that nearly happened in 1997, when the Saints went down to Adelaide in a hard-fought Grand Final at the MCG.

Looking back on his only encounter to date with football's one day of the year, Harvey remembers it as 'the highest and lowest moment, all in one hit'. The passing years have taught him that the wait between Grand Finals can seem like an eternity when your team is a heartbreak old club like St Kilda, with only one premiership in its long history.

After the 1997 finals loss, Harvey consoled himself with the thought that another chance at the flag would come soon. But all that came was another St Kilda slump to the bottom of the ladder, more instability at the club, a succession of coaches and the departure of quality players Tony Lockett, Matthew Lappin, Barry Hall, the Wakelin twins and Peter Everitt, as hope gave way to despair.

Arresting the Saints' slide down the ladder while players jumped ship and the club lurched from coach to coach, president to president, proved an impossible task, even for a player of Harvey's calibre and integrity. Leadership did not come easily to a quiet, introspective man, who preferred to let his football skills speak for him. Nor was he helped by the injuries that suddenly began to plague his otherwise super-fit body. Badly torn quadriceps, chronic groin problems, strained calves and hamstrings and a knee reconstruction in 2001 saw him watching from the sidelines more often than leading the Saints on the playing field during a horror stretch that cost him the best part of three seasons.

As the long breaks between games took the sharpness from Harvey's form, many began to wonder if his footballing days were numbered and his skills irrevocably diminished. Football followers wondered if they would ever again see the sublime skills, hard running and endurance that were the hallmarks of Harvey's game.

Among the great sights in football during the 1990s was Robert Harvey rollicking through the middle, dishing out handballs to teammates, delicately side-stepping opponents as if they didn't exist, creating space seemingly out of nowhere. One football writer described his on-field demeanour thus:

> Harvey would bound out of the centre, riding on the balls of his feet, the Sherrin held in both hands, eyes searching, and the men around him would appear to grind almost to a standstill ... the would-be tacklers evaded by that trademark jink – a kind of swaying of the upper body – or that rugby-style sidestep – a 90-degree change of direction that sacrificed neither balance nor pace.

Harvey is simply a 'genius', according to John Beveridge, who singles out Harvey's evasive skills, the turn of the hips, the ability to find space, his aerobic capacity, the ground he covers and the vast number of possessions he amasses. 'Harvs can get the ball in the heaviest traffic,' says Beveridge. 'It's a gift. He possesses an acute awareness and great confidence in his ability to shake a tackle, which he's done more than any player over time.'

As one of the fittest and most committed players in the AFL, Harvey's run of injuries has baffled sports medicine experts. The popular theory is over-training. Legend has it that after a particularly hard training session Harvey would jog twenty kilometres home from the Moorabbin ground. His dedication to fitness has given Harvey exceptional aerobic skills but has also contributed to his injury problems. 'If he was unhappy with his level of training, he would do more on his own, over and above the normal workload,' says Beveridge, 'You could say that at certain times in his career, he probably trained too much, and that may have contributed to him being injury-prone – the odd tear here and there.'

Over time, those running St Kilda's training program have advised Harvey to slow down and look after his body. He now trains smarter and spends extra time in stretching exercises. 'I've learned that there's more to football,' says Harvey, 'You have to listen to your body. At 31, I've finally got the message.'

For a player who avoids the limelight, it was somewhat ironic that Harvey's first Brownlow medal win, in 1997, was shrouded in controversy. The Western Bulldogs' Chris Grant polled one vote more than Harvey, but Grant had received a week's suspension during the season for striking, rendering him ineligible for the award. It was the first time such a dilemma had arisen, and at the awards ceremony several league officials made a point of congratulating Grant first. There was even some jeering when Harvey received the medal. Harvey himself declared that, 'In a way, it's a hollow victory.' The doubters were silenced the following year, when Harvey won his second Brownlow, this time gaining the highest number of votes of any player, suspended or otherwise.

Harvey's coaches and peers are united with the umpires who award the Brownlow votes in their admiration. Harvs's first coach at St Kilda, Darrel Baldock, recalls his initial impressions:

> You could virtually see from the first minute that Robert Harvey was going to be a top footballer. He had the natural ability and the right temperament to make it. I've never seen anyone so young just jump immediately into senior football.

Stan Alves concurs: 'I think he is an outstanding player. His area of improvement has been quite astronomical. He is the equal of anyone in the game in winning the ball.'

The last word can go to Harvey's current coach, Grant Thomas, who rates Robert Harvey as a 'pro's pro'. In Thomas's words, he is:

a deep thinker, who leaves no stone unturned in his preparation and even pushes himself too far in his quest to be the best. Along with Baldock and [Ian] Stewart, he's at the top of the tree of St Kilda greats. He's also the most humble footballer I've ever met. He shies away from accolades. He's the complete, selfless team-player.

Peter Weiniger is a Melbourne journalist, author and lecturer, who has followed the Saints since Alan Killigrew won the Best and Fairest.

'Robert Harvey: Poise, perseverance, humility' draws on information from Russell Holmesby's *Heroes with Haloes*, the *Sunday Age* (18 May 2003) and the AFL website.

31

ROBERT HARVEY
Just Another B. O. G. Performance

by Stephanie Holt

Robert Harvey, future Brownlow medallist. We'd heard it so often, it had become a cliché, those extra three words tacked on the end of Harvs's name whenever the commentators had a moment of silence to fill or the columnists needed an extra line of copy. And the thing with clichés is, the more you hear them the truer they become. But no amount of 'expert' opinion ever won anyone a Brownlow Medal. No, you have to earn one of those.

One moment last year stands out. Round 11 at Subiaco. Harvey's got the ball round on the boundary. John Worsfold slinks over the line, blood rule, caught by the camera with a sprung-bad look on his face. It looks like the Saints have lost the momentum; but Harvey's about to steal it back. Slow towards the man on the mark, then instantly up a couple of gears, baulks, dodges, round he goes and slips through a perfect goal. Rubbing salt in the wound. Cool and classy as they come. Never put a foot wrong, and it's just one highlight in a match-winning, history-making thirty-five-possession game.

I'm entranced by that thing he does. The way he stops the play around him, weaving and twisting through bodies caught in freeze frame, like that old TV ad with Paul Cronin holding forth in a crowded bar about drinking and driving. Except what Paul Cronin could teach Harvey about football you could write on the back of a Brisbane Bears balance sheet circa 1990. What Harvey could teach him about footy – and accounting, for that matter – would fill a book.

So when my pulse is racing, and I'm taking savage drags on a botted last-quarter fag, hoarse from 100-odd minutes of shouting, all it takes is for Harvey to get his hands on the ball and the tension melts away. Others might be mercurial, thrilling, freakish. Others might make as big an impression off the field as on. Harvey, he's just so good you don't have to think twice. Just another 30-possession day at the office. Just another hundred minutes of the perpetual motor machine. Just another B.O.G. performance.

I've seen a lot of great Saints in my time, and I've loved many more besides, in that way you do, refusing to be shaken from the shaky claims to greatness you're making for, well, most of the first eighteen. But as time sorts out the real champions, I know I'll look back with a sense of pride and priviledge that I could go week in, week out and watch players like Barks and Plugger, Nicky and Harvs.

So roll out the clichés for Robert Harvey. Grace under pressure. Poetry in motion. Actions speak louder than words. All-time great. And lets not forget the one that says it all: Robert Harvey, Best and Fairest.

Stephanie Holt is a writer and editor specialising in art, football and other topics of vital cultural significance.

'Robert Harvey: Just Another B. O. G. Performance' was originally published in St Kilda fanzine *Marching In*, no. 5, in 1998.

32

WAYNE CAREY

by Michael Winkler

Great Men are not always great men. JFK was a pants man. George Orwell was a curmudgeon. Bing Crosby was a bad father. Richard Wagner was an anti-Semite. The tide of history hasn't washed away the sins of these men – but even the harshest revisionists are too smart to suggest that Kennedy wasn't a fine politician, that Orwell couldn't write, that Bing couldn't sing or that Wagner couldn't compose. I wonder, though, if posterity will smile on Wayne Carey.

I suspect that future generations will recall Carey's off-field indiscretions more easily than his on-field dominance. The gloss of football greatness tends to fade faster than the stink of immorality. He'll remain the punchline to a thousand pie-night gags, while his status as a modern great could be pushed into the background. Whether or not we owe Carey leniency as a man, football history demands we remain clear-eyed in assessing his worth as a player. Because as a player, in his prime, he was a gun.

Carey is not just the best player the Kangaroos ever had, he also probably saved the club from extinction. The quickest route to oblivion for a footy club is consistent lack of success; the second quickest route is supporter apathy. Carey helped make the Roos a force but, more importantly, he gave them a face. It was a face that millions of footy fans wanted to slap, but that was preferable to the indifference that could have seen the cash-poor Roos go under. Following Newton's law, the equal and opposite reaction to the loathing that Carey inspired in supporters of other teams was the pride he instilled in loyal Roos.

For the royal-blue-and-white faithful, Carey provided an identity, something the club desperately needed. He played during a decade when mergers with Fitzroy or Footscray were rumoured, when the 'North Melbourne' moniker was dropped, when overtures were made towards both the Canberra and Sydney markets, when despised 'big brother' Carlton bought sufficient shares in the Roos to make a takeover seem possible. When even the most rusted-on fan could have wondered what the club stood for, Carey provided the answer.

For a dozen years, Carey was North Melbourne and North Melbourne was Carey. When he appeared in the Adelaide Crows strip for the first time, it was an assault on the senses. It may not have been as seismic as Barassi donning a Blues guernsey, but it still seemed like a massive transgression.

North, Carey. Roo Boys, Roo Boy. Few things are as evocative of footy in the '90s as Carey in a Roos jumper under lights at the MCG on a Friday night. This monolithic man would prowl the forward half of the ground, terrorising backmen, taking marks, kicking goals. And winning.

The soundtrack to this quintessential 1990s footy imagery is, of course, the incomparable Bruce McAvaney on Channel 7. I once asked McAvaney which player he loved calling most, and his answer would surprise no-one:

> Wayne Carey. He's a bit like Carl Lewis for me. Lewis is the best athlete, and I think Carey is the best footballer I've seen, in terms of making a difference. I think I've seen the greatest player of his generation at his peak.

Of Carey's 244 games at Arden Street, 184 were as skipper. He is fifth on the league's list of most matches as captain. He emulated Noel Teasdale and David Dench by winning four North Melbourne Best and Fairest awards, and was runner-up three times. He kicked fifty or more goals in seven seasons, and his status as the Kangaroos' leading goalkicker is a mantle he will retain for a long time to come. In twenty-one finals matches for the Roos, Carey kicked fifty-nine goals. In 1996 he was premiership captain and his club's Best and Fairest and leading goalkicker. Carlton's Stephen Kernahan is the only other player to have achieved this treble. In 1999, Carey was premiership captain, club leading goalkicker and all-Australian captain.

He has been named all-Australian seven times, and in four of those years he was captain. Both achievements are unmatched by his contemporaries. He is one of only two players to have twice won the AFL Players

Association most valuable player award – arguably the truest test of a modern player's worth.

Carey is a prolific goalscorer. He has kicked seven goals or more in thirteen matches. As 2003 began, he ranked seventeenth in the all-time record for career goals. Only one true centre half-forward, Stephen Kernahan, was ahead of him (also ahead of him is Bernie Quinlan, who played much of his career at centre half-forward). Carey has averaged 2.75 goals a game – better than sharpshooters such as Quinlan, Kevin Bartlett and Peter Daicos – while his 62% accuracy compares favourably with Gordon Coventry, Doug Wade and Gary Ablett. His best bag was in 1996 when he booted 11.2 in a big win over Melbourne. Even more remarkable was his 10.5 in a losing side against Essendon in 1999.

As crucial as Carey's own goalscoring was the amount of space and opportunity he created for his fellow forwards. In the first half of the 1990s, John Longmire thrived on Carey's presence, while secondary forwards Corey McKernan, Craig Sholl and Mark Roberts were spared the opposition's best defender. Throughout Carey's career at North, the likes of Anthony Rock, Brett Allison, Brent Harvey, Peter Bell and Shannon Grant prospered at his feet.

Barassi's rudimentary 1970s Kangaroos strategy – 'long bombs to Snake Baker' – was reinvented in the 1990s by Denis Pagan as 'long bombs to Duck Carey'. The Kangaroos' forward line was cleared out so that there was yawning space in the attacking 50-metre arc. Midfielders could aim towards it, knowing that Carey would sprint back with the flight of the ball unimpeded by onrushing defenders. Centre half-forward? He was effectively a spearhead, but standing in the regular centre half-forward position. Opposing defenders were sucked up the ground, and Carey's direct opponent (or, often, opponents) would have to combat him on their own. Other North Melbourne players knew Carey would be the primary target, and that he would always provide a contest. If he didn't pluck the ball from the air, he would help create room for them to run past the pack.

This game plan became known as 'Pagan's Paddock'. It was an unattractive but brilliantly effective ploy that enraged the purists, symbolic of the almost umbilical relationship between coach and captain. 'Here are my eggs,' Pagan seemed to be saying, 'and here's my one basket. What are you going to do about it?'

In 1999, 2000 and 2001 a *Herald Sun* footy fan survey voted Carey the sport's most hated player – and that was *before* the scandal that ended his Arden Street tenure. The antipathy came because he was a winner who didn't mind throwing his weight around. And because he seemed arrogant.

Carey is a patrician footballer, completely secure in his own ability and happy for everyone to know it. But then, Haydn Bunton was said to be well aware of his superiority, as were Bob Pratt and Laurie Nash, and no-one ever accused Dermott Brereton or Ted Whitten of undervaluing their own worth. Brereton once wrote in the *Age*:

> In my time in football, there have been only three or four players who've exuded such confidence. Leigh Matthews went about things in his quiet, assured way, Gary Ablett had an unwavering confidence in his ability, but Carey surpasses them both in that regard ...
>
> Because of his aura, [Carey] retains the ability to get into the head of the opposition and mentally dominate them. It does not matter if he's on one leg, they will always fear him.

As a footballer he can be compared to the great Whitten, an exercise that diminishes neither of them. Although there are enormous differences between the two, not least in their off-field habits, both were titans who were at their best in the hardest position on the field, both were happy to use low-level violence to achieve their aims, and both were shining stars in unloved teams.

Carey is, for all intents and purposes, stateless. He grew up in the freakish sporting cradle of Wagga Wagga in New South Wales. (In the one decade, that Riverina town provided an all-Australian captain in Carey, an Australian cricket captain in Mark Taylor, and an Australian rugby league skipper in Laurie Daley.) At 15 Carey followed his elder brother, Dick, to Adelaide, and at 16 he debuted for North Adelaide. He played for Victoria in the under-17 national championships, and has played senior football in state teams representing both South Australia and New South Wales – but interstate contests never interested him. He seemed content to simply make the all-Australian team instead.

In 1988 Carey played in an under-19 flag side at North Melbourne, under coach Pagan. The following year he made his senior debut but also suffered a dislocated left shoulder, an injury that was to shadow his career. In 1990 he announced his arrival as a player by coming second in the club's Best and Fairest, but in 1991 he damaged his right shoulder.

However, his ability as both a player and a leader was obvious. Pagan's appointment as coach in 1993 coincided with Carey's elevation to the captaincy. At 21 years, 304 days, he became the second-youngest skipper in VFL/AFL history.

Before reaching a hundred games, Carey had been named all-Australian skipper, played for two states and won two club Best and Fairests. The legend was starting to grow. Commentary-box boosters dubbed him 'King Carey', while his teammates continued to call him 'Duck'. Opposition barrackers habitually collapsed the two into something comparable to 'Duck-King Carey'.

The opprobrium of opposition fans reached new heights in 1994 when Carey's playing style – always physically expansive – crossed the line into brutishness. The season was barely half over when he'd faced four charges at the tribunal. He was cleared of attempted eye gouging and charging, before copping two- and then three-week suspensions for striking offences. He was singled out for some stinging criticism by then-AFL heavy Ian Collins. In match after match Carey crashed into the back of opponents, hit people borderline-high, roughed them up. It was as if he was groping in the dark, trying to find a limit – waiting for someone to say 'stop'.

Still, no-one doubted Carey could play footy. He was bigger than most, stronger than most, faster than most, and more skilful than almost any. He had various trademarks: running with the flight of the ball and seizing possession as he charged towards goal; taking crunching pack marks; dribbling six-pointers off the outside of his boot in a manner that would have made Peter Daicos proud. His supreme athleticism and anticipation got him to a large number of contests. As often as not, it would buy him an extra half-second, too; at these times he could look almost leisurely. And, all the time, he had that swagger. That leisurely swagger. That infuriating, unshakeable belief in his own superiority. He never seemed to believe that he – and, by extension, his team – could be beaten.

In the 1994 Preliminary Final, Carey played a mighty solo hand against Geelong, with fourteen marks and 6.4 in a brilliant effort that saw the Roos miss the Grand Final by a kick. In 1996 he was irresistible. He accumulated 200 marks and eighty-two goals during the season, and closed it by hoisting the premiership cup.

In 1997 the rigours of playing the game's toughest position started to tell on him. He dislocated his shoulder in the opening game against

Melbourne and didn't get back until round 13. After North lost the Preliminary Final, he had shoulder and knee surgery.

In 1998 he was once again the leading mark-taker in the game, with 193, won his club Best and Fairest and skippered his team to the Grand Final, but missed out on the Brownlow, after starting as favourite. He played in the Grand Final, but was well held by Peter Caven in the second half as Adelaide upset the Roos for the flag.

Carey showed his steel in 1999 when, despite missing five games with a groin injury, he became the Kangaroos' all-time leading goalkicker and the club's first dual-premiership captain. His body continued to let him down in 2000, when he battled groin and shoulder problems, but he still placed second in the club's Best and Fairest. In 2001 he played only fourteen games, and didn't play at all in 2002.

There is a weighting attached to the deeds of the greats. The bar is set so high that the extraordinary becomes expected, and an average game is rated as a failure. Truly great footballers also have to contend with not just the toughest opposition player but often, in the case of forwards such as Carey, with two or even three opponents. This has been the lead in Carey's saddlebags since he first caught the footy world's attention, and it makes his achievements all the more laudable.

Carey could be quelled – most notably in some of his highly anticipated battles against West Coast hard nut Glen Jakovich. The two were beautifully matched in terms of height, strength and attitude. Carey had an edge in athleticism, but often chose not to use his running ability. Instead he would get suckered into a body-on-body battle with Jakovich, as if his machismo wouldn't let him play it any other way. It was a bit like Muhammad Ali and his disastrous habit of absorbing punishment in order to disprove the knockers who claimed he couldn't take a punch. Outsiders couldn't understand why Carey would do such a thing, but Jakovich knew – and Carey probably knew, too. Each man wanted his victory to come on a level playing field, such was their respect and their rivalry. Carey didn't just want to beat Jakovich; he wanted to beat him at Jakovich's game.

Other clubs knew Carey's worth. After seeing Port Adelaide defeated in a 1999 Qualifying Final, coach Mark Williams took time away from mourning his team's demise to pay tribute to the North Melbourne skipper, who took eleven marks and kicked six goals on a wet day. 'I thought we saw one of the best players of all time today,' Williams marvelled. 'He stood up and single-handedly won the game.'

In 2000, Collingwood coach Mick Malthouse speculated that Carey might be the best player he'd ever seen. After watching his man stomp all over the Magpies, Pagan agreed and said, 'I reckon I have looked in all my dictionaries, looked in all my Roget's [thesaurus] and I can't find any more adjectives to describe him.' 'Magnificent' was the one settled on as best fitting the task. Also in 2000, an AFL Players Association survey rated Carey the most intimidating player in the league. (Interestingly, four of the survey's five most intimidating players were Kangaroos: Carey, Glenn Archer, Mick Martyn and Byron Pickett. Barry Hall, then at St Kilda, completed the five.)

A footballer's worth to the sport is made up of more than his achievements on the paddock. Carey brought disgrace to his club on more than one occasion; finally, and most seriously, through his dalliance with the wife of his football lieutenant, also one of his best friends. While Carey should carry the blame, the Kangaroos and especially Pagan could ask themselves some tough questions. Insiders say that for a long time there was one set of rules for Carey and another for everyone else.

The affair between Carey and Kelli Stevens came to light during Glenn Archer's 30th birthday party on 10 March 2002. 'For the wellbeing of all concerned, I have ceased my career with the Kangaroos,' was how Carey informed the world that the AFL's strongest player–club link had been severed. At the time he was believed to be the highest-paid player in the game. *Business Review Weekly* estimated his annual income at $1.5 million.

The sordid saga did nothing for Carey's standing as a person, and put a question mark over his worth as a clubman, but it didn't diminish his eminence as a player. Most rival clubs expressed strong interest in him, once he was on the market. Adelaide chief executive Steven Trigg reported that he consulted his players before signing up Carey, and that Mark Ricciuto responded with, 'He's the greatest player of the last two decades, and he'd be fantastic for our club.' Former Adelaide player Darren Jarman, now a match committee member, said 'I hated him because he was so bloody good. I'm still dirty on him for winning that final against us in 1994 when I was at Hawthorn.' Jarman didn't forget what Carey could do on the field. No-one who played against him ever will.

By the end of the 1990s, the dynamic duo of Pagan and Carey had earned the Roos unofficial Club of the Decade status, having played in six Preliminary Finals and three Grand Finals, and won two flags. For a struggling outfit operating out of ramshackle premises, it was an incredible effort. Carey was named captain of the North Melbourne Team of the [20th] Century.

Five hundred and eighty-three days after his last match in a Kangaroos guernsey, Carey played his first league match for Adelaide. He strutted around Adelaide's home ground as if born there, kicked four goals, snaffled multiple marks and made his teammates walk a little taller. His team won, as Carey teams tend to do. He looked as if he expected nothing less.

Michael Winkler is a Melbourne writer who has worked in radio, television, print and the internet.

33

JAMES HIRD
Real Men Do Cry

by Michael Winkler

There wasn't a lot of talent on offer in the 1990 national draft. Geelong took Stephen Hooper with the first pick, James Cook went to Carlton with the second, and David Donato was claimed by Fitzroy with the third. Essendon was kept busy, claiming Todd Ridley (at 13), then Richard Ambrose (21), John Fidge (24), Glen Hoffman (37), Jarrod Carter (51) and Stephen Fry (65) – only one of whom (Ridley, who managed twenty-five games) ever played for the Dons. Then, with their penultimate choice, the 79th draft pick overall, Essendon gambled on an injury-prone kid from Canberra.

It turned out to be a gamble worth taking. It's hard to believe now that seventy-eight footballers could have been preferred to James Hird, who twelve years later was named the third-greatest Essendon player of all time, and the best since John Coleman's knee buckled in 1954.

The old cliché suggests that if you open up a footballer's skull you'll find a Sherrin. That's intended as a compliment. But open up Hird's skull and you'd find a brain, not a footy; open up his thorax and you'd find a heart and a set of lungs of extraordinary size and efficiency. He's perhaps the smartest footballer in the game. He may also be the most courageous. His stamina, mental and physical, is something to be marvelled at.

Hird has won both a Brownlow and a Norm Smith medal, a double that only Greg Williams shares. As well as winning Essendon's Best and Fairest three times, the Essendon captain has skippered the all-Australian team and the Australian International Rules team, won the Jim Stynes medal for best player in a series against Ireland, and topped Essendon's goalkicking twice.

All of this, one suspects, means precious little to him. What matters to Hird is that he played in Essendon's flag-winning sides of 1993 and 2000; that he has played in three pre-season premierships; and that he has captained his club since 1998. Along with every other player, Hird claims to value team glory above individual rewards. I have an unshakeable suspicion that Hird is more sincere about this than pretty much anyone else.

It seems bizarre to describe James Hird – a multimillionaire part-time merchant banker – as a 'football socialist', but no player in recent memory has displayed such inherent understanding of, and ferocious commitment to, Marx's famous words: 'From each according to his ability.'

Hird never baulks at the notion that if he gives his all he will be contributing more than those around him. His only hurdle seems to be understanding that others might not share his instinctive conflation of *Das Kapital* and Australian Rules. Selflessness is the rock on which his game is built. If others don't subscribe to his notion of sacrificing everything for the common good, he is not so much disappointed as perplexed.

Because of the level of commitment – and sacrifice – that Hird has made his personal benchmark, he can expect physical woes for the rest of his life. While he has been blessed with a frame big enough – just – to play a key position, and an engine that allows him to buzz around the midfield for 120 minutes, the trade-off is a fragility at odds with his physical recklessness. One reason Hird was taken so late in the national draft was a serious hip injury sustained as a teenager, and he has been stricken with a succession of significant injuries in the years since, yet he continues to attack the ball every bit as fiercely as he did when a rookie.

There is an Italian proverb that asks, 'Why live like an invalid to die as a healthy man?' It's a viewpoint ingrained so deeply in Hird it might be plaited through the strands of his DNA.

Team success, Hird's great motivator, came almost immediately after his move from ACT club Ainslie. In 1991 he played in Essendon's under-19 premiership. In 1992 he played at half-forward in a Reserves premiership team that included Terry Daniher, Mark Mercuri and Sean Denham.

Hird made his senior debut in 1992, in an opening-round loss against St Kilda, and then sat out most of the season, recalled for the last three home-and-away matches when it was clear the Dons had missed the finals. Early the next year he announced his arrival as a senior player by kicking five goals against Richmond in Essendon's pre-season premiership win. He finished the year as centre half-forward for the 'Baby Bombers', the famous flag side that included seven players under 21. When he started 1994 in similar fashion, as part of Essendon's pre-season premiership side, Hird must have thought further success was imminent. Instead, he had to wait until 2000 to experience the ultimate success again.

Real men do cry, it seems. The two strongest images of the great Bomber do not show him in full flight on the field but in tears on the wrong side of the boundary line.

The first of those indelible images came in the second quarter of Essendon's round 2 match against the Kangaroos in 1999. Hird hobbled to the bench and sat there weeping tears of pain, frustration and helplessness. His body had let him down again. Bomber fans were numbed, wondering if the curse of Coleman and Neale Daniher had returned to claim another Windy Hill prodigy. At the age of 26, it seemed entirely possible that Hird's brilliant career could be over, after several injury-wrecked seasons.

From 1994 to 1996 Hird barely missed a match, and in 1996 he was rewarded with the Brownlow medal. But by the 1997 pre-season, he had turned his ankle, returned too quickly from the injury and, as a consequence, sustained a stress fracture of the navicular bone in his foot. He played only seven games in 1997 due to the stress fracture and a calf injury, and only thirteen games in 1998, a year plagued by hamstring injury. Hird's 1999 was effectively over after just one match, when the pain of his foot's latest stress fracture led to those Friday night tears at the MCG. A planned comeback late in the season was aborted when the pain returned to his foot. 'If I didn't [stay positive], what would [I] do?' he said at the time, 'You'd go and top yourself, wouldn't you?'

The second of those indelible images came at the end of the following season. The siren had sounded on the final game of 2000. Essendon were premiers; Hird was the premiership captain. But this supreme team player broke away from his mates as they ran their victory lap, jack-knifing his body across the MCG fence into the arms of his wife, Tania, and baby daughter, Stephanie. He sobbed, and they sobbed with him. His body shuddered with the emotion of the moment. Somehow, against unthinkable odds, his dream had come true.

At the start of the year, few had expected much from the brittle Bomber who had played just twenty-two of a possible sixty-nine matches in the previous three seasons. The pre-season knockers had written him off, and Dermott Brereton – a good judge of both centre half-forwards and injured champions – had accused him of not playing his part as captain, and effectively blamed Hird for his own injuries.

Defying his critics, Hird had started the 2000 season by piloting his side to a pre-season flag, the club's first since 1994. Other achievements followed: he became the inaugural winner of the Anzac medal, for his

James Hird, plays football not because it's easy but because it isn't, *courtesy of Sport the Library.*

efforts against Collingwood on Anzac Day (an honour he would repeat, in another emotional comeback from injury, in 2003); and he polled sixteen votes in the Brownlow, to finish equal seventh in a season in which he missed five matches through finger and buttock injuries.

Come the Grand Final, Hird's awesome attack on the ball made him a simple choice for Norm Smith medallist. As the Bombers devastated Melbourne, Hird had twenty-nine touches, took seven marks, pumped the ball inside the attacking-50 on ten occasions, and cleared it from the defensive-50 six times. He wouldn't rest until his team had won the flag, but once that goal had been achieved, he didn't seem to know what to do with himself. When he hoisted the premiership cup, his roar of triumph was so heartfelt, even primitive, it was frightening.

Those of us who ranked Hird at the top of the footballing tree had one fervent wish when his golden 2000 ended: that he would retire. It was impossible to imagine a better season than the one he had just completed. He was smart, with a life away from the game and a family who deserved more of his time. If he were to pull the plug then and there, he might not end his life a sporting cripple. Surely his football journey was over.

How little we understood James Hird. Of course he came back. Of course he was there through the heartbreak of 2001, and the physical torture of 2002, and there again for 2003. It didn't make sense. But ponder the words of boxer Kostya Tszyu, a sportsman of rare self-knowledge:

> The important thing for anybody in their career is not to finish on top. It doesn't mean anything. It is to finish on the finish line, because sometimes you finish and you are not on the finish line. If you do this you are going to be disappointed for yourself because you haven't gone to the end of your career.

Hird wasn't ready to go. He was a dual premiership player and had long ago fulfilled his destiny by becoming club captain. (His only captaincy experience had been with the Ainslie under-13s, but his character was such that he had been considered a certainty to be made Essendon skipper, following leaders of rare quality in Terry Daniher, Tim Watson, Mark Thompson and Gary O'Donnell.) It wasn't unfulfilled goals that kept Hird playing the game; he hadn't expended the desire to play football and to represent the club.

Others have made far more of Hird's Essendon lineage than the player himself. Allan Hird, his grandfather, played 102 games for the Dons, was a half-back in their 1942 flag side and became club president. James's father, Allan Hird Jr, played four games in the red and black during 1966–67. But perhaps the strongest 'family' ties the young Hird felt were to the older-brother figures of Daniher, Watson, Thompson and O'Donnell. They were the men he most wanted to emulate and impress.

In 2002, just when it looked like the most dramatic travails of his rollercoaster career were behind him, Hird sustained the worst injury of his career. In round 6, against Fremantle at Subiaco, he was running with the flight of the ball and collided with teammate Mark McVeigh. The impact with McVeigh's knee caused Hird multiple facial fractures, which required the surgical insertion of seven plates. 'He's medically fine, but a bit sore and sorry for obvious reasons – like he would be with a truck hitting him,' reported Essendon doctor Bruce Reid.

It is worth reflecting on players of heedless courage. To what extent do they have to take responsibility for their own welfare, and to what extent do those around them have a duty of care? After the Darren Milburn–Steven Silvagni incident at the end of 2001, Milburn was roundly vilified for running through the Fullback of the Century, when Silvagni should surely have shared the blame. At the very least, Silvagni neglected to protect himself, which wasn't in the overall interests of his team. But what can a team do with players for whom flinching – let alone judiciously pulling out of a physically dicey contest – is anathema?

Hird quite rightly refused to apportion any blame to teammate McVeigh, but couldn't bring himself to believe his own courage had been misplaced. In contrast, he made a lot of the nudge he'd received in that game from a Fremantle opponent, Matthew Pavlich. In his 2002 memoir, *Challenging Times*, Hird writes candidly about the injury, the pain, and his subsequent battle to regain confidence. (His value system ensures that the book is weakened by a very pronounced blind spot: Hird will only write about his teammates in flattering terms.)

Hird's legend grew when he returned to footy, against the Western Bulldogs, after just eight weeks out of the game. It says a lot about the man that he was Essendon's best player in that match, cruising across the half-back line, hoovering up possessions. He completed the season wearing a headguard reminiscent of Noel Teasdale's helmet in the 1960s, and at the end of the year was named Essendon's most courageous player of 2002. The award was somewhat less than surprising.

You sense that James Hird plays football not because it's easy but because it isn't. As a youngster he was habitually tagged with adjectives like 'brilliant' and 'gifted'; better words for his latter years would be 'persistent' and 'courageous'. His impassioned outburst after the 2000 flag about wanting to keep the players together and not wanting team success to lead to a fracturing of the group was a very public display of his team-first orientation.

Opposition supporters used to goad Hird as a 'pretty boy', for his blond hair, or 'Professor', because his worldview extended beyond the half-back flank. Ultimately, it dawned on them that no player goes harder at the ball and such taunts only underline the ignorance of the taunter. The last time I saw Hird play, an opposition barracker labelled him a 'try hard'. Which was pretty accurate. (Only in Australia could that be regarded as an insult.)

Hird will play on until he doesn't need to play footy any more. His best might be behind him now, but it's hard to imagine a player more likely to take a telling mark or kick a crucial goal or wrest possession – or even a match – through sheer force of will. Watching him, you can only wonder: Dick Reynolds and John Coleman must have been some sorts of players to rank ahead of Hird as the greatest Bombers of all time.

Michael Winkler is a Melbourne writer who has worked in radio, television, print and the internet.

34

MICHAEL VOSS
From Midfielder to Forward, a Lethal Move

by Robert Walls

Nearing 28 years of age and with just over 200 games under his belt, Michael Voss, consistently rated by media and his peers as the AFL's finest player, is in his prime. But are we seeing him evolve into a new role? It's only five games into a new season but the signs suggest that Voss is heading to the third and final stage of his career. And that is to the forward line, to be a permanent forward.

Back in 1992, when Voss debuted for the Brisbane Bears, he was a lightly framed winger. For the next couple of seasons, he played mainly on the wing and half-back flank. He was kept out of heavy traffic and used more as an outside running player. As the games racked up and the muscles and confidence grew, Voss was elevated to important midfield roles. He played centre and ruck-rover, and rested briefly on a half-forward flank. He thrived on the physicality of it all, enjoyed the bash-and-crash, the constant tests of courage, and the chance to go head to head with a Paul Kelly, Greg Williams, Anthony Stevens or Andrew McLeod.

The leader of the midfield gang for Brisbane through the mid '90s was Craig Lambert, who had such a positive effect on young Voss. Lambert led the way with the one-percenters: hardness, voice, niggle and analysis. Voss watched and listened and learnt quickly.

Today, the Brisbane skipper is quick to rate Lambert as the most influential teammate he has played with. Lambert, who now so astutely coaches the Lions midfield, retired at the end of 2000, battered but proud. By then, Voss was a Brownlow medallist, repeat all-Australian and poised to captain the next two premiership teams.

When you think of Voss the midfield champion, you see the quick centre breaks, the bone-crunching tackles, the bullet-like long handballs and the balance and poise of a super-fit athlete. What you haven't seen is a lot of goals being scored. Throughout his career, he has averaged less than one goal a game. Last year, Voss managed an average one and a half

Michael Voss, the champion of Brisbane's all-star mid-field, *courtesy of Sport the Library.*

goals a game, his best return. This year, the average has risen to two goals per outing.

There are reasons for this. In the mid to late 1990s, Voss and Lambert were the engine room. They thrived on the heavy work. The support wasn't there as it is now. Today, Brisbane boasts the best and strongest group of midfield players the game has seen. Voss can push forward knowing the Scott twins, Brownlow medallists Akermanis and Black, the gifted Nigel Lappin, gritty Norm Smith medallist Shaun Hart and the ever-improving Luke Power will control things in his absence. But I believe the main reason Brisbane's captain is spending more time up forward is because his wise old coach, Leigh Matthews, sees a lot of himself in Voss.

Matthews, like Voss, was the best player of his era, and some say of all time. Matthews, like Voss, made his name as a midfielder. Both won a string of club Best and Fairests (Matthews eight, Voss four so far). Both started as 17-year-olds and captained premiership teams. And, because of the fearless way they played, both copped a physical battering.

Matthews finished playing at 33. Most of his last five playing years were spent deep in the forward line where the Hawthorn star averaged an amazing three goals a game. Matthews knows Voss could do the same. Playing as a near-permanent forward will extend Voss's career.

There's no doubt he would be a star there – his overhead marking strength, accurate kicking and innate ability to read the play would give defenders nightmares. From skinny winger to muscled midfielder to goalkicker. The evolution of our game's best is exciting to see.

Robert Walls played for Carlton, has coached Carlton, Fitzroy, Brisbane and Richmond, and is now established as one of the most astute commentators on today's game.

'**Michael Voss: From Midfielder to Forward, a Lethal Move**' first appeared in the *Age* in May 2003.

35

WHAT LIFTS MICHAEL VOSS ABOVE DROSS

by Martin Flanagan

In the second quarter of the match at Optus Oval last week, there was a moment, as occurs in modern football, when one team seemed to be dragging the other like a speedboat drags a man on skis.

Carlton was doing the dragging and Brisbane was being sped to its doom. I can't say where and when the change occurred, but suddenly Michael Voss was in the middle of the action, standing between wing and centre where his teammates in defence could spot him, not only to direct the ball to but also to run past and collect it. For twenty minutes, as the game was won and lost, he directed traffic like a policeman.

Voss is a great player. There aren't many great players – never have been. It's a word that should be used sparingly. Most people now put the number of great current players at four: Nathan Buckley, James Hird, Voss and Andrew McLeod.

I fear we may have seen the best of Hird, whose body has taken a terrible pounding over the years, and I wonder if we will ever see the likes of Andrew McLeod as he was in Adelaide's Grand Final wins. The genius of Malcolm Blight on those occasions, I always thought, lay in entrusting his best player to create the winning pattern for the team. Playing under a coach who insists on a rigid pattern of play, as McLeod now does, radically reduces the scope of what he can create and order.

In recent weeks, Hawthorn captain Shane Crawford has been under the spotlight. Crawford is not a great player. That is not a derogatory statement, as it puts him in the class of players such as Jason Akermanis and Simon Black. A very good player can be, as Crawford frequently has been, inspirational. He can break one line, reappear moments later and break another, having followed his kick by running at speed.

But great players have the capacity to think beyond their own game and think for their whole team. What is more, in Voss's case, the whole team trusts him to do so. When they're in trouble, the Lions look to Voss, who works out a solution and they play accordingly. Voss's greatest feat to date was winning the 2002 Grand Final in the last ten minutes of a mighty match.

A Hawthorn supporter, a theatrical type known to me as Myles na Gopaleen, recently asked me if I thought the standard of football generally had dropped off this year. He was good enough to concede that, with the eight now dominated by interstate clubs, this could be a Melbourne-based perception.

I don't know if it's dropped off – I've seen good games this year – but I do think the quicker the game becomes, the more erratic it gets. Designed for acceleration and speed, football teams are like drag racing machines with their front wheels scarcely touching the ground. More and more, they have to be skilfully driven.

The other problem they share with drag racers is that they can be hard to stop and send in another direction. You also need some mechanism for slowing down other teams when their engine is running better than yours, particularly if it's one of those frenetic spells when a match is being won and lost. Both the teams getting blown around this year, the Western Bulldogs and Hawthorn, lost players at the end of last season who provided them with such a mechanism.

At the Dogs, it was Tony Liberatore, burrowing into packs, clamping the ball to bodies, holding up play, giving his teammates a chance to recover their composure. If I were to give the position he played a name, I'd call it the anchor. In a slightly different way, the player who did that for Hawthorn was Daniel Chick.

I saw a Hawthorn match last year against the Kangaroos at the MCG. Chick was playing at full-forward on Glenn Archer. I sat behind the goal, near an overweight young Hawthorn supporter who tempted fate by shouting insults at Archer of a most personal nature.

Archer was red hot, but Chick continued to lead him to the ball, taking the inevitable punishment when caught by Archer. Chick absorbed the fury of the Kangaroos' most intimidating player; meanwhile, around him, his young teammates made merry, devouring the opposition. Watching the Hawks that day was like watching one long, collective intuition.

So that's what I ask when I look at football teams now. Do they have a driver? Do they have an anchor? What makes Voss such a great player is that he can do both, and the rest of what everyone else does besides.

Martin Flanagan writes for the *Age*. His books include *Southern Sky, Western Oval, The Call* and his recent memoir *In Sunshine and in Shadow*.

'**What Lifts Michael Voss above the Dross**' first appeared in the *Age* in 2003.

36

THE ART OF
NATHAN BUCKLEY

by Kevin Childs

The five fundamentals for success in war also apply to football. The first is moral influence, the second the weather, then there is the ground, followed by command, and finally doctrine. Moral influence, as defined in *The Art of War*, results in harmony with the leader, the willingness to follow him, no matter what the danger. The weather, of course, must be studied to adjust one's style of play, just as the terrain – rough or smooth, slippery or firm – must be examined. As for command, Sun Tzu, in this 2500-year-old classic, talks of the leader's qualities of wisdom, sincerity, humanity, courage and strictness. By doctrine is meant organisation, control and assignment of appropriate ranks. All generals know of these five matters, Sun Tzu writes: 'Those who master them win; those who do not are defeated.'

What happened to Nathan Buckley in 2003 is that he realised the role of moral influence. This was seen in his inspirational role and the way he talked of it. The weather and terrain were almost always mastered, and there is no doubting his command, while his control, where possible, exhibited an elevated doctrine. Yet Collingwood was beaten too often, at least in the first half of the season. Then again, a captain does not an entire team make.

At the time of writing, another season was in the balance and Buckley's lifelong aim of a Grand Final win seemed elusive.

He does not draw solace from winning everything else. No matter that he is among that little bunch whose football prowess is acknowledged, often grudgingly, by even the most virulent of opposition barrackers, and who are not only outstanding in their own performances but are also capable of lifting their teams to new heights.

Nathan Buckley's career evolved to that level. As an iconic figure, he has a website contrived by passionate fans, including songs dedicated to him and a cringe-worthy interview, while thousands of kids love their guernseys with his no. 5. He features in internet jokes and has his own tabloid column (worthy, at best). He has the life, the wife and the personal record, but it is a shadow without the substance of a premiership. There is a daunting irony that back-to-back flags have gone to the team that recruited him in 1993, the Brisbane Lions, a team he forsook for the greater fame and passion of Collingwood, while a pair of premierships have been won by another side he spurned, North Melbourne.

That is all in the ruck of a sporting life. To his tough-as-a-Mallee-root comrade, Scott Burns, Buckley is simply the best player in a decade, outranking the sublimity of a Hird and the dynamism of a Voss. Follow Buckley during a game and you follow the ball, as so often he seems positioned for it to squirt to his keeper's gloves of hands, and then he invariably delivers it with skill and devastating impact. Seldom was this more so than a third of the way into season 2003.

Again and again in the rampage that overran the previously exuberant St Kilda in round 9, Buckley showed élan. Then, again, in the searing last minutes of the match against Adelaide at AAMI Stadium, Buckley set up the goal that won the game. How simple that sounds, yet when you are a single point behind in the seventh game of the season, having lost three, nothing is simple. The Magpies had trailed all night. They had lost to Essendon at the MCG on Anzac Day, and the previous week the proud Bombers had been cleaned up by a rampant Adelaide at its home stadium.

The scoreboard at quarter time against Adelaide spelt four goals down. Collingwood was being neutered in almost every phase, with anti-hero Wayne Carey goaling twice, then scoring again to give Adelaide a nine-point half-time lead. In the third quarter Adelaide made the difference twenty-seven points, until Buckley hit back with his only goal of the game, followed by two from teammates, all in just four minutes, to draw it back to nine points. The Crows were eleven up entering the final quarter. And it seemed over when Carey booted his fourth goal.

Again it was back to a seemingly impossible twenty-three points, then the astonishing rebuttal of five goals in seven minutes.

The last of the goals was the stuff of dreams. As Adelaide coach Gary Ayres reflected, Collingwood's ability to take the advantage from stoppages made a difference. Thirty-one minutes into the quarter Buckley, a chain on a sprocket, willing his boys to win, grabs the ball from a stoppage and fires it into the embrace of the inimitable Chris Tarrant, while behind him defender Ben Hart is suddenly bum down on the drizzle-soaked grass. The hooter blares. Tarrant goals in a shot unseen by coach Mick Malthouse, his eyes shielded in fear.

From shadow to reality, a season is alive again.

Buckley, in the manner of many sportspeople, could never be accused of being excessively articulate. When, early in 2003, he was asked by commentator Tim Lane whether the milestones of the previous year – turning 30, marrying and playing in his first Grand Final – had changed him, he opined that actual events did not change one, but over the course of life 'different things come up' and, yes, the final six months of 2002 were the most eventful of his life. His age also meant that he was now closer to ending his playing days 'and you need to find other interests that are going to keep you filling your time, I suppose ...' But he cut short that area of speculation by getting back on message, saying that he was focused on his football and wanting to get the best out of it.

His seniority meant that his role as the 'go to' player would decline, which in turn would be likely to have an effect on his consistency, one aspect of his game that had slipped in 2002. 'Above all other things, I think, my career's been based on consistency, and being able to maintain what I hope is a high level for that period is something that I'm very proud of.' Amen

Buckley is courageous, but he has publicly fretted about the possibility of having to have painkilling injections. He notes that today the game is faster, bodies more finely tuned and the grounds harder. Interestingly, he rates those factors as having more impact on players' health than the painkillers that are injected. His memory of these jabs is clear. The day before a home game against Adelaide at Victoria Park in 1994 he saw Scott Wynd, then in the Bulldogs' reserves, but a Brownlow medallist just two seasons earlier, on a table getting a syringe for a tendon tear on his jumping leg. Next day there was the strange matter of Mick McGuane's groin strain. A miscued painkiller that deadened some leg nerves. Mick had not trained and it was assumed he was not in the side. Then in the first ten minutes or so he had about five touches, with every kick dribbling along the ground. So much for injections. Under Mick Malthouse, said former Richmond great Barry Richardson, Buckley added leadership to his armoury and what some call 'inside toughness' to his outside running game.

Of course, while he may be tough on the inside, he is no oil painting, with features that show the results of footy's batterings and hair so spiky that a joke has him using it to impale taggers. Still, in a TV interview Buckley was brave enough to venture an opinion on his appearance: 'I think I'm very beautiful on the inside.'

Beautiful or not, Buckley has certainly moved his focus to helping young players. This, he says, gives him a greater sense of self-worth around the club than he used to get from playing. Of course he still gets it from

Nathan Buckley, no oil painting but a picture of a champion, *courtesy of Sport the Library.*

playing, but helping the youngsters has been elevated to an equal, if not more important, level. He is determined that the glass is half full, sounding so positive about that one lost Grand Final, which held such sweet promise. Terms such as 'helpless' and 'desperate' do not surface. Instead he says, 'Each individual will deal with it as they see fit, and they've got to make sure it's going to have a positive effect in some way.' His pluses are that he was 'very proud' and similarly very proud of the team's effort that day. They had played their best. And had a real crack. So, using this double dose of pride, he talks of taking the positives and also turning negatives into positives, when the pain had clearly blown his heart wide open.

Just as coach Mick Malthouse famously wept after this loss, so did Buckley, in the quiet times. 'It's just desolation and complete despair,' he has said. A loss had not been contemplated, so how to react? 'It's pretty much a void feeling, and one you don't want to experience too often.' Focused on victory, they felt only the beating of a huge wound.

Buckley's Grand Final despair was demonstrated when he threw aside his Norm Smith medal for best afield, won over another outstanding captain, Brisbane's Michael Voss. For some, Buckley's decision to discard the medal as he left the dais was tacky and insulting, reminiscent perhaps of the great Peter Moore, a Magpies Brownlow winner, who threw his runner-up medal to the crowd. The next day Buckley's medal was still in his footy bag, but now it's in a cupboard 'with all the other stuff I've accumulated along the footy journey'. That includes a Jack Oatey medal for best on ground in the SANFL Grand Final ten years earlier (the same season he won the Margery medal), five Copeland trophies as Collingwood's best and fairest, and six all-Australian selections.

The 2002 season had its trials. In round 6 the tribunal cleared Buckley of a striking charge. Two rounds later a wrestling charge was withdrawn. Seven rounds later, Buckley showed that for the length of an eye blink he is capable of losing control and that anyone who crosses him may regret it and became the first AFL footballer reported for wiping blood on an opponent. Near the end of the first quarter of Collingwood's upset loss to Geelong by twenty-eight points at the MCG, Buckley's tagger, Cameron Ling, had hit him, drawing blood from above the eyebrow. Buckley, in what the tribunal ruled was a deliberate and calculated act to exploit the blood rule, made what he called a split-second decision as he was leaving the ground under the blood rule, to wipe the blood on Ling, who crossed his path. Buckley knew Ling would then also be sent off. Buckley said at the tribunal that nothing could justify his attempt to use a loophole to get a player off the field. Having passed an HIV/hepatitis test some two years before, and having been in a monogamous relationship, he was sure his blood did not endanger anyone. Ling explained: 'We were all saying a fair bit to him – we were egging him on, "Get off the ground," but not as nice as that.' The tribunal suspended both for one game in a night when Barry Hall got five and Jason Akermanis two.

Even including this aberration, Buckley's journey has been remarkably straightforward. He is incapable of deviating from the utterly clear view he espoused on arrival at Collingwood in November 1993: 'I'm hungry to play in finals.' Given the formidable drive of Collingwood, and its passion for finals, it is chastening to contemplate what followed. Only a year later Buckley was in a side that vanished from contention by two points to a rampant West Coast on its way to premiership glory, but a decade and 182 games with the Pies later, Buckley has played in just one AFL Grand Final. Small wonder that the loss was so painful. Never mind the cupboard full of Best and Fairest trophies. The years kept rolling on, he laments, with nothing to show for them.

A hamstring injury kept Buckley out of the 2002 Qualifying Final against Port Adelaide, evoking memories of times when he wondered whether events were ever going to turn around and he would play in a Grand Final. After 1994 the downward tilt of the club seemed irreversible, encompassing its longest patch outside finals action, from 1995 until 2002, and including the bile of a second wooden spoon, in 1999. From 1995 to 1999 the club finished tenth, eleventh, tenth, fourteenth and sixteenth. Character building does not come any more painful. As shown by David Williamson's play *The Club*, set in the Magpie milieu, when defeats mount, cliques form and plots are laid. So it was at Collingwood. The club lost its way. Buckley chose the term 'very un-Collingwood' to describe the scheme to replace coach Tony Shaw with Damian Drum during the 1998 season.

In a newspaper interview, Buckley reflected:

> I don't think we dealt with that [speculation over Shaw's future] very well. Perhaps we weren't as upfront and honest with each other within the club as we should have been. That was more of a reflection of things on a higher level.

So the fish, as often is the case, was rotting from the head, and as Buckley tells it, this putrefaction at a higher level induced Channel 9's Eddie McGuire to move in as club president. This change, always said to be unconnected, was eventually followed by the decision of the AFL to switch football broadcasting rights from the long-held embrace of Channel 7 to a witches' brew of Nine and Ten, with the third-rating commercial channel somehow emerging with finals rights, much to the towering rage of McGuire's boss, Kerry Packer.

This media embrace was on show when Buckley married on the night before News Year's Eve, 2002, at St Ignatius Catholic Church in Richmond, with the reception at the profoundly vulgar Crown Casino. He and Tania Minnici had been a couple for a considerable time. The passionate Pie manager of an Italian-style restaurant in Fitzroy St, St Kilda, will show the casual visitor just where Bucks sat when he popped the question. Like other stars, usually of the screen, Buckley used muscle to deflect any paparazzi after the rights to the wedding snaps were flogged off to a gossip magazine.

By pre-season 2003 Buckley was fired up in the Wizard Cup, notably gathering nineteen possessions and kicking four goals in the thirty-seven-point semi-final drubbing of Geelong.

He carried this into the season proper, with thirty possessions against Carlton, in the second round. Of those, twenty-seven were effective. Against Geelong a week later he amassed ten kicks, seven handballs, five marks and five tackles, even though he was off the ground for about a quarter.

Barry Richardson has noted that Buckley's peers unhesitatingly rate him a champion because of his consistency, professionalism, amazing endurance and ability to counter up to three taggers in most games. The rise of tagging of key players over the last two decades led former Sydney Swans coach Rodney Eade to nominate Buckley as just one of three great players who could realistically hope to limit a tagger, working off them and winning possessions. Andrew McLeod and Michael Voss are the others. Eade has found that players who have to deal with a shadow week in and out must be mentally tough as well as physically fit. Most nominated Buckley as the best kick they had seen. Judged as so outstanding by some of the wisest of judges, Buckley still looks to that one great goal. Any real fan would hope he gets it. Wouldn't they?

Kevin Childs is a leading Melbourne journalist and communications consultant. His profile of Tom Hafey appeared in *Footy's Greatest Coaches* in 2002.

37

ANDREW MCLEOD
Keeping His Cool in Chaos

by Michelangelo Rucci

Andrew McLeod had so much going through his mind, yet the 1997 Norm Smith medallist was still as cool as the match-winning centreman had been to stake an indisputable claim to the title of best afield in the Grand Final.

There was the inevitable pandemonium in the changerooms, but McLeod – who can create space amid chaos on the field – had found a corner where he dropped his head, for the first time, and listened to the jangle of an AFL premiership medal hitting his Norm Smith medal. At 21, the pint-sized package of pure genius had followed the path of his idols from the Northern Territory – Richmond's Maurice Rioli and Essendon's Michael Long – to the MCG on Grand Final day and continued the tradition.

McLeod was only six when Rioli won the Norm Smith playing in the Tigers' losing 1982 Grand Final team. He had only started playing league football in the SANFL at Port Adelaide in 1993 when Long carved apart Carlton with his striking run from the midfield in the Bombers' last premiership. 'The last two guys who had come from the NT to play in a Grand Final had won the Norm Smith, so that put the pressure on me at the start,' said McLeod, who throughout the month-long finals series had been reading faxes from former Brisbane NT recruit Michael 'Magic' McLean reminding him to 'keep going and show a bit of flair'.

But McLeod, now worthy of emulating McLean as the 'Magic Man' of the AFL, is so cool under pressure. He started at his preferred half-back flank, mopping up everything that came his way while making Matthew Lappin look out of sorts. And at the thirteenth minute of the second quarter, he was called to replace his skipper, Mark Bickley, in the midfield where – as he had done against the Western Bulldogs the previous Saturday – he turned the game.

Not bad for a lad who Fremantle passed up three years before, when they had first hold on his obvious talent, in a trade for taller forward Chris Groom from Adelaide.

Not bad for the most consistent member of the league's best defence, who did not collect a much-deserved all-Australian jumper and received just one – one! – Brownlow medal vote.

Not at all bad for the most improved graduate of Malcolm Blight's football academy, who six days after rising to football's ultimate plateau would be honoured as dux of the Class of '97 and wear the golden jacket of Adelaide's club champion for the first – but not only – time.

Always humble, McLeod did not hide his disappointment at being overlooked as an all-Australian in his third and best season of AFL competition. But he did not need to make an issue of that bewildering oversight or his lack of acknowledgement in the Brownlow votes: the Norm Smith medal and a premiership medallion was the ultimate answer back.

'Well done to all the guys who did get in the all-Australian team, but I was pretty disappointed, as were a lot of other guys, at not making that team,' McLeod said. 'But these two medals cap it off. They're just special. It's unbelievable; it's fantastic. I really can't believe it.'

'I'd rather win these than perhaps get an all-Australian jumper or Brownlow votes. Congratulations to Robert Harvey on winning the Brownlow medal, but I'm sure he'd rather have these,' added McLeod, as he held his collection of medals with pride and appreciation.

His words were sincere, as was his sympathy for the beaten Saints. As the final siren still echoed around the MCG to announce Adelaide had won its first premiership, McLeod headed straight for St Kilda veteran Nicky Winmar, who lost his father to cancer on the eve of the big match. 'I just went up and said I was really sorry for what had happened. Everyone feels for him,' said McLeod. 'Us Aboriginal guys are very close and we do feel for Nicky.'

McLeod had his own inspiration in a cancer victim. He had remembered the encouragement Adelaide timekeeper Wally Smith had constantly offered him at West Lakes. McLeod had seen him on television, very much weakened by cancer, appealing to the Crows to bring him back the premiership cup, while he remained bedridden in an Adelaide hospital. 'I felt really emotional, I really felt for him,' said McLeod.

That day put McLeod's name among the greats of VFL/AFL Grand Final history, and gave him a medal not even his greatest idol, Essendon's Flying Dutchman Paul Van Der Haar, could win. So did it mean he was now one of the league's best?

'No way,' said McLeod, maintaining his stoic modesty:

Tony Modra, Tony Lockett, those guys, they're sensational. I'm just out there doing my job, trying not to be too flairy. Maybe it will change how some people see me, but you can't put me up there with those great players.

Had it been his best game? 'I don't know,' McLeod responded. 'I was too busy worrying about what was going on the scoreboard to think about my game.'

If the ultimate test of a footballer's worth is his ability to perform in the ultimate game then let us declare here and now that Andrew McLeod is the best player in the AFL. By the age of 22, McLeod had twice proven himself by winning the Norm Smith medal as best-afield in an AFL Grand Final. The second time, the genuine package of magic did it on one leg.

But McLeod's hands with their precise jabs of the ball, his eyes with their extraordinary vision, and his mind with its uncanny sense of where the ball will fall next make the mercurial Crows midfielder a star.

It is six years since McLeod was first seen at Alberton after he headed south from Darwin, where he developed that lovely style of nursing and running the ball through rugby. Those who saw him said 'This boy will be everything – not anything, everything.'

With just seventy-nine AFL games on his record, McLeod, after two Grand Finals, walked away – or limped away – with more prizes than anyone else: two premiership medals, two Norm Smiths. In that order, said McLeod. 'The Norm Smith medals are a bonus if you're playing well. The premiership medal is the ultimate. I'm prouder to have a second premiership medal than a Norm Smith medal.' McLeod joins Hawthorn defender Gary Ayres as a dual winner of the Norm Smith.

In 1998, for the second consecutive year, McLeod had changed the tone of the Grand Final when thrust into the midfield. He finds the ball, moves the ball, puts himself at the right place at the right time – and brings team-mates into play with the most precise delivery. It is always the right option.

The previous year, on two sound legs, McLeod moved from half-back to the middle after half time to destroy St Kilda with thirty-one disposals. In the following Grand Final, McLeod moved to the midfield just before half time to cut apart the Kangaroos, with fifteen kicks and fifteen hand-balls. His actions – all so smooth and so enthralling that it seems time freezes around him – say it all.

And it was not conceit or smugness that left McLeod reluctant to speak of his achievements ahead of the team at the end of the Grand Final. 'I was a bit lucky. Got a few kicks,' he said as he was presented as the 1998 Norm Smith medallist. McLeod tired during the finals of hearing how North Melbourne was its captain, Wayne Carey, dubbed the best player in the AFL. 'What about us?' McLeod said. 'We've got a great team here. They've got a couple of champions in their team. We've got a team full of champions here.'

But McLeod stands out as the champion of champions. To have thrived in his first Grand Final put the football world on notice. To have done it again twelve months later after a year of annoying leg injuries – first having a bit of cartilage taken from a knee, then a nasty thigh strain and in the prior month fluid on and pain through the knee again – says McLeod is special, very special. 'Andrew McLeod is writing his own foot-ball history,' Adelaide coach Malcolm Blight said. 'Where that goes to is entirely up to him, but I've got a fair idea it'll be okay.'

Five years later, while Blight watched from the tropical reaches of north Queensland, McLeod enhanced his reputation of making Grand Finals his particular stage when, in the 2003 pre-season Wizard Cup Grand Final against Collingwood, McLeod. Although his right knee was degenerating from wear and tear, his smooth, tearaway pace from con-gested packs was undiminished. With taggers shadowing him tighter than ever, his mind still read the play quicker than others. He collected twenty-four disposals, Adelaide won its first pre-season title, and again McLeod – making a statement about team success ahead of individual honour – had the premiership medal draped above his Michael Tuck medal won for being best-afield. 'It is certainly something I will look back on fondly after I have finished playing,' said McLeod of the Tuck medal, 'You don't go out there to win individual things. I was just in the right place at the right time.' Symbolic of how he plays, many would say.

Michelangelo Rucci is the chief football writer at the *Advertiser*, where he has written of the most dramatic changes in South Australian football since 1983, and author of *Dynasty*, a book on South Australian football legend Fos Williams and the Port Adelaide Football Club.

'Andrew McLeod: Keeping His Cool in Chaos' is a revised version of articles that appeared in the *Advertiser* following the Crows' 1997 and 1998 premierships.